Praise for *Work Out Your Salvation*

Butner's theology of the market is a risky endeavor. Previous attempts fall into serious theological error by sacralizing the market, instrumentalizing the Trinity, or invoking "common grace" to justify existing social relations. With judicious insight, Butner avoids these errors and produces a remarkable achievement—a theology of the market that helps us reconsider its place in the divine economy. Combining in-depth knowledge of economics and theology, this work is a must-read for anyone who works in the intersection of faith and business.
—D. Stephen Long, Cary M. Maguire University Professor of Ethics, Southern Methodist University

Dr. D. Glenn Butner superbly utilizes market design and experimental economics research to show that markets are what we make of them. He then demonstrates how theology can help us steer markets away from moral corruption toward moral improvement. Readers will not fail to see the value of solid economic research and thoughtful theological considerations to major issues of our day.
—Dr. Robert C. Tatum, Cary Caperton Owen Distinguished Professor in Economics, University of North Carolina Asheville

Butner has greatly contributed to the literature on Christian theology and economics. He develops a number of theological themes too often neglected by economists. Moreover, his ability to see the complexity of different market mechanisms, and to draw upon a wide variety of social science literature, has helped him craft an argument that brings nuance and clarity to a topic too often dominated by polemics and ideology. I will be turning back to this book in my work for years to come.
—Steven McMullen, professor of economics, Hope College, and editor of *Faith & Economics*

This wholly original book intervenes with wit and rigor in conversations about moral agency and moral formation, sin and salvation, Trinitarian theology, and, not least, economic ethics. D. Glenn Butner succeeds admirably in his nuanced aim, neither to defend nor to deride markets, but to help us see them more clearly, urging Christians to recognize our own agency in shaping markets as they, inevitably, shape us.

—Kate Ward, associate professor, Marquette University, and author of *Wealth, Virtue, and Moral Luck: Christian Ethics in an Age of Inequality*

How should Christians respond to living in a society where most economic activity occurs through markets? D. Glenn Butner explores this question with theological, philosophical, and empirical analysis, avoiding both blind support and easy criticism of capitalism. He examines how markets shape us and how intentional design might transform them. Butner offers a theological framework that centers on God's redemptive work, seeing markets as a space where divine and human agency intersect. This work is a welcome exercise in faith seeking economic understanding.

—Jules Martínez-Olivieri, visiting professor of theology, Interamerican University of Puerto Rico, and author of *A Visible Witness: Christology, Liberation, and Participation*

WORK OUT YOUR SALVATION

WORK OUT YOUR SALVATION

A Theology of Markets and Moral Formation

D. GLENN BUTNER JR.

FORTRESS PRESS
MINNEAPOLIS

WORK OUT YOUR SALVATION
A Theology of Markets and Moral Formation

Copyright © 2024 by Fortress Press, an imprint of 1517 Media. All rights reserved. Except for brief quotations in critical articles or reviews, no part of this book may be reproduced in any manner without prior written permission from the publisher. Email copyright@1517.media or write to Permissions, Fortress Press, PO Box 1209, Minneapolis, MN 55440-1209.

Library of Congress Cataloging-in-Publication Data

Names: Butner, D. Glenn, author.
Title: Work out your salvation : a theology of market and moral formation / D. Glenn Butner, Jr.
Identifiers: LCCN 2023031120 (print) | LCCN 2023031121 (ebook) | ISBN 9781506479415 (print) | ISBN 9781506479422 (ebook)
Subjects: LCSH: Capital market—Religious aspects—Christianity. | Commerce—Moral and ethical aspects. | Social responsibility of business.
Classification: LCC BR115.C3 B88 2024 (print) | LCC BR115.C3 (ebook) | DDC 332/.0415—dc23/eng/20231018
LC record available at https://lccn.loc.gov/2023031120
LC ebook record available at https://lccn.loc.gov/2023031121

Cover design and illustration: Ashley Muehlbauer

Print ISBN: 978-1-5064-7941-5
eBook ISBN: 978-1-5064-7942-2

Printed in China

For Mom and Dad,
with gratitude for your support through the many years of
education that made this book possible

Contents

	Acknowledgments	xi
	Introduction	1
Part I: Economics		**13**
1.	Markets and Moral Formation	15
	Trust and Deception in Markets	19
	Perception and Motive in Economic Agents	24
	Just Outcomes and Mechanism Design Theory	29
	Once More on Market Design: The Kidney Exchange	32
	Markets and Moral Formation	35
2.	Method in Theological Economics	37
	The Positive/Normative Distinction in the Study of Economics	38
	Method in Theological Economics	49
	The Plank in My Own Eye	57
3.	What Is a Market?	59
	Markets and Their Makers	62
	Markets as Imagined Spaces by Design	63
	The Design of Exchange Mechanisms	65
	The Design of Information Flows	69
	Market Design and Market Participants	72
	Legal Regulation of Goods in the Market	75
	Two Examples of Market Design	76
	Amazon and Corporate Market Design	76
	Governments, Economists, and the Design of Markets for Pollution	79
	Market Design and Economic Ethics	82

CONTENTS

Part II: Theology — 85

4. Providence and Creaturely Agency — 87
   - A Noncontrastive Account of Transcendence — 89
   - Divine Transcendence, Human Causation, and the Economy — 92
   - Concurrence, Human Freedom, and Moral Responsibility — 96
     - Human Action as Voluntary — 98
     - The Reality of Human Causal Power — 98
     - Human Acts as Contingent — 99
   - Concurrence and the Problem of Evil — 102

5. Sin and Grace — 105
   - Relevant Aspects of the Theology of Sin — 106
     - Social Sin and Collective Actions — 107
     - Social Sin and Structures of Sin — 109
     - Social Sins and the Social Dimensions of Moral Personhood — 113
   - Sin and Moral Formation in Markets — 114
   - Common Grace — 117
   - Common Grace within Markets — 121
     - Common Grace and Special Grace — 122
     - Common Grace and the Risk of Racism — 125
   - Sin, Grace, and Markets — 128

6. The Trinity and the *Ordo Salutis* — 129
   - A Flawed Well-Trod Path in Trinitarian Theology of Economics — 130
   - A Trinitarian Theology of Divine Action — 134
     - Inseparable Operations — 135
     - Appropriations — 137
     - Missions — 138
   - Communion with the Trinity in the *Ordo Salutis* and the Market — 139
     - The Father's Providence, Culture, and Society — 141
     - Justification in the Son and Identity — 142
     - Sanctification in the Holy Spirit and Norms of Behavior — 146
   - Points of Intersection between Theology and Economics — 149

Part III: Theology and Economics   **151**

7. The Father's Providence and the Context of Markets   153
   The Context of Markets and Moral Formation   155
       Wealth, Poverty, and Moral Formation   156
       Economic Inequality and Moral Formation   159
       Culture and Moral Formation   163
   Spirituality and Divine Providence   166
   Market Design as a Faithful, Hopeful, Loving
       Response to the Father's Providence   169
       Scripture's Critique of Wealth and Economic Inequality   170
       Market Design and Inequality   173
       Christian Challenges to a Culture of Commodification   176
   Providence and Moral Formation in Markets   178

8. Markets, Discrimination, and Identity in Christ   181
   Discrimination in Markets   184
       Experiments on Discrimination in Markets   185
       Christian Identity and Unity in Christ   193
       Moral Formation in Racialized Markets   197
   Market Design and Discrimination   199

9. The Sanctifying Spirit and the Market   205
   Sanctification in the Holy Spirit   207
   Incentives and Moral Formation   209
   The Holy Spirit, Liturgy, and the Means of Grace   215
       Liturgies in Moral Theology   216
       Liturgies and the Varied Social Norms of Markets   221
       Technology and Social Action   227

Conclusion   231

Bibliography   235

Name Index   255

Subject Index   259

Acknowledgments

This book is the product of over a decade of reflection, and as such there are many who deserve my sincere thanks for their contributions to my thinking. This project began as a dissertation, though it has been so substantially revised that its resemblance is minimal even as its research question and basic impulses are identical. I am therefore greatly indebted to D. Stephen Long, my dissertation director and a strong influence on my thinking who was always gracious and insightful in his guidance of my work, even as it remained underdeveloped in many areas. Thanks also must go to the late Fr. Joseph Mueller, may he rest in the peace of Christ, who advocated for me to have permission to continue working with Steve even after he had left to teach at Southern Methodist University. Without his advocacy, the project (and likely the degree) would have been abandoned. Fr. Robert Doran, who has also recently joined the church triumphant, graciously stepped in to serve as the on-site director. He ensured a robust development of my trinitarian thought. Thanks also to Marcus Plested and John Davis, who served as readers on a project well outside their normal areas of study. I also must acknowledge that I would not have gone into a doctoral program without the encouragement of Randall Styers at UNC and Sujin Pak at Duke Divinity School.

Many have graciously offered input as I have wrestled with these ideas. In the initial dissertation, Gene Schlesinger, Kirsten Guidero, Myk Habets, Jordan Ballor, Dylan Pahman, and Daniel Bell each provided helpful feedback (sometimes without their knowing it, as Steve Long coordinated peer review). Since graduation, I have striven to better incorporate the lessons I learned from Fr. John Thiede on liberation theology. Christina McRorie provided helpful feedback at a conference hosted at Sterling College in 2018. At the invitation of Steven McMullen, I was able to test my thoughts on the use of the Trinity in a theology of economics in *Faith & Economics*. As I began writing in earnest, several scholars offered research or provided feedback, including

ACKNOWLEDGMENTS

Roy Millhouse, Daniel Lee Hill, Conor Kelly, and especially Jules Martinez. As always, my colleague and friend Tim Gabrielson put himself at my disposal for all questions related to biblical studies. Sheb Varghese, a new colleague, provided helpful input near the end of the project. Without the extensive work of Laurel Watney and Mikki Millhouse at Sterling College's Mabee Library, I could not have put forward the massive revision of my dissertation found in this book. I am grateful for such wonderful feedback, even as I admit any continuing shortcomings in this text are my own.

This is my second book with Fortress Press, and I am thankful for the opportunity to work with such a quality team, including my friend Ryan Hemmer, Sonua Bohannon, Chloe Wertz, and Marissa Wold Uhrina. I am thankful for great marketing and editing and the patient editing needed to make this work clean and polished. Once again, the team has designed a great cover, too.

Above all, I want to thank the members of my family that supported me in my lengthy education and subsequent writing process. Without my wife, Lydia, I would have never completed or attempted a doctoral program. Her emotional and, at stages, financial support was vital to my success. My parents, David and Renee Butner, were also a tremendous support through years of school. It is with deep appreciation for their love, support, and encouragement that I dedicate this volume to them.

Introduction

In the economy as much as in politics and culture, we are all potentially influencing each other as moral agents, whether we know it or not.
—Christina McRorie[1]

In a fascinating study, economists found participants from fifteen small-scale societies for a series of experimental economic games designed to test fairness, cooperation, and altruism. The study was a first of its kind because most cross-cultural economic experiments use university students who largely come from industrialized large-scale societies with similar economies. In contrast, participants in this experiment came from societies with a range of economic development. Some participants came from foraging societies that rarely traded with anyone outside of the family, while others participated in a significant degree of regional exchange as part of growing agricultural societies. Still others were fully integrated into the globalized capitalist economy. Each game was designed to allow a participant to distribute money using various mechanisms to the various players of the game. What is striking about the set of experiments is that researchers found that in some societies, participants distributed the money almost equally, while in others, they were much more likely to keep a significantly larger portion of the money for themselves. These differences were found to correlate with the economic and

---

1 Christina McRorie, "Markets as Moral Contexts: An Account Based in Catholic Theological Anthropology," in *Democracy, Religion, and Commerce: Private Markets and the Public Regulation of Religion,* ed. Kathleen Flake and Nathan B. Oman (London: Routledge, 2023), 163.

social interactions participants faced in daily life. In societies where interaction with others through a market is frequent and culturally reinforced by standards of fairness, distribution was likely to be fair. In cultures where there is limited economic exchange and/or few cultural norms enforcing fairness in such exchanges, distribution was far less equitable. The economists concluded that "economic choices... are shaped by the economic and social interactions of everyday life." Simply put, some economies mold individuals to be fairer, and others apparently do not.[2]

How can we make theological sense of this research? Christians have always lived in a wide range of societies, adopted a vast range of cultural values, and exchanged within a wide variety of economies. Presumably, Christians in different economies would be more or less likely to develop fair patterns of exchange and altruistic behaviors, at least if the findings of this study can extend across time. What is most puzzling is the question of how these differences in economy relate to the work of God. Christians claim that sanctification is the work of the Holy Spirit, and yet this study—and many like it—suggests that regular economic exchange under certain conditions may foster virtue. This study of cultural influence on fairness in economic exchange is only one of the hundreds of similar experiments that economists using emerging economic methods such as experimental economics, behavioral economics, and game theory have performed in recent decades. Many of these studies suggest similar variability in the ethical outcomes of economic interactions. Some economic systems and exchanges seem to result in positive moral formation but others in malformation.

Perhaps the matter can be put another way if we start with a theological question: What does it mean for a person to daily be transformed and sanctified toward the end of participating in the communion of the Father, Son, and Spirit in a world where that person's daily life primarily consists of participation in a market economy? Such gracious participation in the divine life is, after all, part of what Jesus Christ makes available to the believer. In him, we are becoming "participants of the divine nature" (2 Pet 1:4)[3] such that we may become one in love as the Father, Son, and Spirit are one in their love of one another (John

---

[2] Joseph Henrich et al., "In Search of *Homo Economicus*: Behavioral Experiments in Fifteen Small Scale Societies," *American Economic Review* 91, no. 2 (May 2001): 73–78.

[3] Unless otherwise noted, all Scripture citations are taken from the New Revised Standard Version. Copyright © 1989 National Council of the Churches of Christ in the United States of America. Used by permission. All rights reserved worldwide.

17:20–23). Our current participation in the life of God is itself an anticipation of that last day, when not only will we "see [Christ] as he is" (1 John 3:2), but we will also see the Father face to face (Rev 22:3–4), something the Scriptures repeatedly affirm is impossible in this current life (e.g., Exod 33:20; 1 Tim 6:16).

While Christians share the hope of participation in the divine nature, holiness, and love, it is often unclear how to be a participant in these realities today while also participating in a market economy. What do such theological statements have to do with our labor or our choice of occupation; with our financial investments, savings accounts, or credit card debt; with the way that we manage and evaluate our employees; or even with our purchasing decisions at the mall or at the nearest Walmart? Many recognize that each of these human endeavors is laden with certain moral obligations prohibiting laziness and dishonesty in the workplace, fraudulent financial practices, or exploitative management techniques. Most Christians could easily list a number of moral laws to be observed in the marketplace, but one must wonder whether such rules are the best way that Christian faith relates to markets, the spaces where the average citizen in the industrial and postindustrial world exerts most of their economic interactions. Do our daily interactions in markets as consumers and producers, investors and debtors, have any direct bearing on our participation in God's redeeming work in drawing us into ever-increasing participation in the divine life?

In this globalized age, much of the world is characterized by markets, the spaces of exchange between individuals, companies, and governments in the economy.[4] Theologians and economists who analyze markets recognize that they can play a formative role for participants, but they disagree on the nature of this formation. Some theologians view markets as a source of vice, one that corrupts the sort of moral formation that the Holy Spirit brings about in Christians through sanctification. Consider, for example, Daniel Bell, William Cavanaugh, and James K. A. Smith, who are significant representatives from a viewpoint aptly called ecclesial ethics. This perspective emphasizes the formative nature of worship as a basis for ethics[5] and then identifies ways in which culture can be counterformative, shaping a human in a manner contrary to ecclesial liturgical practices. For example, James K. A. Smith sees "globalized capitalism" as a "rival liturgy" with a "rival discipleship" that forms us

---

4 Chapter 3 will dedicate more time to defining this term in detail.
5 See especially the essays in part I of Stanley Hauerwas and Samuel Wells, ed., *The Blackwell Companion to Christian Ethics* (Malden, MA: Blackwell, 2004).

in a manner inappropriate for Christians.⁶ Two examples will illuminate the practices that ecclesial ethicists critique. William Cavanaugh points to the example of a twenty-year-old college student in Nebraska who sold advertising space on his forehead for $37,000. Cavanaugh sees this as an example of how modern consumerist capitalism leads to inordinate detachment such that "*anything* can be sold: healthcare, space, human blood, names ('Tostitos Fiesta Bowl'), adoption rights, water, genetic codes, the rights to emit pollutants into the air, the use of one's forehead."⁷ By way of contrast, Cavanaugh argues that Christian participation in the Eucharist leads to attachment to the body of Christ, replacing detachment for the sake of consumption with attachment rooted in participation in Christ (1 Cor 10:16–17).⁸ Daniel Bell points to the example of Mardi Gras. "One does not naturally or instinctively expose oneself on camera or perform sex acts on strangers in the middle of a crowded street," Bell writes.⁹ Mardi Gras is a "thoroughly capitalist experience. The actions on display there are carefully nurtured and encouraged for the sake of capitalist accumulation."¹⁰ In particular, Bell believes these acts are a byproduct of capitalism's deficient theology. Capitalist anthropology rooted in the *homo economicus* views humans as decidedly individualist, characterized by a freedom from constraint to choose in the pursuit of self-interest whatever they might want as a temporary reprieve for an ultimately insatiable desire.¹¹ Bell claims that capitalist practices such as Mardi Gras are designed to foster such desire and to provide the freedom from constraint that allows individuals to pursue whatever ends they see fit. As Smith, Cavanaugh, and Bell see it, markets—especially capitalist markets—are a major hindrance to Christian moral formation.

Ecclesial ethicists raise serious concerns about the role markets play in moral formation, but they do so with at least three blind spots. First, they tend to neglect the fact that markets are quite variable. Daniel Bell's critique of capitalism, for example, is technically only a critique of the Chicago and

---

6 James K. A. Smith, "The 'Ecclesial Critique' of Globalization: Rethinking the Questions," *Faith and Economics* 56 (Fall 2010): 14–15.

7 William T. Cavanaugh, *Being Consumed: Economics and Christian Desire* (Grand Rapids, MI: Eerdmans, 2008), 34–35.

8 Cavanaugh, *Being Consumed*, 54.

9 Daniel M. Bell Jr., *The Economy of Desire: Christianity and Capitalism in a Postmodern World* (Grand Rapids, MI: Baker, 2012), 57.

10 Bell, *The Economy of Desire*, 58.

11 Bell, *The Economy of Desire*, 93–103.

Austrian schools of economic thought, not of capitalism per se. Bell consistently critiques leading Chicago and Austrian school figures without considering many variant forms of capitalism.[12] While Bell does at times offer greater specificity, condemning, for example, the "the neoliberal economic vision," as a whole, his work speaks of "capitalist theology."[13] Given the wide range of forms of capitalism, never mind the variety of markets available, it would not obviously follow from an accurate condemnation of the *homo economicus* as advocated by the Chicago and Austrian schools that there is no theologically acceptable form of markets; I will largely avoid using the loaded term *capitalism*. Second, ecclesial ethicists generally ignore studies of the sort discussed above, but experimental studies can greatly clarify where, when, and how markets go wrong, leading to problematic moral formation. Third, the accounts given by ecclesial ethicists often leave the reader with a vague sense of how to actually make changes to improve markets. Ecclesial ethicists

---

12 See especially Bell, *The Economy of Desire*, 94–117, where Bell summarizes what he calls "capitalist anthropology." In point of fact, his quite accurate critique of the *homo economicus* focuses primarily on a handful of like-minded theologians and economists. Bell cites Friedrich von Hayek in twenty-four notes (n. 8, 10, 16, 20, 21, 25, 26, 38, 39, 48, 51, 55, 59, 60, 68, 71, 74, 77, 82, 83, 87, 92, 93, 94), Michael Novak in thirteen notes (n. 1, 5, 15, 17, 80, 81, 88, 91, 95, 96, 98, 99, 100), Adam Smith in nine notes (n. 29, 30, 41, 57, 61, 63, 72, 73, 76), and Milton Friedman in seven (n. 3, 6, 18, 28, 32, 37, 57). Also making noteworthy appearances are Margaret Thatcher (n. 7), Frank Knight (n. 35), James Buchanan (n. 31), and Gary Becker (n. 36, 40, 57). While Bell does mention other perspectives on occasion, citing Amartya Sen twice (n. 24, 40) and mentioning the "new institutionalism," it is clear that his criticism applies mainly to an associated group of economists connected with the Mont Pélerin Society, founded by Friedrich von Hayek. Friedman and Knight were founding members of the Mont Pélerin Society, an initially small organization designed to promote the liberal political and economic ideals of a free society through the interaction of a number of major academic figures. The first meeting's convocation was explicitly and self-consciously in the spirit of Adam Smith, and major neoliberal figures such Novak, Buchanan, and Becker continue to join the society's ranks up to the present. Hayek, Friedman, Becker, and Buchanan are, in fact, former presidents of the society, whose ideas were greatly influential on Thatcher. The group Bell criticizes is closely knit indeed. For a helpful discussion of the society, see Richard Crockett, *Thinking the Unthinkable: Think-Tanks and the Economic Counter-Revolution, 1931–1983* (London: HarperCollins, 1994), 100–121. A similar point could be made for many theologians who are critical of "capitalism."

13 Bell is aware of the limited scope of his analysis, defending his position on the grounds that neoliberal economic theory is the dominant and majority position. Bell, *The Economy of Desire*, 22–24; cf. Bell, *The Economy of Desire*, 101. Even granting this, however, it seems a methodological mistake to continue to discuss "capitalism" and not "neoliberalism." "Capitalist Theology" is the title of chapter 4.

might provide certain examples of alternative markets such as Church Supported Agriculture,[14] or they might call for works of mercy,[15] yet one cannot help but feel underwhelmed at times with the proposals offered.

Not all theologians and ethicists are as skeptical as those within the ecclesial ethics approach. Others believe that markets foster virtue. Consider Deirdre McCloskey, who argues for the *doux commerce* thesis, a term coined by Albert Hirschman to describe the sort of arguments found in Montesquieu, Condorcet, and Paine to argue that commerce softens or polishes the commoner, making them moral.[16] "Commerce, the French said, is a sweetener,"[17] writes McCloskey, in the sense that "capitalism has not corrupted our souls. It has improved them."[18] McCloskey explores this improvement through the lens of virtue ethics, arguing that capitalist exchange depends on and produces virtues. Part of this production of virtue is indirect: capitalism produces enough wealth to provide for the leisure time and material resources that allow for the pursuit of education, culture, and virtue.[19] Partly, capitalism directly fosters virtue because these are "good for business" as much as they are "good for life."[20] McCloskey acknowledges—at least in a limited way—certain faults of capitalism: consumerism, injustice, overemphasis on utility. Yet she does not consider these problems insurmountable. While it may well be the case that consumerism is troubling and fueled by forms of capitalism, she claims it is also true that a market economy could adjust in the long run were the majority of consumers to suddenly adopt a frugal lifestyle.[21] Though economists have long limited virtue to prudence, recent developments in game theory destroy a prudence-only perspective on economics.[22] Yes, capitalism ought

---

14 Cavanaugh, *Being Consumed*, 87.

15 Bell, *The Economy of Desire*, 187–213.

16 Albert O. Hirschman, "Rival Interpretations of Market Society: Civilizing, Destructive, or Feeble?" *Journal of Economic Literature* 20, no. 4 (December 1982): 1464–66. Hirschman focuses on early modern political and economic thinkers, but many contemporary Christian ethicists and theologians adopt a similar perspective. See especially Michael Novak, *The Spirit of Democratic Capitalism* (Lanham, MD: Madison Books, 1991), 92–95.

17 Deirdre N. McCloskey, *The Bourgeois Virtues: Ethics for an Age of Commerce* (Chicago: University of Chicago Press, 2006), 30.

18 McCloskey, *The Bourgeois Virtues*, 23.

19 McCloskey, *The Bourgeois Virtues*, 24–25.

20 McCloskey, *The Bourgeois Virtues*, 294.

21 McCloskey, *The Bourgeois Virtues*, 456.

22 McCloskey, *The Bourgeois Virtues*, 117, 127–28. McCloskey particularly points to Vernon Smith's work.

to take blame for the systemic evils it may foster, but we ought to also credit it for the systemic good it nurtures. In any event, many of the evils attributed to capitalism are a result of human nature, not capitalism itself.[23] In the end, McCloskey is confident that the ultimate fruit of capitalism is virtue, not vice:

> You can choose to disbelieve if you wish some of the things said to go along with the capitalist revolution of the past two centuries, such as the emerging global village, the rise in literacy, the progress of science, the new rule of law, the fall of tyrannies, the growth of majority government, the opening of closed lives, the liberation of women and children, the spread of free institutions, the enrichment of world culture. But if only a few of these alleged consequences were justified, then capitalism itself would be justified. And not by bread alone.[24]

Like the ecclesial ethicists, the *doux commerce* thesis encounters problems. Again, insufficient attention is paid to the variability of moral formation in markets. In particular, McCloskey tends to assume that most virtues are enhanced by markets. Here again, the *doux commerce* thesis ignores empirical and experimental studies, which have shown that markets do not affect all virtues in the same way. A survey of the literature connecting virtue, vice, and capitalist markets provides results that are far more ambiguous. Johan Graafland surveyed seventy-three studies that consider the impact of market participation on virtue, uncovering several important findings.[25] First, empirical studies, which are already troubled by a number of methodological challenges, are sparse. More than half of the studies considered are theoretical only. Second, empirical studies are more pessimistic regarding the market's impact on virtue than are theoretical studies, though both kinds include evidence for and against the *doux commerce* thesis. Third, the impact of markets on particular virtues may vary—there is more evidence of a positive impact on diligence, but markets also foster envy.[26] In other words, "the impact of the market on virtues is too diverse for sides to be taken in the debate on the doux commerce ... thesis."[27] As Graafland notes, McCloskey has to modify the meaning of key Christian virtues such as humility, faith, and hope to make them more clearly compatible with capitalism, but economic literature does

---

23 McCloskey, *The Bourgeois Virtues*, 29.
24 McCloskey, *The Bourgeois Virtues*, 26–27.
25 Johan Graafland, *The Market, Happiness, and Solidarity: A Christian Perspective* (New York: Routledge, 2010), 128–35.
26 Graafland, *The Market, Happiness, and Solidarity*, 128, 132.
27 Graafland, *The Market, Happiness, and Solidarity*, 132.

not justify her broad thesis.[28] Graafland concludes his survey with a more modest proposal: "Up to a certain point more market competition stimulates the development of various virtues. Beyond this point, a further increase in competition tends to eliminate virtues and increase vices."[29] In other words, markets are variable, and particular features of a given market may cause it to produce virtue or vice.

The perspectives and arguments adopted by proponents of ecclesial ethics and by defenders of the *doux commerce* thesis illustrate patterns prevalent across Christian theological and ethical engagements of the economy. First, such theological engagement tends to occur at the level of economic systems, failing to recognize that a given economic system can be modified considerably within the context of specific cultures, institutions, markets, and political contexts. It is relatively easy to find discussion of "capitalism's inability to produce virtue."[30] It is much more difficult to find serious Christian proposals for concrete changes in the design of specific markets, and when such proposals are put forward, they often are not feasible.[31] Second, Christian ethicists can boldly claim that "a good Christian can be, indeed should be, a good capitalist"[32] or, conversely, that "under free market capitalism, only

---

28 Graafland, *The Market, Happiness, and Solidarity*, 105. McCloskey redefines "humility" as a willingness to listen to others, not as considering others better than one's self (Phil 2:3). Faith becomes a secular conviction in some reality beyond the knowable, and hope is the anticipation of a future attainable good. See McCloskey, *The Bourgeois Virtues*, 159, 189–91.

29 Graafland, *The Market, Happiness, and Solidarity*, 134.

30 D. Stephen Long, *Divine Economy: Theology and the Market* (New York: Routledge, 2000), 252. I intentionally chose a theologian whose project I am quite sympathetic to and whose influence has been tremendously beneficial toward my own personal and professional development. Long is not someone I easily dismiss, yet I hope to pursue more nuance in this project.

31 Philip Goodchild, for example, proposes "a secondary tier of the economy concerned solely with the production and distribution of effective evaluations." This second tier would circulate an "evaluative credit" that would impact an individual's, a firm's, or an institution's ability to receive money. Phillip Goodchild, *Theology of Money* (Durham, NC: Duke University Press, 2009), 243–44. Goodchild's proposal would require the development of a second currency system, of new institutions equivalent to central banks that would distribute this currency in a centralized manner, and of a global transition toward this end nearly simultaneously, for any change of this nature to the monetary system of a large country like the United States would have a global impact. This proposal lacks any feasibility.

32 Jay W. Richards, *Money, Greed, and God: Why Capitalism Is the Solution and Not the Problem* (New York: HarperOne, 2009), 8.

the rational pursuit of profit and growth counts ... [and] Christian political theology faces a crisis of relevance."[33] Much less frequently do such ethicists engage with experimental data showing the variability of moral outcomes possible in markets.

Despite tendencies toward universal evaluations of economic systems, there is a continuous strand of theological analysis that offers a subtler treatment of moral formation in markets. One of the stronger examples of this minority trend is Christina McRorie, who summarizes her perspective on moral formation in markets as follows:

> When market settings facilitate or encourage us to make good choices, they are also facilitating or encouraging us to become good persons, and thus supporting our ability to receive grace and experience freedom. Where markets do the opposite, they are in turn inhibiting our (correct) moral formation and militating against our ability to receive grace and be truly free. And, because markets are not self-instituting, this further implies that those who design, limit, or in any morally significant way shape the markets in which we act are thus possibly influencing our character, and possibly either mediating grace to us or working against its mediation.[34]

McRorie recognizes that markets are not "necessarily all the same,"[35] and she intentionally seeks to balance the optimism of the *doux commerce* theory and the pessimism of a more critical analysis of markets. Instead, McRorie insists that "markets are at least as complex, ambiguous, and variable as any other moral setting."[36]

This book resists common simplified treatments of markets as beneficial or harmful by appealing to the variability of markets and thus the variability of the possible influences that markets can have on moral formation. Drawing on the field of experimental economics, I will provide evidence for how different possible features of markets can have different results in terms of moral formation. Utilizing the tools of the field of market design, I will also offer an account of ways in which markets are intentionally structured in different manners. With the aid of theologians like McRorie, who offer nuanced accounts of theological economics, and, often, with the additional help of

---

33 Philip Goodchild, "Capitalism and Global Economics," in *The Cambridge Companion to Christian Political Theology*, ed. Craig Hovey and Elizabeth Phillips (Cambridge: Cambridge University Press, 2015), 219.
34 McRorie, "Markets as Moral Contexts," 168.
35 McRorie, "Markets as Moral Contexts," 168.
36 McRorie, "Markets as Moral Contexts," 176.

theologians who have not directly addressed the economy, I will provide a theological analysis of such market design with the intention of providing numerous specific tools for developing markets that better contribute to Christian moral formation.

Christians are faced with a basic paradox at the foundation of their theological self-understanding. On the one hand, Scripture tells the Christian to "work out your own salvation with fear and trembling" (Phil 2:12). Much of Christian life occurs in markets, including labor markets, where Christians seek employment; various markets for goods, where they buy their clothing, groceries, or houses; and financial markets, in which they invest for retirement or from which they borrow when buying a house or pursuing a college education. Therefore, working out our salvation requires us to understand how the transformation that salvation brings about is carried into these market contexts. On the other hand, we read that "God is at work in you, enabling you both to will and to work for his good pleasure" (Phil 2:13). The emphasis on the activity of God demands a theological account of the moral formation and malformation that occur in the economy that can explain God's agency in and through markets. The thesis of this book is that human economic activity in markets is also the triune God's concurrent work that can contribute to the transformation of Christians, but the extent to which this transformation is impeded or enhanced by markets is based in part on the contexts in which markets occur and on the design of particular markets. While both the choices that individual persons make in markets and the unpredictable distribution of divine gifts to the faithful play a tremendous role in the moral development of Christians, this study will primarily focus on the context of markets without denying the significance of God's transformative special grace or the moral responsibility of each human being.

I will proceed in three parts. Part I focuses on the discipline of economics. In chapter 1, I survey the results of experimental economics to begin to demonstrate the variable effects that markets can have on moral formation. This chapter will also lay the groundwork for the more detailed analysis in part III. Chapter 2 addresses the common distinction in economic theory between positive economics, thought to be purely descriptive, and normative economics, which concerns ethics and value judgments. If this distinction remains in its most robust form, theological analysis would be excluded from many of the results of experimental economics. Therefore, I seek to deflate the positive/normative distinction in order to defend the need for theological analysis of markets. In chapter 3, I move to define markets with greater precision, including especially the fact that markets are designed by governments, economists, corporations, and other interested parties.

Part II emphasizes theology with the goal of providing an account of God's work in and through markets. With this end in mind, chapter 4 provides an account of divine and human agency rooted in the doctrine of concurrence, which allows us to consider human economic activity as simultaneously the result of divine providence. Chapter 5 offers an account of common grace and social sin with the goal of providing a theological framework for analyzing various possible market designs and the results of experimental economics. Chapter 6 clarifies divine agency in a trinitarian idiom. In particular, through appropriation or by appeal to the divine missions, I attribute providence to the Father, justification and union to the Son, and sanctification to the Holy Spirit. These attributions provide concrete theological loci to connect to the results of experimental economics.

In part III, I turn to the task of synthesizing the economic and theological content that is explored in the earlier parts of the book. Chapter 7 considers the contexts of markets, showing experimental evidence that culture, socioeconomic class, and inequality of wealth affect the ways that markets contribute to or impede moral formation. Drawing on a spirituality of the Father's providence, I suggest market design as a means of improving the contexts in which markets occur. In chapter 8, I consider the identity Christians have in Christ as fundamental to proper moral agency. Surveying experimental audit and correspondence studies, I argue that when markets are designed to encourage or allow discrimination, they both undermine proper Christian moral development and bring about unjust outcomes for groups facing discrimination. Once again, market design provides a means of improving the justice of outcomes and the corresponding influence of markets on moral transformation. Chapter 9 provides an account of sanctification in the Holy Spirit as faith working through love. Love requires motivations oriented toward the intrinsic good of the object of love, but experimental studies have shown that the use of incentives in markets can undermine such intrinsic motivations. Chapter 9 also explores the role of social norms and of technology in contributing to or resisting sanctification.

Taken together, the three parts of this book will demonstrate the variability of markets and provide a theological framework for analyzing markets as potential sites of God's concurrent work through common grace, even as they are perpetually fraught with social sin. I attempt to be ecumenical, but at times my own reformed proclivities will be evident. Nevertheless, this project is intended as a step forward in precision, scope, and nuance in discussions of the formative role of markets, but it is certainly not the last word. The last word will only be given when Christ returns and the full plan of God in markets and in all the other dimensions of creation is made clear. Until then, I present these arguments in fear and trembling, with the hope that God may use them to help the church work out its salvation more fruitfully.

PART I

Economics

CHAPTER 1

Markets and Moral Formation

"Does capitalism work?" is the wrong question to put to capitalism. It is the wrong question because it is rather obvious that capitalism works. . . . Instead of asking, Does capitalism work? we ought to ask, What work does it do?
—Daniel M. Bell Jr.[1]

In the early 1980s, Ruth Ames and Gerald Marwell conducted eleven experiments to test what is known in economic theory as the free rider problem.[2] According to conventional theory, a public good is something that can be used by numerous people simultaneously but in a context where it is difficult to exclude anyone from benefiting from this good. Persons who choose to benefit from these goods without contributing toward their costs are called "free riders."[3] Those who go to free public fireworks shows in the next town over or look up information on Wikipedia—both public goods—but never donate to support the show or website are free riders. National defense is another public good. Suppose a nation funded its military through donations or through private purchases of a defense share. If the nation were invaded, both those who paid and those who did not would benefit from any defensive measures, but those who did not pay would do so as free riders. There are many other

---

1 Bell, *The Economy of Desire*, 84.
2 Gerald Marwell and Ruth E. Ames, "Economists Free Ride, Does Anyone Else? Experiments on the Provision of Public Goods, IV," *Journal of Public Economics* 15 (1981): 295–310.
3 Neva Goodwin et al., *Microeconomics in Context*, 2nd ed. (Amonk, NY: M. E. Sharpe, 2009), 22.

possible examples. The free rider problem serves as a helpful starting point for our analysis because many public goods are morally desirable, at least at first glance.[4] In the examples above, Wikipedia can contribute to learning, civic events to the development of community and family enjoyment, and though the ethics of war and peace is far too complicated to address in this context, it is at least probable that any peace provided by the deterrent effects of the presence of a standing military would be a positive thing. Marwell and Ames's studies can therefore provide a preliminary piece of evidence for the formative nature of markets.

Marwell and Ames's experiments revealed that the free rider problem was generally much smaller than anticipated, with one notable exception. An experiment conducted among economics graduate students manifested the free rider problem much more significantly than any other experiment. Furthermore, surveys conducted after the experiments found that the economics students were "half as likely as other subjects to indicate that they were 'concerned with fairness' in their decisions during the experiment."[5] Ames and Marwell reached two widely discussed and debated conclusions about this anomaly: first, those who received some training in economics tended to think differently than other subject groups, and second, this measurable difference is either learned by students of economics or demonstrable of a tendency among more selfish—perhaps economically "rational"?—individuals to select economics as a major.

Subsequent studies have uncovered mixed evidence regarding the nature and validity of Marwell and Ames's conclusions. In a noteworthy experiment, Carter and Irons performed tests using an ultimatum bargaining experiment.[6]

---

4 A full analysis would require a theological explanation of which goods are made accessible through a given public good, moral analysis of the means used to obtain those goods, attention to the effect of such means on virtue formation, and consideration of possible alternative ways of securing the same desirable moral ends.

5 Marwell and Ames, "Economists Free Ride," 169. Other studies have found that studying business or economics may shift notions of fairness. Richard Thaler, for example, surveyed consumers to see if they would consider various examples of price gouging acceptable or unfair. For instance, raising the price of snow shovels in a snowstorm may be a rational equilibrium response to a rise in demand. Participants untrained in economic rationality consistently found price gouging in such contexts unfair, while MBA students were much more likely to consider such pricing fair. Richard H. Thaler, *Misbehaving: The Making of Behavioral Economics* (New York: Norton, 2015), 128.

6 John R. Carter and Michael D. Irons, "Are Economists Different, and If So, Why?" *Journal of Economic Perspectives* 5, no. 2 (Spring 1991): 171–77.

In this standard economic experiment, one subject receives a sum of money that must then be split with a fellow participant. The subject can offer any fraction of the sum to their partner, but if the partner turns down the offer, neither individual keeps any money. According to standard game theory, a division of economic theory that considers such interactions typically under the assumption that participants will act rationally in the sense of maximizing earnings and/or utility, the subject should offer a minimal amount to their partner. The partner should then accept because any amount is better than no reward. Carter and Irons found that economics students acted differently, offering less money and also accepting less than peers majoring in a different discipline. Economists did think differently.[7] However, Carter and Irons detected no difference between first-year economics students and those in later years and therefore concluded that differences in mindset are not learned through the study of economics but rather reflect natural tendencies among those who select an economics major.

On the other hand, Frank, Gilovich, and Regan performed a number of experiments to reach the opposite conclusion of Carter and Irons.[8] One test performed at the beginning and end of a semester addressed whether students would perform "dishonest" actions for a higher payout if there was no risk of repercussion. This test showed that students at the end of a semester of economics training tended to be more dishonest than those without economics instruction during the semester, especially in courses with a strong emphasis on game theory and utility-maximizing rationality. In another study, Frank, Gilovich, and Regan found that economics students tended to fail to cooperate in the prisoner's dilemma, a form of game requiring cooperation for optimal outcomes—more on this later—as predicted by economic theory. Furthermore, they failed to cooperate more often than non-economics

---

7 Questions remain in the discipline of experimental economics concerning whether this represents a decline in fairness or whether those who share resources at any level do so merely for strategic reasons, according to some principle of egoism. So we must be aware that such experiments may not evaluate fairness as much as a certain mental strategy. However, there is some evidence that fairness is truly considered in the game, given that a variation of the game called a "dictator game," in which the second player cannot reject an offer, still results in some money being shared. David J. Cooper and John H. Kagel, "Other-Regarding Preferences: A Selective Survey of Experimental Results," in *The Handbook of Experimental Economics*, vol. 2, ed. John H. Kagel and Alvin E. Roth (Princeton, NJ: Princeton University Press, 2015), 219.

8 Robert H. Frank, Thomas Gilovich, and Dennis T. Regan, "Does Studying Economics Inhibit Cooperation?" *Journal of Economic Perspectives* 7, no. 2 (Spring 1993): 159–71.

students. In a sample of students from a variety of majors and years of study, successful completion of the game through cooperation increased as students neared graduation, with one exception: "This trend is conspicuously absent for economics majors."[9] While economics majors may not become more selfish during their studies, they also do not become more altruistic, as is the case in other disciplines. It seems that the formal study of economics may indeed influence behavior by changing the way its students experience the world.

Taken together, these studies suggest that learning to think according to economic theory may lead to a loss of trust and of the virtue of justice. Of course, we must immediately qualify this claim. The studies provide explicit statements of the students' stated motives and of outcomes, and the experimental outcomes differ. Economists, and theologians interpreting economists, can track behavior and self-reported motives but not internal dispositions. Furthermore, these studies lack data over a sufficient period to adequately track the development of vice or virtue on any large scale.[10] It is unlikely that economic experiments will provide irrefutable evidence of the development of virtue or vice. Nevertheless, the above studies do provide some evidence that those who learn to operate in markets according to the ideal of many economists may be malformed in their mental processes from a moral standpoint, nor are these isolated studies. A considerable amount of economic, sociological, and psychological literature demonstrates a formative effect on economic interactions, motives, and outcomes. The cumulative weight of these studies demands a more nuanced treatment of market interactions than those offered by either the *doux commerce* theorists who endorse markets so cheerily or the ecclesial ethics approach that so often villainizes markets entirely. Apparently, markets can contribute to or impede moral formation, as an extensive array of studies has shown.

---

9 Frank, Gilovich, and Regan, "Does Studying Economics Inhibit Cooperation?" 168.
10 For a fuller account of these limitations, see Graafland, *Market, Happiness, and Solidarity*, 110–11. Experimental studies in the development of virtue in economics face additional methodological problems that challenge the discipline of experimental economics in general. Specifically, many question the extent to which conclusions reached in the artificial laboratory setting of an economic experiment will correspond to outcomes of real-world economic interactions. Unfortunately, external validation from real-world economic interactions is difficult to produce, so many studies presently lack such backing. See a more robust discussion in Ana Santos, "Experimental Economics," in *The Elgar Companion to Recent Economic Methodology*, ed. John B. Davis and D. Wade Hands (Northampton, MA: Edward Elgar, 2011), 49–50.

TRUST AND DECEPTION IN MARKETS

Proponents of the *doux commerce* thesis frequently appeal to the need for trust in market economies. Thus, Michael Novak claims that democratic capitalism is founded on "basic trust."[11] Brent Waters makes the more modest claim that local markets rely on and develop trust, while global markets lack sufficient direct relationships, therefore relying on "verification and coercion" instead.[12] Economists make similar claims. Ginny Choi and Virgil Storr surveyed eleven different studies that show a positive correlation between trust and positive economic performance in such areas as gross domestic product (GDP) growth, low transaction costs, and strong financial markets.[13] Of course, correlation cannot prove causation. If there is a causal link, the causal influence could run in either direction—strong markets might produce trust, but it may also be the case that trustworthy individuals foster strong markets. Choi and Storr argue that a market economy incentivizes trustworthiness. A reputation for being trustworthy may cause a rise in potential partners in economic transactions.[14] This explanation seems plausible on consideration. Businesses, at least, seem to accept the connection between trustworthiness and economic success, which is why various companies from Midas to State Farm attempt to depict themselves as trustworthy businesses. One can conceive of a market that drives participants to develop honesty, integrity, and prudence required to survive, and there is considerable experimental evidence that this increase in trust is precisely what happens in a market economy.[15]

---

11 Novak, *Spirit of Democratic Capitalism*, 123.

12 Brent Waters, *Just Capitalism: A Christian Ethic of Economic Globalization* (Louisville, KY: Westminster John Knox, 2016), 135.

13 Seung Ginny Choi and Virgil Henry Storr, "Can Trust, Reciprocity, and Friendships Survive Contact with the Market?" in *Economics and the Virtues: Building a New Moral Foundation*, ed. Jennifer A. Baker and Mark D. White (Oxford: Oxford University Press, 2016), 221–22.

14 Choi and Storr, "Can Trust, Reciprocity, and Friendships Survive," 222. Choi and Storr also note that trust may reduce transaction costs as firms must spend less time investigating potential business partners.

15 Experimental economists have developed several standard games to test fairness and trust. In the dictator game, discussed briefly above, one player is given a sum of money and offered the chance to donate a portion of their choosing to an anonymous second player with whom they will never interact. In the ultimatum game, discussed in the introduction, one player can divide a sum with another, who can accept the offer or reject it. If rejected, no player gets money. In the trust game, one player is given a sum of money. That player can then give any portion of the money to a second player. All given

Nevertheless, other experimental evidence suggests that markets also lead to certain restricted forms of deception. George Akerlof and Robert Shiller's *Phishing for Phools* is an entire book dedicated to such deception. Whereas the word *phishing* normally refers to an internet scam designed to trick someone into disclosing information, Akerlof and Shiller extend its meaning to apply to any economic interaction where one party attempts to lure another party into an action (e.g., a purchase, an investment, or a contract) that is contrary to their best and real interests. Akerlof and Shiller identify three different types of phishing that may trap an economic agent into making bad decisions: (1) psychological phishing—targeting emotions—occurs when phishing triggers a person's emotions to "override the dictates of his common sense"; (2) psychological phishing can also exploit cognitive biases; and (3) phishing may exploit an information asymmetry, a situation where one economic agent possesses information that the other lacks.[16] Akerlof and Shiller argue that phishing can increase a company's profits, so markets will naturally push economic agents toward such opportunities for profit until no remaining opportunities are available. In Akerlof and Shiller's minds, it is a fundamental premise of market economics that economic agents will pursue opportunities for profit until no unclaimed opportunities exist. In other words, "the free-market system exploits our weaknesses automatically."[17] Their book surveys a number of examples of phishing where companies deploy strategies that increase their economic competitiveness but decrease the wellbeing of their customers. According to free market principles, a company that avoids profit-making from phishing opportunities will be at a competitive disadvantage to companies that pursue such phishing. Shiller and Akerlof focus on loss of customer health or personal wealth, but they fail to consider the impact of such phishing efforts on the moral formation of employees of phishing firms, who must be trained to successfully entice customers through phishing. Intuitively, such phishing

---

money is tripled. Then the second player can return any sum of their choosing to the first player. In each of these experimental games, participants from societies with a market economy demonstrate higher levels of trust and a fairer final earnings distribution than participants from non-market economies. Jason Brennan, "Do Markets Corrupt?" in Baker and White, *Economics and the Virtues*, 239–40.

16 George A. Akerlof and Robert J. Shiller, *Phishing for Phools: The Economics of Manipulation and Deception* (Princeton, NJ: Princeton University Press, 2015), xi.

17 Akerlof and Shiller, *Phishing for Phools*, 2–3.

must undermine the development of trustworthiness, honesty, and even love toward others.

Anna Bernasek offers a balanced approach toward the two sides of the market. On the one hand, "pervasive integrity is fundamental to our enormous, fast-moving economy. . . . Without integrity, the economy would not function."[18] Here, Bernasek points to the sorts of studies noted by Choi and Storr that indicate a correlation among trust, integrity, and economic performance. One need only imagine an economy mired in corruption and dishonesty to recognize the need for integrity. Yet Bernasek notes that integrity is something we must invest in by fostering "self-reinforcing systems that promote greater integrity and wealth."[19] As it turns out, investing in integrity can be quite challenging.

Economists in the discipline of game theory have recognized the need to foster cooperation and have performed considerable research on the subject. The most famous example of the need for cooperation is the game known as the prisoner's dilemma, mentioned briefly above. Designed to model the interrogation where detectives lacking sufficient evidence to convict interrogate two culprits of a crime separately, the game recreates the temptation facing such prisoners in the face of a plea bargain. When offered a bargain, each prisoner can remain silent, which will result in the best outcome provided that the other prisoner is also silent. The prisoner can also take the plea bargain, receiving a reduced sentence while the other prisoner would get a full sentence. If, however, the prisoner remains silent but the partner confesses, then the first prisoner will receive a full sentence. Frequently, the prisoner's dilemma results in self-interested behavior where both parties confess in order to receive a plea bargain. From the standpoint of game theory, this is the rational choice that maximizes each player's expected outcome—mutual plea bargains attain what is called Nash equilibrium, the predicted stable outcome of the game that maximizes utility for participants. However, game theorists have shown that if the participants play this simulation repeatedly with one another over any period of time of unknown length, at least for the participants, then the rational strategy and Nash equilibrium involve both

---

18 Anna Bernasek, *The Economics of Integrity: From Dairy Farmers to Toyota, How Wealth Is Built on Trust and What That Means for Our Future* (New York: HarperStudio, 2010), 11.

19 Bernasek, *The Economics of Integrity*, 16.

players remaining silent during each iteration of the game.[20] Experiments on the prisoner's dilemma using human participants have shown that trust is higher than anticipated—or, from the standpoint of game theory, than rationally justified—in single-iteration games, where 40–50 percent of participants remain silent. Unfortunately, experiments have shown that human participants do not often pursue the rational strategy for repeated iterations of the game—participants tend not to trust other players and to accept the plea bargain more than is rationally ideal.[21] This failure to reach Nash equilibrium has led to various efforts to discern how to develop cooperation in repeated games. Let us consider one example of such efforts.

In 1986, a team of psychologists performed a two-step experiment to evaluate previous findings that groups are more prone to competitive behavior in games than are individuals. The experiment first had individuals participate in the classic prisoner's dilemma. Following the prisoner's dilemma, participants took part in a second game designed to test self-interest. As Insko and Schopler note in their thorough evaluation of the study, "the idea was to expose subjects to a situation in which competitiveness did or did not occur prior to their participation" in the second game.[22] The second game is known as mere categorization, and like the prisoner's dilemma, it had already been studied by various psychologists. The game divides participants into two groups based on purported preferences for the art of Klee or Kandinsky as determined by participants viewing several pieces of art and responding. Groups were then asked to allocate money to unidentified members of their own groups and of other groups. Insko and Schopler explain, "If the group-on-group play of the [prisoner's dilemma] created a belief in the appropriateness of competitiveness, that belief should carry over to the mere-categorization situation where competitiveness less obviously occurs [as was known from previous iterations of the game]."[23] The second experiment revealed that participants

---

20 For a more thorough explanation of the prisoner's dilemma and infinitely repeated versions of the game, see Martin J. Osborne, *An Introduction to Game Theory* (New York: Oxford University Press, 2004), 14–18, 419–24.

21 Siang Yew Chong et al., "The Iterated Prisoner's Dilemma: 20 Years On," in *The Iterated Prisoner's Dilemma: 20 Years On*, ed. Siang Yew Chong, Xin Yao, and Graham Kendall (Singapore: World Scientific Publishing, 2004), 2–6.

22 Chester A. Insko and John Schopler, "Categorization, Competition, and Collectivity," in *Group Processes*, ed. Clyde Hendrick (Newbury Park, CA: Sage Publications, 1987), 234.

23 Insko and Schopler, "Categorization, Competition, and Collectivity," 234.

who worked in groups during the prisoner's dilemma game and who therefore saw more self-interested outcomes were significantly more self-interested in the mere-categorization game, allocating much more money to those who shared their preferences for art. This outcome is now discussed under the label of the discontinuity effect.

There are two possible explanations for the discontinuity effect. The first is known as the schema-based distrust hypothesis, which posits that groups are more likely to expect an outgroup to act selfishly and therefore are more likely to respond to this expectation by acting selfishly themselves. While plausible, this explanation does not adequately explain why groups in a mere-categorization game who are primed through group participation in the prisoner's dilemma to see self-interest as acceptable act more selfishly than groups who are not primed in this way.[24] Therefore, a second explanation is needed: the social support for shared self-interest hypothesis. This hypothesis suggests that group members support one another in acting selfishly.[25] Specifically, we might speak of social norms as the basis for such outcomes. If self-interest is a social norm, it will become more readily manifest in social situations, especially in the context where that norm has been strengthened or highlighted as in the two-stage experiment just discussed. In other words, experimental economics and game theory have uncovered evidence that selfishness can be fostered in the context of social norms treating self-interest as socially acceptable. Conversely, experiments have shown that trust and fairness can be fostered in a similar manner by establishing a similar social norm.[26]

Institutions can also play a role in fostering integrity, trust, and honesty. Private-sector companies like Yelp, Google, or Angi that allow customers to publicly report on a company provide reinforcement for the need for honesty in business. Firms that also self-regulate through association with the Better Business Bureau have further institutional support for trustworthiness. Experimental economics has uncovered evidence that economic interactions in a context with fair legal systems will reduce cheating and dishonesty—an

---

24 Incidentally, this explanation may help reveal why groups participating in the prisoner's dilemma act in a more self-interested way in the first place.

25 Gary Bornstein, "A Classification of Games by Player Type," in *New Issues and Paradigms in Research on Social Dilemmas*, ed. Anders Biel, Daniel Eck, Tommy Gärling, and Mathias Gustafsson (New York: Springer, 2008), 28.

26 Cooper and Kagel, "Other-Regarding Preferences," 241.

intuitively plausible claim as it is.[27] We can reasonably conclude that societies could contribute both internal constraints (i.e., norms) and external constraints (i.e., institutions) to foster trust and cooperation. Of course, Christians must adamantly oppose any reduction of moral formation to such social factors, denying the role of the Holy Spirit and of personal moral responsibility, but theologians must also wrestle with the question of how such social factors relate to the inner work of the Holy Spirit in sanctification.

PERCEPTION AND MOTIVE IN ECONOMIC AGENTS

In 1998, two economists conducted a study in ten day care centers in Israel to determine the effectiveness of the practice of fining parents who were late in picking up their children. After spending a month establishing a baseline measure of how many parents were late to pick up their child, six of ten day care centers studied implemented a small fine for parents who were more than ten minutes late. The remaining four centers instituted no fines and served as a control group. In the month following the implementation of the new fines, late child pickups at centers with the new fines steadily increased before settling at a new level roughly twice as high as the level prior to instituting the fine. Meanwhile, in the control group, instances of late pickups remained unchanged. What is particularly fascinating about the study is that the six day care centers that implemented a fine removed it after twelve weeks with no noticeable reduction in late parents. It seems that the behavior of the parents was permanently changed.

When planning the study, Uri Gneezy and Aldo Rustichini assumed the standard economic position that implementing the fine would deter late pickups due to increased costs for arriving late. When their predictions failed, they had to develop a new explanation for the results. Therefore, the authors posit that "the introduction of the fine changes the perception of people regarding the environment in which they operate."[28] They assume an implicit contract between parents and the day care center prior to the announcement

---

27 Alessandra Cassar, Giovanna d'Adda, and Pauline Grosjean, "Institutional Quality, Culture, and Norms of Cooperation: Evidence from Behavioral Field Experiments," *Journal of Law and Economics* 57, no. 3 (August 2014): 821–63.

28 Uri Gneezy and Aldo Rustichini, "A Fine Is a Price," *Journal of Legal Studies* 29, no.1 (January 2000): 3.

of specific fines such that parents fear the imposition of a significant fine or perhaps more significant consequences such as the elimination of the child from the day care system. Once a fine is introduced, the expected, or feared, cost for parents decreased, causing the cost of late pickups to be less than the benefits. In this theory, late parents operate according to the standard models of rationality of economic theory, which Gneezy and Rustichini are able to map using game theory and a model describing equilibrium within this game.[29] While they consider the standard equilibrium model tenable, the authors note that "a completely different interpretation" is also possible, one based on "social norms." Prior to implementing the fine, parents perceived any teacher who remained late with children after regular hours as a "nice and generous person" who should not be taken advantage of by parents who were late. After implementing the fine, parents understood teachers who remained late due to parental tardiness to be operating within the same market structure where childcare can be bought at the given price as much as desired. In other words, implementation of a fine results in a shift from focusing on moral duty to focusing on exchange by price mechanism, what we could call a *market*. After this shift, the market social imaginary remains dominant, even after the elimination of a fine. As the authors note, "Once a commodity, always a commodity."[30] There is some evidence, to be produced below in a discussion of framing, that the second hypothesis is the better explanation.

Here, then, is a moral concern uncovered by experimental economics: consumers may de-emphasize moral duty as a motive for action in the context of a price mechanism.[31] This shift in the perceptions of parents in the studied day cares leads to acts based on cost-benefit analysis. In this case, parents shift their understanding of what is happening at a day care, no longer thinking in terms of duty but rather thinking in terms of price. Many Christian theologians and ethicists have critiqued capitalism's ability to commodify virtually anything, and in Gneezy and Rustichini's study, they appear to have empirical basis for these concerns. In the introduction, I have already noted William Cavanaugh's critique of detachment from commodification. Consider also the work of Vincent Miller, who argues that ideological critiques of consumerism fall short because they ignore the nonintentional aspects of consumerism

---

29 Gneezy and Rustichini, "A Fine Is a Price," 11–13.
30 Gneezy and Rustichini, "A Fine Is a Price," 14.
31 This is known as the crowding-out effect, which will be discussed more extensively in chapter 9.

and because capitalist societies are able to commodify dissent in a way that actually reinforces the basic problem.[32] Drawing on a wide range of cultural critics, sociologists, and economists,[33] Miller suggests that a consumer culture is one in which "elements of culture are readily commodified."[34] Consumerism demands an ever-increasing amount of goods but makes these goods interchangeable and, thus, hollowed out.[35] In order to overcome these tendencies, Miller argues that economic agents must be resituated in the economy and the religious community in roles that exceed that of consumer by becoming involved with production processes, by reconnecting commodities to their production process, and by re-embedding religious practices and doctrines in communities and traditions.[36]

Miller rightly identifies a problem associated with market economics.[37] Markets allow for the (relatively) unrestrained exchange of commodities, but such exchange requires the ability to treat objects, ideas, methods, and institutions as tradable institutional facts. Following the terminology of John Searle, an "institutional fact" is a fact where the "attitude that we take toward the phenomenon is constitutive of the phenomenon."[38] Specifically, a certain attitude toward a phenomenon institutes the possibility of certain

---

32 Vincent J. Miller, *Consuming Religion: Christian Faith and Practice in a Consumer Culture* (New York: Continuum, 2004), 18.

33 Miller particularly draws on Henri Lefebvre, Guy Debord, Jean Baudrillard, Karl Marx, and Frederic Jameson.

34 Miller, *Consuming Religion*, 72.

35 Miller, *Consuming Religion*, 77.

36 Miller, *Consuming Religion*, 184, 189, 195.

37 Bruce Rittenhouse challenges Miller's basic understanding of consumerism and commodification, arguing that Miller proposes several different explanations for consumerism that are self-contradictory. Rittenhouse notes that many existing theories of the reasons behind consumerism lack empirical backing. He argues instead that consumerism is essentially an alternative religious way of securing life against "the existential threat of meaninglessness." Rittenhouse points to studies that show an increase in consumption when consumers are shown images of death, guilt, and suffering, providing some evidence for consumption as meaning-making. Rittenhouse's appeal to consider empirical data is helpful, but his empirical critiques of existing theories of consumerism and his specific critique of Miller neglect the fact that there may be multiple causal factors behind consumerism. This book will provide a number of pieces of experimental and empirical evidence suggesting that consumerism, detachment, and commodification can be brought about by various factors. See Bruce P. Rittenhouse, *Shopping for Meaningful Lives: The Religious Motive of Consumerism* (Eugene, OR: Cascade Books, 2013), 48, 133, 147.

38 John R. Searle, *The Construction of Social Reality* (New York: The Free Press, 1995), 33.

actions.[39] Money is an obvious example—we must acknowledge a piece of paper to be money for it to count as money. If Americans ceased recognizing the dollar as currency and switched to an economy entirely based on Bitcoin, a five-dollar bill would only be a piece of paper, a historical curiosity but not something that could be used in a financial transaction. If counted as money, paper facilitates the action of making a purchase, saving value, or paying a laborer. Searle argues that institutional facts take the form "X counts as Y in context C." So a specific piece of paper (X) counts as money (Y) in the context of a financial transaction in a nation-state where the specific money is recognized as legal tender (C).[40] To connect Searle to the above discussion, Miller is concerned that in the context C of a market, too many X-objects can count as Y-commodities. Similarly, Gneezy and Rustichini discovered that when Israeli day cares started charging fines for late pickups, the context C switched from one of moral obligation to one of a financial transaction, such that late pickups (X) no longer counted as social or moral infractions (the old Y) but as legitimate purchases (the new Y).

Behavioral economists have recently studied the sort of phenomenon explored by Gneezy, Rustichini, Searle, and Miller using the concept of framing. In behavioral economics, framing describes a change in the context (C) of a transaction, resulting in different outcomes, some of which are pertinent to theological concerns about commodification and the related potential decline in moral duty as a motive in social interactions. In a classic study by Tversky and Kahneman, participants were asked to choose between two hypothetical solutions to the supposed outbreak of a rare disease infecting six hundred patients. In this imaginary scenario, treatment program A would result in two hundred patients living and four hundred dying, with absolute certainty. Treatment program B had a one-third chance of saving all six hundred patients and a two-thirds chance of all patients dying. From the standpoint of rational choice theory, the expected probabilistic value of each program is the same: two hundred patients on average live. What Tversky and Kahneman found, however, is that when presented with plans in terms of how many patients were expected to live, participants preferred the risk-averse program A. When participants were presented with potential casualties, they preferred program B. The authors found comparable outcomes across a wide range of experiments, prompting them to conclude that "individuals might have a

---

39 Searle, *The Construction of Social Reality*, 26–28.
40 Searle, *The Construction of Social Reality*, 46.

different preference in a different framing of the same problem."⁴¹ In short, the way you present a decision impacts the choice that will be made—as, for example, in deciding whether to pick up your children from day care on time.

For the economist, these findings threaten a number of basic assumptions in economic theories of preferences and decision-making, but the findings are also significant for ethicists given evidence that certain forms of framing may trigger a sense of moral obligation in decision makers.⁴² Dan Ariely ran a number of experiments where business students were given an exam and various kinds of opportunities to cheat, including being given an answer sheet with bubbles prefilled in, opportunities to change answers, etc. Classes given these opportunities consistently reported higher scores than classes that were not given these opportunities, suggesting that cheating did occur. Ariely then repeated experiments about cheating, except the new test opportunities included an initial question that required students to transcribe the Ten Commandments prior to completing the rest of the tests. For those classes whose assignments were framed in the context of this biblical moral code, all evidence of cheating was eliminated. Similar results were found for transcribing the university code of ethics.⁴³ Based on these outcomes, we have reason to doubt that Gneezy and Rustichini's original findings about the permanence of a loss of moral duty in preschool settings. The fines at day cares reframed late pickups as a financial transaction, but dropping the fine did not offer an alternative framing narrative. I hypothesize that if parents were asked to sign some moral commitment to resist tardiness, then tardy pickups might return

---

41 Amos Tversky and Daniel Kahneman, "The Framing of Decisions and the Psychology of Choice," *Science*, New Series 211.4481 (January 30, 1981): 457. See the additional discussion in Kevin Sontheimer, "Behavioral versus Neoclassical Economics: Paradigm Shift or Generalization?" in *Handbook of Contemporary Behavioral Economics: Foundations and Developments*, ed. Morris Altman (London: Routledge, 2006), 248–49.

42 Indeed, moral considerations go far deeper than this, especially if Tversky and Kahneman's work on framing is set within the larger context of their research. Christina McRorie notes the following areas in which ethicists should respond to the findings of behavioral research: (1) a need to incorporate external prompts such as framing into any evaluation of moral agency, (2) a need to develop organizational strategies that would address the "situational anatomy" behind various ethical decisions in order to optimally encourage moral outcomes, and (3) the need to nuance existing moral theories—McRorie focuses on virtue ethics—in light of the influence of various behavioral factors such as framing. Christina McRorie, "Rethinking Moral Agency in Markets: A Book Discussion of Behavioral Economics," *Journal of Religious Ethics* 44, no. 1 (March 2016), 201–2.

43 Dan Ariely, *Predictably Irrational: The Hidden Forces That Shape Our Decisions* (New York: Harper, 2008), 206–8, 212–13.

to prestudy levels. Of course, further experimentation is required, but here again we have some reason to believe that steps can be taken to mitigate the negative effects of commodification and the corresponding loss of a sense of moral obligation. These steps cannot stand on their own as a complete Christian response to commodification, but they do suggest that such a response may not require a complete repudiation of markets.

JUST OUTCOMES AND MECHANISM DESIGN THEORY

Some economic experiments have revealed that participants want to appear fair to other participants and to the experiment designer more than they want to *be* fair. Games that mitigate the need to display fairness publicly show a decline in outcomes that have a fair distribution.[44] Appearance is no doubt related to the findings of another variant of a game known as the dictator game. In the normal version of the game, one player decides how to distribute a sum of money between themselves and another player, who has no say in the matter. In this experiment, single "dictators" could choose between an equitable split or one that benefited themselves considerably more. Only 26 percent chose the unfair distribution. Experimenters then ran a variant of the game where two dictators had to decide the outcome. If either of them chose the equitable outcome, then that was how the money was split. Both had to choose the unfair distribution in order to receive it. Surprisingly, in the context of this diffusion of responsibility where each player could rely on the other to do the right thing and where neither would bear the guilt alone for an unfair distribution, 65 percent of the teams chose the unfair distribution.[45] These experiments reveal that the outcomes of economic interactions often depend on the type of mechanism used to establish the economic outcome. Where individuals have clear, undiffused responsibility and where they are publicly visible when making their choice, they are more likely to bring about fair economic outcomes.

It is quite common for theological critics of capitalist markets to make their case based on the unjust outcomes that capitalism fosters. Consider, for example, representatives from Latin American liberation theology, though we could easily consider many other schools of thought here. Jon Sobrino

---

44 Cooper and Kagel, "Other-Regarding Preferences," 246–47.
45 Cooper and Kagel, "Other-Regarding Preferences," 249.

is quite clear on this point: "the manifestation of antilife" is a "historical product of human wills," those wills that sanction and develop a "capitalism of dependence" that exploits Latin American countries and particularly those who are impoverished for the enrichment of the Global North.[46] Even a second-generation liberation theologian like Jung Mo Sung, who generally looks more favorably on markets than his predecessors do, can describe capitalism and its market logic as requiring "human sacrifices," such as those who die as a result of poverty or those who die due to wars designed to protect capitalist markets from communist incursion.[47] For many Latin American liberationists, capitalist markets harm those who are poor for the benefit of those who are rich, requiring correction through government intervention and the use of socialist policies.

Theologians who would defend capitalism, on the other hand, are quick to point to data that suggests capitalism is helping those who are poor. Jay Richards offers a typical response to the claim that markets produce unjust economic distributions: relative inequality is not necessarily evil, he says, but absolute poverty, where people struggle to live, is.[48] He states, "If we really want to help the poor, we need to get our eyes off decoys and focus on the real problem—*poverty*—and its only known solution: creating wealth."[49] On this reading, liberation theologians rightly are outraged at poverty but wrongly diagnose the problem. As Chad Brand and Tom Pratt argue, "A marketplace of commerce is necessary to the production of adequate wealth for access to it on a wide enough basis to reach all people."[50] Capitalism produces wealth, and wealth is the best means of fighting poverty—"a rising tide lifts all boats," as Kennedy once argued. There is no actual rising tide, theologians like Joerg

---

46 Jon Sobrino, *The True Church and the Poor*, trans. Matthew J. O'Connell (Maryknoll, NY: Orbis, 1999), 166.

47 Jung Mo Sung, *Desire, Market, and Religion* (London: SCM, 2007), 90–91. Unlike his predecessors, Sung recognizes that there is a role for markets and for wealth generation through markets. Therefore, he argues that there is a need to transition liberation theology from a contestatory theology criticizing capitalism to an administrative theology that recognizes the need to use markets in some contexts to generate wealth. See Sung, *Desire, Market, and Religion*, 100–154.

48 Richards, *Money, Greed, and God*, 87–92, 104–9.

49 Richards, *Money, Greed, and God*, 110.

50 Chad Brand and Tom Pratt, *Seeking the City: Wealth, Poverty, and Political Economy in Christian Perspective* (Grand Rapids, MI: Kregel, 2013), 29.

Rieger respond.[51] And so the argument circles back and forth in seeming endless dispute.

Contrary to many theological debates, it is not clear that markets automatically produce just or unjust outcomes. In fact, many specific features of a given market determine the nature of the outcomes for different participants in that market—small changes may shift outcomes from being unjust to being just. Nowhere is this as clear as in the emerging discipline of market design. As Alvin Roth, a Nobel-Prize-winning founder of the discipline of market design, summarizes, "Market design helps solve problems that existing marketplaces haven't been able to solve naturally."[52] Take, for example, the case of access to financial markets among those who are extremely poor. To my knowledge, economist Muhammad Yunus was not drawing on the formal theory of market design, but he illustrates what this theory is about when he intentionally designed a new financial market for those who are impoverished. Access to financial markets provides individuals with the opportunity to take out loans, which in turn can be used to open or expand businesses and thereby increase income. Unfortunately, financial markets have historically been closed to those who are poor for many reasons. Small loans do not cover the transaction costs of writing loans at traditional institutions like banks. Those suffering under absolute poverty lack collateral to secure the loan. Often, they are unable even to sign their names on loan documents.[53] There is a clear problem here: poor people would benefit tremendously from access to loans, yet they are unable to access typical financial markets. Yunus responded to this problem by designing a new sort of financial market: microfinance. Poor people could receive loans without collateral. Lending was typically made to

---

51 Joerg Rieger, *No Rising Tide: Theology, Economics, and the Future* (Minneapolis: Fortress, 2009). Rieger appeals to "the logic of the downturn" to claim that much financial growth is a result of enthusiasm in financial markets that often lacks a basis in reality. Rieger is not convinced that economic data truly shows adequate gains in the elimination of absolute poverty. From my standpoint, Rieger's economic analysis is underdeveloped, but a more compelling case can be found in Joseph E. Stiglitz, *Making Globalization Work* (New York: Norton, 2007). Regardless, one objective of this work is to reorient the conversation away from such macroeconomic concerns.

52 Alvin E. Roth, *Who Gets What—and Why? The New Economics of Matchmaking and Market Design* (Boston: Houghton Mifflin, 2015), 7.

53 Yunus's initial conversations with bankers about obtaining credit for those who are poor is quite illustrative of the problems faced by poor people. See Muhammad Yunus, *Banker to the Poor: Micro-Lending and the Battle against World Poverty* (New York: Public Affairs, 1999), 45–57.

groups, and group members all had to repay loans in order to be eligible for future loans. Such group lending led to accountability and high repayment rates on uncollateralized loans so that loan programs could continue. Offices and paperwork were abandoned in favor of field workers, cutting transaction costs. Suddenly, finance was available to those who were impoverished, with demonstrable success, though even here positive outcomes were not automatic.[54]

Microfinance is not a silver bullet—additional work is required to help those who are absolutely poor, and microfinance does not work in all situations. In particular, it struggles to foster the emergence of a middle class, an important component of a healthy economy. Yet this example illustrates my basic claim. Though the simple presence of capitalist financial markets does not automatically help those who are absolutely poor in all circumstances, with intentional market design, markets *can* be oriented to helping those who are impoverished, with demonstrable success. Here again, we find that the outcome of markets is contingent on a number of factors. Markets do not automatically lead to exploitation, but it is also true that a rising tide may not raise all boats.

ONCE MORE ON MARKET DESIGN: THE KIDNEY EXCHANGE

Another example from market design theory will illustrate the complexity of moral formation in the marketplace. One of the great supposed successes of market design is the implementation of kidney markets. Alvin Roth played a central role in designing the New England Program for Kidney Exchange, a market designed to facilitate the exchange of kidneys between potential donors and recipients. The market arose because many family members are willing to donate kidneys to a sick family member who needs a transplant, but often such family members are not a match and are therefore unable to

---

54 See the discussion in Dean Karlan and Jacob Appel, *More than Good Intentions: How a New Economics Is Helping Solve Global Poverty* (New York: Dutton, 2011), 65–98. Karlan and Appel survey a number of economic studies that reveal that microcredit can provide financial security, encourage community development, and considerably increase the profits of small businesses. These benefits are not automatic, and not all poor people will benefit from access to microfinance markets. Most significantly, though, evidence suggests that direct mentoring in business principles can play a significant role in increasing the efficacy of microfinance.

donate their kidney. In response to this problem, economists built a market that could match pairs of patients and their willing family donors such that the donor from one family could provide a kidney to the patient in another and vice versa.[55] Eventually such matching developed into a complex, multiparty matching system involving dozens of patients. In order to facilitate such exchanges, economists had to develop a matching mechanism. The matching mechanism for such donations drew on several existing algorithms and a model for equilibrium in a certain type of game theory simulating the housing market. With such models in mind, economists could construct a donor-matching system and facilitate the exchange of kidneys on a market in New England.[56] This project saved the lives of many medical patients who would otherwise have died. From a purely consequentialist perspective, this appears to be a clearly moral outcome. Yet things are more complicated than they seem.

The theological response of D. Stephen Long is typical of the skepticism many theologians would express. Long is concerned about a "market for bodily organs," for "even if this mechanism facilitates more efficient exchanges . . . something seems to have been lost."[57] Efficiency is gained, but virtue is lost, in particular "the virtue of charity toward friend and neighbor."[58] In part, Long's objection stems from a misunderstanding—he appears to assume that such a market is based on the price mechanism, merely seeking to find a price at which a donor would be willing to sell a kidney instead of give one out of love. In fact, selling organs is illegal in the United States, so the market for kidneys does not involve prices at all.[59] Thus, the problem isn't the commodification of organs, nor is the problem the reduction of moral obligation to self-interested reception of payment. Nevertheless, Long's questions about efficiency do raise some important issues.

Consider two different possible formations of the market for organs. The first is known as a trading cycle, which involves several parties committing a

---

55 Alvin E. Roth, "The Art of Designing Markets," *Harvard Business Review* 85, no. 10 (October 2007): 118–26.

56 Tayfun Sönmez and M. Utku Ünver, "Market Design for Kidney Exchange," in *The Handbook of Market Design*, ed. Nir Vulkan, Alvin E. Roth, and Zvika Neeman (Oxford: Oxford University Press, 2013), 93–94.

57 D. Stephen Long, Nancy Ruth Fox, and Tripp York, *Calculated Futures: Theology, Ethics, and Economics* (Waco, TX: Baylor University Press, 2007), 61–62.

58 Long, Fox, and York, *Calculated Futures*, 61.

59 Roth, *Who Gets What?*, 31.

simultaneous trade. For the sake of illustration, consider three individuals—Matthew, Samantha, and Ricardo. Each needs a kidney, and each has a willing donor, but Matthew's wife has a kidney that is a match for Samantha, not for Matthew. Samantha's sister can only give to Ricardo, and Ricardo's son is conveniently a match for Matthew. In this market, each donor can give a donation to another out of love for their relative, who will receive a kidney in return. As Roth notes, surgeries must be completed simultaneously: "With non-simultaneous surgeries, in a conventional exchange between two pairs, a donor might renege and leave the potential recipient in the lurch."[60] In other words, Matthew's wife might donate to Samantha, but Samantha's sister backs out, so no one else receives a kidney. Simultaneous surgery is key here. Note several features of this exchange. First, the emphasis on simultaneity is rooted in a lack of trust, which this system may perpetuate. More in line with Long's concern is that the love shown is different from the virtue of charity that Long considers. A donor gives a kidney to a stranger not out of love for the stranger as a neighbor but in the self-interest of not losing a close loved one. The outcome is lives saved, but moral formation in the process might be problematic.

An alternative form of kidney exchange known as the transplant chain may allow for a different sort of moral formation. A transplant chain begins with "living potential donors interested in giving a kidney to anyone who needed one."[61] Under such circumstances, the first kidney given is an act of love (*caritas*), unconditionally given to an as-of-yet unknown neighbor. When the recipient of such a kidney is already registered for the trading-cycle market paired with a potential donor, that donor has a decision to make. Their loved one no longer needs a kidney and they are under no obligation to give, but through the market, the donor can still find a match and often chooses to do so. In fact, Roth describes one such chain that began with a donor giving in an act of love and continued for thirty-seven different patients, ending with a recipient who did not have any potential donor to continue the chain.[62] The response evoked in a transplant chain is not based on a lack of trust. It, in fact, prompts those who had delayed giving a kidney in the hope of reciprocation to move away from required reciprocation to a gratuitous gift in response to a gratuitous gift, imaging the gratuitous gift of Christ's life for the Christian, which is the basis for Christian love (1 John 4:19). Further analysis is certainly possible, but the distinction

---

60 Roth, *Who Gets What?*, 43.
61 Roth, *Who Gets What?*, 41.
62 Roth, *Who Gets What?*, 43–45.

between chain and cycle kidney markets reveals that even a market with positive moral outcomes like saving lives may have different impacts on character formation given the particular market process designed and implemented.

MARKETS AND MORAL FORMATION

We have seen considerable economic evidence for the fact that markets and economics can shape participants in morally significant ways. Evidence suggests that under certain circumstances, markets can foster trust and trustworthiness, but they also tempt individuals to pursue profit through manipulation and deception. The moral formation that occurs through market interactions is often heavily influenced by institutions, social norms, and the conditions under which such interactions occur. Economic exchanges in a market context can also affect the desires and motives of individuals. The behavioral economic concept of framing reveals that the specific nature of the influence on desires depends on the conceptual framework within which an economic interaction is interpreted. Evidence suggests that it may be possible to nudge individuals toward virtue or vice through such framing efforts. Such factors cannot be taken so far as to undermine human agency and responsibility; human beings retain freedom and moral agency.[63] Similarly, the outcomes of economic interactions in a market are neither automatically just nor automatically unjust—capitalism may be able to generate wealth, but considerable effort is required to ensure that poor people benefit from such wealth production. Finally, the discipline of economics itself can have an impact on moral formation. The study of economics, particularly those forms influenced by utility maximization and rational choice theory, may cause a decline in concerns about fairness and a loss of trust, or at least it may hinder growth in such areas where growth is fostered by other disciplines. Yet the emerging field of market design opens the potential for designing markets that are more likely to produce moral outcomes and a positive formation of virtue. In short, this chapter has shown that there is a considerable reason from the discipline of economics to analyze markets theologically, recognizing that it is unlikely that capitalism and markets are as moral as defenders claim or as immoral as critics charge.

---

63 On this point, see McRorie, "Markets as Moral Contexts," 165–66.

CHAPTER 2

Method in Theological Economics

In truth there is no such thing as a value-free discipline. The attempt to make economics value-free was utterly doomed.

—Shlomo Maital[1]

At first glance, theology may seem to have little to do with economic theory. Perhaps theology deals with questions of belief, morality, and value, while theoretical economics deals with questions of fact rooted in empirical data. Even given the discoveries of behavioral and experimental economics, we might argue that these experiments have merely discovered natural characteristics of human nature, will, or society given certain context and conditions. The fact that certain economic interactions may affect the way people act, what they desire, or how they conceive of economic interactions does not automatically mean that these interactions can appropriately be the subject of theological study. The purpose of this chapter is therefore to make the case that theology can appropriately be applied at every step of economic analysis because all steps are value-laden and because theology can speak truthfully of reality.

Two primary obstacles confront any theologian attempting to address the theology of economics. The first obstacle is the risk of reducing the role of theology to establishing which moral values ought to be pursued within economic policies and market design. On this account, economics uncovers facts about the economy, and then experts from the disciplines of theology and

---

1 Shlomo Maital, "Moral Sentiments: Behavioral Economics and the Ethical Foundations of Capitalism," in Altman, *Handbook of Contemporary Behavioral Economics*, 214.

ethics can offer input on how to act given these economic studies. Therefore, the first half of this chapter will consist of a critique of a strong version of the fact/value distinction that would lead to such conclusions. I will argue that the economy is a social phenomenon such that there are no autonomous facts that the discipline of economics can uncover apart from any value-laden perspective. While I certainly do not intend to reject the notion of fact or truth, it will become clear that such ideas cannot be divorced from questions of value. This should be no surprise to Christians, given that the ultimate standards of goodness and truth converge in the divine nature (Mark 10:18; John 14:6).

A second obstacle for any theologian is to incorporate economic theory and discoveries into a theological analysis without becoming captive to any non- or anti-Christian philosophical or theological assumptions latent within that theory. Many leading schools in the theological study of economics succumb to such problems. I will illustrate the risks by referring to economic personalism and Latin American liberation theology, particularly in the methodology deployed by Clodovis Boff. These examples will reveal that any theologian analyzing the economy must recognize that all economic analysis takes place within certain intellectual and affective commitments that will ultimately shape the economy through any study of that economy. Unfortunately, the scope of this book prevents me from fully addressing this question.

This chapter is the most technical in the book, given that it delves quite deeply into the philosophy of economics and into theological methods. Those who accept my conclusions in the above paragraph may opt to skip this chapter without losing the major arc of the analysis. However, for those who remain skeptical that theology should have any voice in the analysis and construction of economics, this chapter will be an indispensable preamble for the larger argument of the work. Similarly, I hope that the scholar or student who is interested in the finer details of how to incorporate theological analysis into economics will benefit considerably from this chapter. So read on or skip to the next chapter, as led by God or by marginal utility analysis.

THE POSITIVE/NORMATIVE DISTINCTION IN THE STUDY OF ECONOMICS

If we accept a common distinction in economic textbooks, then we have reason to believe that theology has no place in evaluating economic theory.

The distinction between positive and normative economics might be used to exclude theology from economic analysis from the start. In its simplest form, the distinction between positive and normative economics is put forward as a distinction between "the actual" or positive behavior of markets and "the desired" or normative behavior of markets.[2] In other words, positive economics provides scientific analysis, while normative economics offers ethical analysis. We might interpret economic method to offer an open door through this distinction: economists admit the need for ethics in normative economics, so theology could contribute in some manner. Perhaps theology can offer ethical principles relevant to welfare economics, for example. However, this distinction also can be used to exclude theology from making a significant contribution to positive economics, which can purportedly seek a factual explanation of the economy without the need for ethical or theological analysis. Such an exclusion would greatly limit the current project.

As a theologian, I believe the scope of theology is considerable. Theology can certainly teach us about values, exploring what is good, holy, or just. However, theology is ultimately concerned with questions of truth, or, more appropriately, with the God who is Truth (John 14:6). Theology purports to offer much in the way of explaining facts about human nature, about the design of the world and the realities of sin. I also hold to objectivist metaethics, a position arguing that ethical evaluations themselves strive after objective moral facts. However, defending any of these claims would take considerable effort, and the form such a defense must take would likely do little to win over any economically minded reader who is informed by the positive/normative distinction in economics. Though I will assume throughout the text that theology and ethics can both provide facts, I will here argue a much more modest claim to dismantle the positive/normative distinction: positive or descriptive economics cannot be completely detached from values and normative economics. Such modest aspirations alone are enough to warrant theologians a seat at the table for any level of economic analysis.

In recent decades, the long-standing distinction between positive and normative economics has come under considerable philosophical criticism. Though it is true that economic theory seeks to discover facts while economic policy is often more attentive to questions of values, it is increasingly apparent that there is no sharp distinction between facts and values in economics.

---

2 Gary S. Becker, *Economic Theory* (New York: Alfred A. Knopf, 1971), 3.

Policies are constrained by factual parameters, and theory is value-laden. This means that theology cannot automatically be excluded from economic analysis because of its ethical dimension. In fact, if values are smuggled into purportedly objective economic theory, this is all the more reason for theologians and ethicists to address economic concerns. In this section, I will survey recent philosophical arguments that undermine a strong version of the positive/normative distinction that would deny theology access to positive economics. By the end of this section, it should be clear that theology can and must have some role in economic analysis if economics is to be done in a Christian manner.

The idea of the positive/normative distinction historically developed in two forms. The first builds on what is often called Hume's guillotine and uses notions derived from logical positivism in the early twentieth century. Hume distinguished between statements of fact describing what "is" and statements of obligation that describe what "ought to be."[3] Hume suggests that there is no way to move from "is" to "ought" and that there is therefore an insurmountable division between statements of fact and statements of value. Such a division assumed, of course, that there are no factual value statements. Logical positivists, drawing in part on Hume's ideas, strengthened the claim by appealing to a verification principle for ascertaining the meaningfulness of statements.[4] This principle of verification went through numerous forms but is perhaps best known as presented by A. J. Ayer. Ayer claimed that there are only two meaningful types of sentences: those analytic statements that are analytically true by definition, such as "all bachelors are unmarried men," or statements that are either directly or indirectly verifiable.[5] All other

---

3 David Hume, *A Treatise of Human Nature*, 2nd ed., ed. L. A. Selby-Bigge (Oxford: Clarendon Press, 1978).

4 John B. Davis, "Economists' Odd Stand on the Positive-Normative Distinction: A Behavioral Economics View," in *Oxford University Press Handbook on Professional Economic Ethics: Views from the Economics Profession and Beyond*, ed. G. DeMartino and D. McCloskey (Oxford: Oxford University Press, 2015).

5 To be directly verifiable, a statement must be an observation-statement, or it must with other observation-statements entail an observation-statement that would not be deducible from these other premises alone. Something is indirectly verifiable if it is not an observation-statement but if, with other verifiable or analytic non-observation statements, it entails an observation-statement that would not be deducible from these other premises alone.

statements, suggests Ayer, are not literally meaningful.[6] It is widely argued that economist Lionel Robbins follows the positivist approach,[7] bequeathing that strain of the positive/normative distinction to subsequent generations of economists when he claimed, "Economics deals with ascertainable facts; ethics with valuations and obligations." According to Robbins, this distinction is based on a "logical gulf" between the two that cannot be overcome.[8] Economics benefits from "verifiability by introspection and observation," while ethics is merely a matter of "thy blood or mine."[9] Paul Samuelson equally adopts the positivist approach in the first edition of his textbook when he distinguishes verifiable "meaningful theorems" in economics from those theories that rely on psychology, philosophy, and ethics.[10] If the logical positivist understanding of the positive/normative distinction is correct, the current project should be abandoned as fruitless, a mere expression of opinion at best and meaningless drivel at worst.

A second form of the positive/normative distinction emerges from the early work of Richard Whately, an economist turned Anglican archbishop who wanted to preserve a religious voice in matters of ultimate concern in the public sphere against "radicals" who wanted the utilitarian-influenced conclusions of political economy to guide all public policy.[11] Whately believed that

---

6 Alfred Jules Ayer, *Language, Truth and Logic* (London: Victor Gollancz, 1949), 13. Later revisions of the verification principle would often grant that these statements may have "grammatical meaning" but not "intelligibility" or "assertory meaning" or any number of comparable terms. The intention, though, is to suggest that these statements are not factual and do not even appear to have any propositional content. This appears to be in line with Ayer's emphasis on "literal" meaningfulness. Ayer would suggest that value statements are simply emotional in nature.

7 Some do object to this interpretation, though Robbins's ultimate position is not particularly important given that other economists—I will note Paul Samuelson below—certainly did follow a more positivist bent. For one recent different interpretation of Robbins, see David Colander and Huei-Chun Su, "Making Sense of Economists' Positive-Normative Distinction," *Journal of Economic Methodology* 22, no. 2 (June 2015): 167–69.

8 Lionel Robbins, *An Essay on the Nature and Significance of Economic Science* (London: Macmillan, 1932), 132. This gulf is expressed as the difference between "is" and "ought." Robbins, *An Essay on the Nature*, 133.

9 Robbins, *An Essay on the Nature*, 132, 134.

10 Paul Anthony Samuelson, *Foundations of Economic Analysis* (Cambridge: Harvard University Press, 1947), 4. Later editions removed this claim.

11 A. M. C. Waterman, "Whately, Senior, and the Methodology of Classical Economics," in *Economics and Religion: Are They Distinct?* ed. H. Geoffrey Brennan and A. M. C. Waterman (Norwell, MA: Kluwer Academic, 1994), 41–60; John Atherton, *Christianity and the Market: Christian Social Thought for Our Times* (London: SPCK, 1992), 104–6.

political economy is concerned with means, but theology is concerned with ends.[12] Political economy would, according to this logic, provide various policy options along with the raw data to assess the effectiveness of these policies, but theology would determine which policy paths were morally permissible and which would result in the theologically desirable economic ends.

Whately's approach is distinct from the logical positivist understanding of the positive/normative distinction because it allows for the possibility of genuine and meaningful theological knowledge playing a role in economics. In fact, some recent theologians still accept a version of Whately's positive/normative distinction. John Atherton suggests it is "one of the great misfortunes of Christian history" that theologians and church leaders have not recognized "the relative autonomy of economic and political thought" maintained through the positive/normative distinction.[13] Chad Brand and Tom Pratt argue that economics is a science that provides economic "laws," which "moral imperatives" cannot logically compel us to question. To challenge such laws would be akin to claiming it a moral imperative to believe that "two-plus-two is five."[14] Ethicists like Philip Wogaman claim that theology's role is only to provide values and a valuation of values (i.e., a ranking of which values are most important) to determine which economic paths are ethically viable.[15]

Despite endorsements from various theologians, even Whatley's interpretation of the fact/value distinction would be disastrous for the current project. On this account, theology might contribute to policy choices not as a meaningless expression of personal preference but by offering genuine truth. However, theology would be barred from having anything to say about the economic "facts" and thereby ultimately from any input in the sort of experimental discoveries covered in chapter 1. Ultimately, Whatley's version of the positive/normative distinction points toward a realm of autonomous facts independent from God—except perhaps insofar as he caused the universe in which they are attained—and an understanding of religious statements as value statements but certainly not as the human accounts of God's factual redemptive acts in the world. If theology is at all concerned about

---

12 Atherton, *Christianity and the Market*, 105.
13 Atherton, *Christianity and the Market*, 108.
14 Brand and Pratt, *Seeking the City*, 836–38.
15 J. Philip Wogaman, *Economics and Ethics: A Christian Inquiry* (Philadelphia: Fortress, 1985), 2, 6, 11.

a God who works in the real world, then theology cannot remain silent on the facts about this world, even if the facts are of an economic nature. Since markets shape human beings in ways that are relevant to God's redemptive shaping of humans, excluding markets from theological analysis would create a substantial problem for anyone seeking to pursue sanctification in a market context. Though theology cannot replace economics as a discipline, it must be able to have input at all stages of economic analysis instead of only providing ethical parameters for policies derived from already developed economic models and theories.

As it turns out, there are strong reasons for doubting that a distinction between positive and normative approaches can perfectly correspond to a distinction between facts and values. Consider a basic neoclassical economic "fact" such as "increases in a price of a good A results in a decrease in demand for that good, *ceteris paribus*."[16] Like any theoretical foundation for any economic description, this claim depends on, to quote Pemberton and Finn, certain "basic assumptions that are value-laden and not value-free. In addition, since these assumptions are starting points, they are unproved and, at least within the science of economics, unprovable."[17] In this case, there is a certain theory of the rationality of various economic agents behind the claim that increases in price reduce demand. Rational agents are those who maximize utility. An increase in price of A—for the sake of ease, suppose A = apples—will allow a consumer on a fixed budget to buy less of other goods if that consumer continues consuming the same quantity of apples. This reduces utility. The rationality of utility maximization indicates that certain consumers will shift to a new bundle of goods away from their current bundle along what economists call an indifference curve in order to buy a different bundle of goods with a lower quantity of apples that provides a higher utility than

---

16 Such a statement would not apply to a good for which there is fixed demand or a price elasticity of demand equal to zero.

17 Prentiss L. Pemberton and Daniel Rush Finn, *Toward a Christian Economic Ethic: Stewardship and Social Power* (Minneapolis: Winston Press, 1985), 123. In fact, there is some statistical data that suggests that increases in price in many circumstances may result in increases in consumption. For example, when nineteenth-century bread prices rose, poor people bought more bread than when prices were low and they had enough money left over after buying the necessary bread to consume meat. High bread prices did not leave adequate funds to buy meat, so excess bread was purchased instead. Jonathan Schlefer, *The Assumptions Economists Make* (Cambridge: Harvard University Press, 2012), 88. Though price increases may result in increased consumption for a number of reasons, economists tend to use the term *Giffin goods* to explain the situation.

that which would be received by continuing to consume the same quantity of apples. In other words, if apples get too expensive, people will start to buy oranges so that they can still afford other foods at the grocery store to which they are accustomed; customers would be less happy leaving the store with apples if it meant they could not also buy steak. The problem with this assumption is that such rationality theory offers an interpretation, not a descriptive "fact" of how economic agents operate,[18] and it is unclear how an economist could even prove that agents were making choices based on utility.[19] Lionel Robbins himself objected to the unverifiability of such utility analysis,[20] and subsequent efforts at theories of "revealed preference" and other alternatives face equal challenges concerning verifiability.[21]

Rationality theories are neither purely factual accounts of economic agency nor purely ethical value statements about how an agent is morally obligated

---

18 Aggregate data of economic decisions is not particularly helpful in demonstrating the truthfulness of rationality theories. This is because microeconomic theories of rationality treat variables like prices, inflation, or unemployment as given—they do not change in these theories. Macroeconomic aggregate data, on the other hand, is what actually determines such variables endogenously. Reza Salehnejad, *Rationality, Bounded Rationality and Microfoundations: Foundations of Theoretical Economics* (New York: Palgrave Macmillan, 2007), 60. Microeconomic demonstrations of individual rationality are also flawed, as is demonstrated in numerous behavioral studies. For example, see Ariely, *Predictably Irrational*. Rationality therefore appears to be more of an assertion than a fact. There are other examples of economic "facts" that appear to be largely assertions. For example, Robert Nelson points out that neoclassical appeals to the "market mechanism" are tautological and not scientifically demonstrated. Robert H. Nelson, *Economics as Religion: From Samuelson to Chicago and Beyond* (University Park: Pennsylvania State University Press, 2001), 58.

19 Preferences, beliefs, and utility are not easily measured, and the three variables themselves are entangled in such a way as to make it impossible to distinguish them. Models are generally grounded on loose empirical observations, not rigorous analysis of data. Roger Backhouse, *Truth and Progress in Economic Knowledge* (Cheltenham, UK: Edward Elgar, 1997), 208.

20 Lionel Robbins, "Interpersonal Comparisons of Utility: A Comment," *Economic Journal* 48 (1938): 625–41.

21 For revealed preference, the problem is rooted in a lack of adequate interpretive rules. For time-sequenced tests of revealed preferences, the researcher has no way of discerning the baseline set of preferences or of discerning whether preferences change for reasons other than the pertinent variables being empirically studied. Apart from these elements, a given interpretation of revealed preferences cannot be conclusively determined to signify one thing as opposed to another. Timothy P. Roth, *The Present State of Consumer Theory: The Implications for Social Welfare Theory*, 3rd ed. (Lanham, MD: University Press of America, 1998), 35–37.

to act. Instead, such theories offer a sort of normative analysis describing how economic agents should act if they desire to be rational according to some definition.[22] The example of economic theories of rationality illustrates what is the case in any sort of description rooted in theoretical analysis: there are unprovable and often value-laden claims underlying the analysis that prevent a sharp fact/value distinction.[23] This is even the case with the philosophical program of the logical positivists, as the verification principle itself appears to be neither empirically verifiable nor clearly analytically included in the definition of *meaningfulness*, at least in any ordinary usage of the term.[24] Any positive description of "facts" would thus appear to depend on nonfacts in a way that undermines a strong distinction between the facts and values of the sort advocated by the logical positivist interpretation of the positive/normative distinction.

Given the unprovable and often value-laden foundations for models and theories, is it not still possible to affirm a pure positive economics that simply avoids using such models and theories? This is the suggestion of Geoffrey Brennan, who believes that "the epistemological autonomy of positive economics may be bought at a fairly high price."[25] Brennan claims that this high price may ultimately require sacrificing so many key elements of economic theory that the remaining elements are no longer particularly useful to the normative theory that now contains most of the material traditionally analyzed by economists. Nevertheless, presumably Brennan would admit that pure data collection on interest rates, expenditures, capital investment, price fluctuations, and so forth could be classified as a positive economics dealing with facts as opposed to a normative economics that is enmeshed with value judgments. However, even this solution faces three very significant problems.

---

22 D. Wade Hands, "The Positive-Normative Dichotomy and Economics," in *Philosophy of Economics*, ed. Uskali Mäki (Amsterdam: Elsevier, 2012), 219–39.

23 I have been using *value-laden* in a somewhat imprecise fashion; at times, there are ethical assumptions that make theory value-laden, while at other times, "epistemic values" concerning what ought to be the case in reasoning are assumed. On varieties of values, see Hilary Putnam, *The Collapse of the Fact/Value Dichotomy and Other Essays* (Cambridge: Harvard University Press, 2002), 30–31.

24 If the verificationist proposes that this is what the definition of *meaningful* should be, one need only disagree to dismiss the entire verificationist paradigm. Alvin Plantinga, *God and Other Minds: A Study of the Rational Justification of Belief in God* (Ithaca, NY: Cornell University Press, 1967), 167–68.

25 H. Geoffrey Brennan, "The Impact of Theological Predispositions on Economics: A Commentary," in Brennan and Waterman, *Economics and Religion*, 168–69.

First, in the real world, there are so many possible facts that could be collected that the selection of specific facts as significant requires certain value judgments that are based on our presuppositions. In this way, our presuppositions shape the outcome of any "factual" analysis by restricting the domain of possible relevant facts and therefore of possible conclusions.[26] Second, even within a specific set of selected data, various categories of description for the data are still possible. A particular economic action can simultaneously be profitable, unjust, unexpected, utility-maximizing, immoral, and culturally aberrant. Choosing one category of description over another will not be a value-neutral exercise.[27] Third, even when we choose descriptive terminology, many terms are what Hilary Putnam calls "thick ethical concepts." These are concepts such as "cruel" or "rude" in which fact and value are entangled. The terms can be used in a purely descriptive way in an accurate and meaningful fashion, but they are also value-laden in a way that suggests there is no sharp fact/value distinction.[28]

Perhaps the positive/normative distinction can be salvaged without resorting to drastic measures like those suggested by Brennan. Mark Blaug argues that we cannot claim that there are no objective statements because that very statement would then be objective, requiring us to lapse into pure subjectivity, a point I certainly concede.[29] Blaug admits that there is "no absolutely watertight distinction between positive and normative economics" but suggests that the distinction is methodological and points to "an ideal at which to aim."[30] While values do tend to seep into positive analysis, the main distinction between positive and normative approaches lies in the fact that positive analysis places a priority on producing and testing falsifiable theories in line with scientific methodology, while normative analysis depends on value judgments that cannot be adjudicated in this manner.[31] Such a methodological distinction appears to offer the hope of evading the problem of unprovable

---

26 Donald A. Hay, "On Being a Christian Economist," in *Christianity and the Culture of Economics*, ed. Donald A. Hay and Alan Kreider (Cardiff: University of Wales Press, 2001), 167.

27 John P. Tiemstra et al., *Reforming Economics: Calvinist Studies on Methods and Institutions* (Lewiston, NY: Edwin Mellen Press, 1990), 69.

28 Putnam, *Collapse*, 35–43.

29 Mark Blaug, *The Methodology of Economics: Or How Economists Explain*, 2nd ed. (Cambridge: Cambridge University Press, 1992), 116.

30 Blaug, *The Methodology of Economics*, 121.

31 Blaug, *The Methodology of Economics*, 119, 134.

foundations in positive economics by suggesting that they may be falsifiable if their predictions are not validated. This methodological dichotomy would then allow for a positive/normative distinction in line with Whately's views, where normative analysis could be open to a different methodology, perhaps one where theology could be utilized.

While plausible at first look, in the end, Blaug's proposal fails because, unlike the physical sciences, economic theories and predictions effect what they predict.[32] The changes in behavior among economics students discussed in chapter 1 provide warrant for this claim, and I will provide further examples later in the chapter. What the influence of predictions on the economy means is that, methodologically speaking, falsification may not be possible. A theory that may not accurately represent the reality described at the time the theory is developed may have influenced that reality in such a way that the representation is far more accurate by the time predictions can be tested. If this occurs, an originally untrue theory will not be falsified but will instead change the world it describes. As D. Stephen Long points out, economists' discussions of facts are often a matter of *poesis*, discussions of "a brute *factum*" forgetful of the associated creative act (*facere*—to make) bringing about such facts.[33] The creative nature of economics results in what James K. A. Smith has aptly called the perpetual "contestability of the empirical."[34]

Here one might stop to object that a theologian making such arguments is overstating the case. John Lunn and Robin Klay, for example, object to what they view as "postmodern" attempts by some Christian economists, theologians, and philosophers to challenge the positive/normative distinction. Lunn and Klay argue that making a statement about historical growth in the money supply and making a statement about how the money supply ought to change in the coming year are clearly two different sorts of statements.[35] This may well be the case, but admitting that economists have different objectives in mind when doing positive and normative analyses, or granting that positive

---

32 Peter L. Danner, *The Economic Person: Acting and Analyzing* (Lanham, MD: Rowman and Littlefield, 2002), vii. Cf. Lorna Gold, *New Financial Horizons: The Emergence of the Economy of Communion* (Hyde Park, NY: New City Press, 2010), 25.

33 Long, Fox, and York, *Calculated Futures*, 103–4.

34 Smith, "The 'Ecclesial Critique,'" 8.

35 John Lunn and Robin Klay, "The Neoclassical Economic Model in a Postmodern World," *Christian Scholars Review* 24, no. 2 (1994): 155. Cf. Blaug, *The Methodology of Economics*, 115.

and normative statements have different intended meanings, does not require an acceptance of the claim that a positive/normative distinction corresponds to a fact/value distinction. Nor, for that matter, does such a difference in intention require that theological ethics can only contribute to economic analysis by providing value parameters after the facts have been described by the economists. I am not after a "postmodern" elimination of objective truth—whatever Lunn and Klay may mean by that particular bogeyman. I merely intend to show that one cannot describe the facts of a social science like economics in a way that is not already value-laden and therefore subject to ethical analysis.

To be precise, I intend only to object to what I will call a strong positive/normative distinction. Such a distinction is one that (a) correlates a positive/normative binary with a fact/value binary, (b) suggests that the facts uncovered by positive analysis are purely objective in the sense of being entirely distinct and autonomous from the researcher and research process, and (c) relegates religion to the realm of values and normative analysis after any factual description has already occurred—provided such normative analysis is even admissible. Such a strong distinction would overly restrict theological exploration into the formative nature of markets. If theology and ethics were reduced to questions of value in normative economics, this study could not explore what a market is such that it may lead to moral formation. It could not evaluate and critique economic theories of rationality, discoveries from experimental economics, or design parameters for a given market in market design theory. In short, theology would be denied a real analytic role.

A weak version of the positive/normative distinction that recognized the problems in a fact/value dichotomy would fit with Lunn and Klay's description of the distinctions without shutting down our current line of questioning.[36] Indeed, some version of the distinction must be maintained, as entirely abandoning it would bring about the suspicion that the economy is infinitely malleable, purely a construct of values divorced from any material constraints. This is not the end I am seeking, first, because philosophically

---

36 For example, Edwin Dolan suggests that positive economic statements are of the form "If policy X, then outcome Y," while normative statements take the form "Outcome Y is good." Provided that positive statements of this form are recognized as potentially performative (i.e., non-objective) and value-laden, and that normative statements are recognized as potentially factual, I suspect Dolan's definition may provide precisely the sort of weak positive/normative distinction that is needed. Edwin G. Dolan, *Basic Economics* (Hinsdale, IL: The Dryden Press, 1980), 14.

speaking, plausible arguments can also be raised against collapsing facts purely into constructed values. Second, and more importantly, because we must remember that God created the material world and called it very good (Gen 1:31). Whatever material or natural constraints come into play in economic modeling, these very constraints are part of the cosmos that the Scriptures claim is waiting in "eager longing" for the final redemption toward which God is working (Rom 8:19). It is not through a denial of the material, historical, or natural constraints of the economy that theology is rendered relevant but rather through a recognition that these material, historical, and natural constraints are inescapably related to God and thus unavoidably the subject of theological analysis.

METHOD IN THEOLOGICAL ECONOMICS

The discussion of the positive/normative distinction may seem too abstract to bear much significance for many readers, some of whom may have moved on to the next chapter. Despite appearances, the stance one takes on the positive/normative distinction often leads to basic commitments that shape theological projects, often for the worse. When theological method accepts as given a certain set of economic data without theological analysis, the theologians deploying this method often incorporate certain assumptions into their theological analysis that may not be consonant with their larger theological positions. In the end, those who allow autonomous economic data to constitute the starting point for their work often reach conclusions that are predetermined because they are latent within the initial data.

The astute reader will immediately note that I am subject to the same risk. No doubt some readers have been frustrated with my surprisingly thin account of virtue, vice, moral formation, or theological method. I admit that I have taken various studies from experimental and behavioral economics at face value, granting their conclusions without considerable analysis. I do not doubt that those who may read this from the perspective of the *doux commerce* or ecclesial ethics positions noted in the introduction—never mind advocates of other nuanced theological positions ranging from distributism to feminist theologies—would raise objections to specific definitions of terms like *virtue, justice, fairness, rationality,* or *trust* as used by the various economic studies cited so far in this work. This is a valid critique, and yet I hope to both deflate it and overcome it in what follows. First, however,

I ought to illustrate how uncritical acceptance of economic data may lead to methodological problems in theology. I will demonstrate these problems with reference to two schools of thought: economic personalism and Latin American liberation theology.

Theologians often express what I have called a strong version of the positive/normative distinction by the use of terms like "socio-analytic mediation"[37] or "methodological individualism."[38] Clodovis Boff's writing on the relationship between the social sciences and theology reveals liberation theology's failure to completely escape Marxist thought, despite many liberationists' sincere efforts to do so.[39] Boff's treatment of the social sciences and theology is so influential among—especially first-generation—liberation theologians that Ivan Petrella can rightly call it "the canonical view of liberation theology's methodology."[40] Like many liberation theologians, Clodovis and his brother Leonardo Boff insist that liberation theology takes a "decidedly critical stance in relation to Marxism" that treats Christ alone as "*the* guide" and resists any "Marxist materialism and atheism."[41] Unlike many liberation theologians, however, Clodovis Boff develops a precise and influential account of how the social sciences relate to theology.

Key to Clodovis Boff's account is socio-analytic mediation, by which he means "the act by which the findings of [the social sciences] are taken up by and in theological practice." The social sciences provide content that is the "material object of political theology," but this material object is "formally

---

37 See Clodovis Boff, *Theology and Praxis: Epistemological Foundations* (Eugene, OR: Wipf and Stock, 2009), 20–66.

38 This terminology is prevalent in economic personalism, as discussed below.

39 Enrique D. Dussel, "Theology of Liberation and Marxism," trans. Robert Barr, in *Mysterium Liberationis: Fundamental Concepts of Liberation Theology*, ed. Ignacio Ellacuría and Job Sobrino (Maryknoll, NY: Orbis, 1993), 85–102. Dussel is more willing than some to claim that liberation theology "accepts and adopts" Marxism, implying use and transformation, particularly a rejection of dialectical materialism (87). Surveying specific liberation theologians, Dussel argues that some use Marx as a mere "instrument," but others take an entire "categorical framework" (91). Yet this adoption of Marxism is only "in a *certain* way" (emphasis in original), never blindly assuming an entire Marxist perspective, and always committed first to the faith.

40 Ivan Petrella, *The Future of Liberation Theology: An Argument and Manifesto* (Burlington, VT: Ashgate, 2004), 26. Petrella here contrasts Boff's "canonical view" with what he calls the "marginal view."

41 Leonardo Boff and Clodovis Boff, *Introducing Liberation Theology*, trans. Paul Burns (Maryknoll, NY: Orbis, 1988), 28.

speaking . . . pretheological."[42] Theology is autonomous from the social sciences in that it has "its own constituents and raison d'être." However, Boff argues that theology is also dependent on the social sciences, particularly because theology is embedded in certain material and historical elements including "conditions of production" and concrete "theoretical and technical tools."[43] Here it appears that Boff is poised to insist, as I have above, that any factual account of the economy contains within it certain commitments to values and certain assumptions about the nature of reality. Indeed, Boff even goes so far as to suggest that there is no "absolutely immediate reading of the real," arguing instead that value-laden theory always relates to facts discussed by empirical analysis.[44] Unfortunately, Boff takes away with one argument the space for theology that he has created with another argument.

The most problematic aspect of Boff's thought is that he tries to divide theological analysis of the social sciences into three temporal stages while still affirming that theology and the social sciences share a "relationship of constitution" with an "organic interchange" between theology and the social sciences. He argues, "What for the sciences of the social is product, finding, or construct, will be taken up in the theological field as raw material."[45] This raw material is "worked" by concepts through cognition to result in theory.[46] In other words, the raw data from the social sciences is hermeneutically mediated through theological concepts to produce theory such as liberation theology. Two problems arise here: First, Boff treats the "raw material" as somehow "already elaborated and transformed" by "cognition"[47] while also claiming that theology can shape this raw material into new theory. This approach fails to recognize that insofar as this raw material already results in historical praxis and is already theoretically understood, it is itself dependent on and indissociable with a social imaginary that makes such praxis and understanding possible. In order for theology to address this data as raw material, theology itself must already occupy an imaginary within which such data is intelligible as relevant material. As discussed above, even the way that data is named or selected as relevant is already value-laden and theological. Any later theoretical reworking of the data will already be captive to prior

---

42 Boff, *Theology and Praxis*, xxiv.
43 Boff, *Theology and Praxis*, 15–16.
44 Boff, *Theology and Praxis*, 21.
45 Boff, *Theology and Praxis*, 3–31.
46 Boff, *Theology and Praxis*, 72–73.
47 Boff, *Theology and Praxis*, 71.

theological commitments and therefore unlikely to truly escape either Marxism or capitalism, depending on the source of the data. In short and despite his disclaimers to the contrary, Boff treats raw data as too separable from ethical and theological values embedded within such data. This objection has rightly been noted by John Milbank and by liberation theologians as part of what Petrella calls the "marginal view."[48]

Boff's methodology is not as transparent as others, so let me illustrate with another problematic methodology: the methodological individualism of economic personalism. The economic personalism especially associated with the (now-defunct) Center for Economic Personalism and the Acton Institute[49] is on the opposite end of the political and economic spectrum from liberation theology. Economic personalists draw on free-market economists, proclaim the virtues of globalization, and decry class analysis in favor of what they call methodological individualism. Despite these substantive differences in content, economic personalists seek the same balance, in this case rejecting Marxism and critically appropriating certain varieties of capitalism.[50] Like liberation theology, personalism ultimately embodies the same fundamental flaws concerning the relationship between fact and value.

Patricia Donohue-White, Stephen Grabill, Christopher Westley, and Gloria Zúñiga's *Human Nature and the Discipline of Economics* is the most focused on methodological concerns of the three major texts emerging from the

---

48 John Milbank, *Theology and Social Theory*, 2nd ed. (Malden, MA: Blackwell, 2006), 253. Milbank objects that Boff reduces theology to the task of "extrapolat[ing] regulatively the significance already implied in the social scientific account." Petrella, *Future of Liberation Theology*, 31. Petrella particularly associates Jung Mo Sung with the "marginal view." He notes that this approach seeks to eliminate hermeneutic mediation because "reality is already interpreted in accordance with liberation theology's values and goals within the socioanalytic mediation, that is, before the theologian moves to the hermeneutic stage."

49 Here, work by Peter Danner and Edward O'Boyle should be distinguished from the writings explicitly associated with the (now-defunct) Center for Economic Personalism. Danner and O'Boyle's works spend less time discussing methodology, so it is less clear whether they commit the same mistakes. See Edward J. O'Boyle, *Personalist Economics: Moral Convictions, Economic Realities, and Social Action* (Boston: Kluwer Academic Publishers, 1998); Danner, *The Economic Person*.

50 In Richard Bayer's words, economic personalism can be seen as "pursuing . . . a critical affirmation of market institutions and practices" that challenges normal individualistic interpretations of capitalism while fully rejecting the collectivism of Marxism. Richard C. Bayer, *Capitalism and Christianity: The Possibility of Christian Personalism* (Washington, DC: Georgetown University Press, 1999), 102.

Center for Economic Personalism. At the foundation of economic personalist methodology is a sharp distinction between the social sciences and theology:

> A theologian reading the chapter "Economic Models of Human Nature" must recognize the autonomy of economics as a discipline and the particularity of the methods appropriate to that discipline. In doing so, the theologian recognizes that, qua theologian, he or she has nothing to say regarding the adequacy of the methods and principles internal to the discipline of economics, including the way in which models of human nature are established and employed. Any critical remarks relative to the models of human nature employed must originate external to the discipline of economics and thus are not criticisms that question the *usefulness* of such models for the purposes of economists.[51]

Such a distinction appears to assume a realm of pure nature fully dissociated from any supernatural *telos* and thus sheltered from the scrutiny of theologians. On this account of the relationship between economics and theology, the economist has access to some domain of facts that lie outside of the purview of any value concerns of the theologian. Admittedly, the distinction between the domains of the theologian and the economist is a bit muddled in its deployment, so the problem may only be apparent. For example, the authors also argue that theology can offer economics a more robust understanding of human nature that provides better predictive accuracy,[52] where prediction is the basis for the "validity of a[n economic] model."[53] Improvements in accuracy seem to suggest that theologians can in fact assess the success of economic models in terms of the internal predictive objective of economists and can comment on the usefulness of particular conceptions of human nature within the field of economics.

---

51 Patricia Donohue-White et al., *Human Nature and the Discipline of Economics: Personalist Anthropology and Economic Methodology* (Lanham, MD: Lexington Books, 2002), 69.

52 Predictive accuracy is a major goal of economic personalism. Gregory Beabout et al., *Beyond Self-Interest: A Personalist Approach to Human Action* (Lanham, MD: Lexington Books, 2002), 3, 12, 104; Donohue-White et al., *Human Nature*, 60, 94. Donohue-White et al. are admittedly confusing here in that they claim both that "if all that economists are concerned about is the predictive power of their models, then personalism cannot offer much in the way of criticism or benefit" (104) and that "an economics that takes into account the fuller picture of the person may in fact render the profession more effective, more predictive, and more realistic" (106). I have chosen to treat the negative assessment of the personalist contribution to predictive accuracy as an aberration of a larger pattern of positive affirmation of the possibility.

53 Donohue-White et al., *Human Nature*, 60.

Regardless of how the statements of economic personalists in this matter are reconciled, two major problems arise from any emphasis on the predictive roles of economic models. The first is that some economists who are internal to the discourse of economics question such predictive accuracy. Katarina Juselius outlines the problem clearly. Most economists follow a theory-first model, where models are taken to data for confirmation and are recalibrated and modified to fit the data if it does not initially confirm the model. The result is an inability to determine empirically which model is correct.[54] Mark Blaug explains that "'calibration' as a method of choosing between macroeconomic theories is, to put it mildly, something of a fraud because it simply cannot fail to confirm just about every model."[55] As the calibration method has become the dominant method in mathematical economics, prediction is far less important in justifying economic models. Even though some personalists like Gregory Gronbacher tone down their predictive aspirations to the level of a "limited degree of prediction,"[56] they insufficiently address the methodological problems that are now the subject of a growing body of economic literature.

Even setting aside the methodological problems facing prediction under the calibration approach, personalists would do well to attend to the phenomenon of performativity. As Michel Callon writes,

> Market laws are neither in the nature of humans and societies—waiting for the scientist, like a prince charming, to wake and reveal them—nor are they constructions or artefacts invented by social sciences in an effort to improvise simple frameworks explaining an opaque and complex reality. They account for regularities progressively enforced by the joint movement of the economy and economics.... These regularities perform behaviors and therefore have the obduracy of the real; yet in turn they are performed by these behaviors and therefore have the contingency of an artefact.[57]

---

54 Katarina Juselius, "On the Role of Theory and Evidence in Macroeconomics," in Davis and Wade, *The Elgar Companion to Recent Economic Methodology*, 405.

55 Mark Blaug, "Ugly Currents in Modern Economics," in *Fact and Fiction in Economics: Models, Realism, and Social Construction*, ed. Uskali Mäki (Cambridge: Cambridge University Press, 2002), 44.

56 Gregory M. A. Gronbacher, "The Need for Economic Personalism," *Journal of Markets and Morality* 1, no. 1 (Spring 1998): 11.

57 Michel Callon, "What Does It Mean to Say That Economics Is Performative?" in *Do Economists Make Markets?*, ed. Donald MacKenzie, Fabian Muniesa, and Lucia Siu (Princeton, NJ: Princeton University Press, 2007), 47.

As models influence policy, as they are incorporated into technology used by firms to make decisions, and as they are taught to business and economics students, they can result in actions that better conform to the models, even if the models themselves initially had limited empirical support. This means that theologians who leave the domain of facts to the economists are inadvertently ceding to economists control of the direct social construction of the economy. I will discuss performativity further in subsequent chapters.

The problem of performation must particularly be kept in mind when considering the personalist objection to the *homo economicus*. Personalists rely on the fact/value distinction when they treat *homo economicus* as a refutable fact, forgetting *homo economicus* also has a normative dimension such that the values affirmed in such a view of human nature can be infused into the economy through the performation of models, as Callon rightly notes. The *homo economicus* is not just a claim about the nature of humanity. It is also a means of disciplining that nature, of gradually conforming it to the utility-maximizing rationality that is the economic ideal. This is certainly evident in the experiment of Marwell and Ames discussed in chapter 1, among others.

A second significant problem reveals that economic personalism too sharply distinguishes between a factual domain that is the concern of economists and a value domain that belongs to the theologian. Many economic personalists—again, particularly those associated with the Center for Economic Personalism—make much of a distinction between methodological individualism and atomistic or moral individualism. Personalists draw this distinction from a number of economic sources, notably Ludwig von Mises and Friedrich Hayek.[58] Economic personalists find allies among economic approaches committed to considering the individual first and to minimizing social considerations. Personalists, many of whom are Roman Catholic, face a considerable challenge given the clear condemnation of "individualism" found in encyclicals like *Quadragessimo Anno* (§46). Here the distinction between methodological and moral individualism comes into play because personalists insist the encyclicals only condemn moral individualism or atomistic individualism.

An example illustrates how the distinction is used. Gregory Gronbacher, one-time director of the Center for Economic Personalism, argues that "moral

---

[58] Beabout et al., *Beyond Self-Interest*, 24–25; Anthony J. Santelli Jr. et al., *The Free Person and the Free Economy: A Personalist View of Market Economics* (Lanham, MD: Lexington Books, 2002), 24–25.

individualism" is "the tendency to refuse participation in community."[59] Methodological individualism has no such commitment to reject community participation. Rather, when coupled with personalist insights, methodological individualism leads not only to "a better economic science but to a humane economy."[60] Whereas moral individualism entails a refusal to morally participate in society, methodological individualism entails the ontological priority of the individual, who exists prior to the nation or any other collective.[61] This ontological priority is inescapable, but it need not entail the problematic moral commitments condemned in the encyclical tradition. Or so the argument goes.

A distinction between method and morality, or between ontology and morality, suggests that values are purely dissociable from the factual world of ontology as uncovered by a value-free science bent on uncovering ontological facts. However, as I have argued above, no such value-free science of the social is possible. To put the matter in the terminology of economic personalism, methodological individualism prioritizes the individual in models that seek to predict and analyze the economy, but the economy itself is a series of actions and habits that are only possible within a certain imaginary. This imaginary is in large part a product of language and symbols. We cannot forget that the mathematics used in economic models is itself a form of language and thus a reality quite capable of contributing to the formation of a social imaginary—more on this next chapter. Moral or atomistic individualism is a manner of posturing oneself within a particular society or economy, but this positioning receives its intelligibility from the social imaginary. It is quite possible that methodological individualism in a society so concerned with the economic can contribute to a culture where moral individualism is more prevalent, but the economic personalists largely disregard this possibility under the assumption that their factual economic science has no bearing on the moral universe within which the economy operates. Here again, too sharp a distinction between positive and normative, or fact and value, causes personalists to become too beholden to forms of individualism they would rather repudiate.

---

59 Gregory M. A. Gronbacher, "The Humane Economy: Neither Right nor Left—A Response to Daniel Rush Finn," *Journal of Markets and Morality* 2, no. 2 (Fall 1999): 256.

60 Gronbacher, "The Humane Economy," 258.

61 Gronbacher, "The Humane Economy," 255–56.

THE PLANK IN MY OWN EYE

The two examples of economic personalism and "canonical" Latin American liberation theology serve to illustrate the practical problems that come with accepting a strong version of the positive/normative distinction: values and ideas that theologians might desire to resist inadvertently can be smuggled in by means of the supposedly neutral data used to begin the analysis. As noted above, I must own my own failings here, given that I have begun this study with a number of pieces of economic evidence. I do not consider this an insurmountable problem. I have demonstrated that under *some* definition of virtues—under *some* definition of justice, or trust, or rationality—outcomes *according to this definition* can change based on the design of market interactions, the social and cultural context within which they occur, the educational background of participants, and various other psychological factors. I have not granted and do not grant that the perspectives offered by such economists on virtue, justice, trust, reason, culture, society, the economy, or human nature are always theologically acceptable. At the end of the day, these studies can serve as a starting point to prove my claim that the economy shapes us in a moral manner and that the way it shapes us can be changed. These studies cannot, however, serve as the starting point for an appropriate theology of economics, nor for a theologically informed economics themselves, at least not without serious and considerable theological analysis that I have no intention of pursuing here. Ideally, if my fundamental thesis is correct, a team of theologians and economists could begin a new series of experiments shaped from the beginning by more explicit theological commitments to begin to explore the possible structures of markets and their influence on a Christian account of virtue formation or sanctification. Sadly, such work is well beyond the scope of this book, and I can only hope to lay preliminary groundwork for such projects, whose existence depends entirely on the somewhat unlikely outcome that economists take interest in these pages. Having argued that theology necessarily has a seat at the table, I have justified the basic perspectives of parts two and three. However, before I move on to theological foundations that will allow me to engage moral formation in the marketplace from a more Christian perspective, it is necessary to explain in more detail what I mean by the word *market*, why markets are the subject of analysis, and to what extent markets can be modified and changed.

CHAPTER 3

What Is a Market?

The way goods or services are exchanged or distributed, one of the key questions that economics aims to address, depends on many factors. Some of these factors are not under our control, but some are, for instance the rules that govern how individuals or firms interact. Those rules are usually not accidental; they have been designed by, among others, policy makers or regulators. Economists usually refer to those rules as the market.
—Guillaume Haeringer[1]

The literature on the theological merits and evils of capitalism is vast yet often imprecise in the objects of its critique. There is general consensus among studies of comparative economic systems that capitalism is an economy based on private ownership and exchange through a market system,[2] but if theologi-

---

1 Guillaume Haeringer, *Market Design: Auctions and Matching* (Cambridge: MIT Press, 2017), 1.

2 Lane and Ersson classify capitalism as consisting of predominantly private ownership coupled with a predominantly market allocation mechanism; they note that "the difficult problem is, however, the extent to which *actually existing institutions* in market allocation or budget allocation come close to the ideal type starting point." Jan-Erik Lane and Svante Ersson, *Comparative Political Economy* (London: Pinter Publishers, 1990), 16. See also Steven Rosefielde, *Comparative Economic Systems: Culture, Wealth, and Power in the 21st Century* (Malden, MA: Blackwell, 2002), 42–43; Rolf Eidem and Staffan Viotti, *Economic Systems: How Resources Are Allocated* (New York: John Wiley and Sons, 1978), 3. Schnitzer and Nordyke use a much more complex definition of capitalism that includes elements such as the profit motive, competition, individualism, work ethic, and limited government. Against the definition offered by Schnitzer and Nordyke, it should be noted that capitalist economies can and in many instances do rely on cooperation instead of

cal treatments of economy are any indication, it is all too easy to forget that both property law and markets themselves can take on varied forms.[3] While theologians often grant a limited variability, few go as far as Ivan Petrella when he argues against his fellow Latin American critics of capitalism that "liberation theology will have to replace its abstract and monolithic view of capitalism with the recognition and analysis of the wide variety of market systems in actual existence in the world today."[4] Drawing on Brazilian social theorist Roberto Unger, Petrella argues that many theologians adopt the idea that there are a limited possible number of economic systems, each of which exists as an indivisible whole governed by law-like principles. Petrella rightly argues that markets can take "many different institutional forms."[5] I base my argument on this claim, arguing that we can design a wide variety of markets that will either foster or hinder moral formation. As Kenneth Barnes notes, "Capitalism is nothing more than the result of countless individual and corporate decisions, and for good or ill, the capitalism we have is the capitalism we have chosen."[6] For this reason, I tend to speak about markets instead of about capitalism or socialism.

It may sound surprising to some readers to speak about designing different forms of markets, but since the days of Adam Smith—and even earlier!—politicians have created markets. For example, in the Methuen treaty of 1703, the British convinced the Portuguese to accept textile shipments

---

competition. They can also be compatible with objectives other than profit maximization. It seems that such an approach too easily confuses capitalism with what is known as "Washington consensus" capitalism. Martin C. Schnitzer and James W. Nordyke, *Comparative Economic Systems*, 3rd ed. (Cincinnati: South-Western Publishing, 1983), 3. Joseph Stiglitz helpfully summarizes the Washington consensus as focused on "downscaling of government, deregulation, and rapid liberalization and privatization." Stiglitz, *Making Globalization Work*, 17.

3 Though I will not focus on theories of property in this book, the point is well made from a theoretical standpoint in Kathryn Tanner's work and from the standpoint of the practical complexities of property law in the work of Hernando de Soto. See Kathryn Tanner, *Economy of Grace* (Minneapolis: Fortress, 2005); Hernando de Soto, *The Mystery of Capital: Why Capitalism Triumphs in the West and Fails Everywhere Else* (New York: Basic, 2000).

4 Petrella, *Future of Liberation Theology*, 97.

5 Petrella, *Future of Liberation Theology*, 94–96.

6 While Barnes's point can certainly be nuanced by exploring who is included in the "we" that is the subject of his statement—after all, many disenfranchised or oppressed peoples may not have had a voice in shaping the variety of capitalism that we have—his larger point remains strong. Kenneth J. Barnes, *Redeeming Capitalism* (Grand Rapids, MI: Eerdmans, 2018), 1.

in return for permission to export port wine to England at a tariff level no higher than that set for French wines. This agreement immediately resulted in a new market emerging for international trade, but it also helped to increase British bullion holdings—Portuguese demand for imported textiles was much higher than British demand for imported wine.[7] Here one could object that this is not an example of market construction but of "deregulation." In point of fact, however, this is more fittingly an example of market design. As Marc Landy and Martin Levin point out, "Market design initiatives, successful or not, embody rules and regulations that are often at least as numerous and complicated as those they displace." It is therefore more proper to speak of regulation shifting from anti- to pro-competition regulations.[8] Such macroeconomic market design occurred in greater scale after the recent fall of the communist bloc. Countries of the former Soviet bloc, like Poland, the Czech Republic, Hungary, and Romania, have markets that were constructed in part by historical circumstances and in part under the guidance of Western think tanks, consultancies, and academic researchers.[9] The complex political process of privatization unfolded within emerging political institutions and a number of national and international interests.[10] In these and other instances, even global markets must be considered at least partly constructed as the byproduct of intentional human agency.

This chapter will explore the various aspects of market design with extensive reference to economic theory and practice. By the end of this chapter, I will demonstrate that, contrary to the myth of the spontaneous and natural market,[11] markets are often designed—if in a decentralized manner—through

---

7 Schlefer, *Assumptions*, 34–35.

8 Marc K. Landy and Martin A. Levin, "Creating Competitive Markets: The Politics of Market Design," in Landy, Levin, and Shapiro, *Creating Competitive Markets*, 5.

9 Roderick Martin, *Constructing Capitalisms: Transforming Business Systems in Central and Eastern Europe* (Oxford: Oxford University Press, 2013), 272–73. Jeffrey Sachs offers a helpful personal account of his involvement in the transition to capitalism in Poland, where he advocated the construction of a market through five pillars of policy proposals as adviser to the Polish solidarity movement: stabilization, liberalization, privatization, a social safety net, and institutional harmonization. Jeffrey D. Sachs, *The End of Poverty: Economic Possibilities for Our Time* (New York: Penguin, 2005), 109–15.

10 Martin, *Constructing Capitalisms*, 79–84.

11 This myth assumes that "a market comes into being whenever acting persons engage in exchanges.... Other things being equal, markets arise naturally and spontaneously." Santelli Jr. et al., *Free Person*, 69. See also the genealogy proposed in John Bolt,

the work of economists, corporate executives, and policymakers, among others. This fact requires that sound moral analysis move from blanket acceptance or rejection of capitalism or markets to a careful analysis of which market formations are moral and which are not. I will make the case by defining markets and then demonstrating how each aspect of a market is subject to various forms of intentional construction, illustrating with a wide range of experimental and actual examples of the principles I discuss. After providing a more extensive illustration of my argument through the two examples of tradable pollution permits and amazon.com, I will conclude the chapter and section with brief reflections on the relationship between market design and moral formation.

MARKETS AND THEIR MAKERS

While it is customary for theologians to debate the merits of capitalism—not to mention socialism or communism—"describing market economies as capitalist tells us little about their real technical and welfare potentials."[12] Further, not all market-based economies are capitalist.[13] For this reason, I will instead focus my analysis on markets, which can be shaped in a wide range of possible ways. I define a market as *an imagined space where participants voluntarily buy and sell goods through a mechanism of exchange based on certain information, including price.* Markets are imagined in the sense that social and cultural factors shape which things a market participant could conceive of buying and selling. Furthermore, those who wish to buy or sell a good must share basic conventions and expectations that make such a transaction possible. Calling markets a "space" is intentionally vague, but I

Economic Shalom: A Reformed Primer on Faith, Work, and Human Flourishing (Grand Rapids, MI: Christian's Library Press, 2013), 46–50. Bolt's claims seem more modest. Where he claims that market construction is not grasped as a whole yet we know many of the parts and can influence growth, he might be pursuing a point similar to my own. Yet I find drawing attention to construction more helpful than drawing attention to spontaneity, even if both are present.

12 Rosefielde, *Comparative Economic Systems*, 43.

13 "Despite the tendency to equate capitalism with the market, it is important to recognize that the market is not particular to capitalism; it may appear in other economic systems, even those proposed as alternatives to capitalism." Antonio González Fernández, *God's Reign and the End of Empires*, trans. Joseph V. Owens (Miami: Convivium, 2012), 38–39.

simply mean to imply that there must be some shared context within which an exchange can occur. The space of a market may be tents and tables at a farmers' market or computer screens, a pit, and telephone and internet lines for a financial market, but some form of infrastructure must create a genuinely shared context of exchange. This infrastructure generally includes material components. Markets also require a mechanism of exchange that can vary. For example, Léon Walras, an important founder of neoclassical economics and the marginalist revolution, imagined markets reaching equilibrium through a "caller" shouting out prices and seeking buy and sell orders.[14] As we shall see, many other market mechanisms are possible. Finally, economists generally understand market participants to be buying and selling according to certain information, decisions, and strategies. In other words, if several individuals threw different sums of money and different objects into a pile, closed their eyes, picked new items and money, and went home, the exchange would not qualify as a market. Market participants make choices for specific reasons based on information at their disposal, though as we shall see, strategies from market participants can vary considerably. Market design is evident in each aspect of the definition of markets.

Markets as Imagined Spaces by Design

In order for a market for a given thing to exist in a particular society, members of that society must be able to perceive that thing as a good—an item that is buyable and sellable. The fact that theologians and ethicists often object to buying and selling certain commodities proves that the commodification of at least some things is contestable; I would argue that all commodities are contestable and could be imagined in alternative ways. Things thought of as goods could be and have been understood in alternative ways. For example, when the introduction explored William Cavanaugh's objections to the detachment fostered by capitalism that was evident in the college student selling his forehead for $37,000, I was providing an example of

---

[14] "The markets which are best organized from the competitive standpoint are those in which purchases and sales are made by auction, through the instrumentality of stockbrokers, commercial brokers, or criers acting as agents who centralize transactions in such a way that the terms of exchange are openly announced and an opportunity is given to sellers to lower their prices and buyers to raise their bids." Léon Walras, *Elements of Pure Economics: Or the Theory of Social Wealth*, trans. William Jaffé (London: Routledge, 1954), 83–84. Walras based his theory of supply and demand on markets of this sort.

one argument that we ought not to conceive of our bodies as commodities.[15] Such arguments are common. Though there are many different aspects of a culture or social imaginary that must be in place in order for a market to exist, in this section, I will restrict analysis to commodification because here is where intentional design is perhaps most evident. Though the culture of a society is too complex to be intentionally directed in significant ways, it is nevertheless the case that in smaller contexts like the commodification of a particular thing, there is evidence of intentional design.

Often economists make concerted efforts to reframe a thing such that it is conceivable as a commodity and then on the basis of this commodification to push for the construction of new markets. For example, economic arguments were decisive in eliminating a military draft in the United States, shifting to the development of a volunteer military force established by individuals willing to enlist at a given price. Economists argued that a volunteer military would reduce costs in detecting draft dodgers and would reduce opportunity costs—a volunteer military force enlists when it is their best source of income or utility, while drafted soldiers might have earned more at higher utility elsewhere.[16] If soldiers enlist for money rather than out of duty, then military service becomes a commodity, something the government can purchase for a market price. The observant ethicist might note that this shifts conscription from the realm of duty[17] to the realm of cost/benefit calculation, the first of many possible ethical implications of market design that I will note.[18]

Another widely discussed example of economists and policymakers working together is seen in the development of individual transferrable quotas (ITQs). Faced with shortages in fish stocks, economists argue that the right to fish might be bought and sold in a market capped at a maximum fishing rate to prevent overfishing.[19] This transition required a shift away from what

---

15 Cavanaugh, *Being Consumed*, 34–35.

16 Beth J. Asch, James C. Miller III, and John T. Warner, "Economics and the All-Volunteer Military Force," in *Better Living through Economics*, ed. John J. Siegfried (Cambridge: Harvard University Press, 2010), 254–57.

17 I grant that this duty is contestable, as is evident in the phenomenon of conscientious objectors. My point is simply that we shift from a question primarily of ethics to one primarily of price and—still value-laden—economics.

18 Asch, Miller, and Warner admit the same. Asch, Miller, and Warner, "Economics and the All-Volunteer Military Force," 256, 259.

19 For example, see Suzi Kerr, James Sanchirico, and Richard Newell, "Fishing Quota Markets," *Journal of Environmental Economics and Management* 49, no. 3 (May 2005): 437–62.

can be called "Olympic fishing," where boats would seek to harvest fish as quickly as possible until the cap was hit and fishing ended for the season, into a market system that was deemed more efficient. Here economists claim that if quotas can be sold, equilibrium would lead the captains or companies who most value the ability to fish to hold the quotas, while others leave the market, preventing "fleet overcapacity."[20] This example of market design raises a second ethical question, for, as Petter Holm notes, the ITQ system fosters a troubling power dynamic—"fisherman-owners now get to decide whether to fish the quota or sell it, without the communities that depend on such decisions for their survival having any say in the matter."[21] Once again, a positive description of something as a market is inescapably connected with certain normative dimensions.

While the two initial examples of efforts to intentionally commodify involve economists and policymakers, there are also examples of economists and business proprietors working together to commodify. For example, economist Julian Simon convinced the (now-defunct) Civil Aeronautics Board in the United States to remove random bumping of passengers from overbooked flights and to institute an auction-based market for vouchers for future airline seats, thereby creating a market to resolve overbooked airline flights.[22] Robert Litan notes that this plan was economically superior, as airlines no longer underbooked flights for fear of accidentally overbooking and having to bump a flier, possibly losing a customer. I would add that such changes also had the ethical benefit of not bumping a passenger with a dire need to be on a flight, a more just outcome, even if only in a smaller degree. It is clear that even at the basic level of markets as imagined spaces, some intentional design occurs.

The Design of Exchange Mechanisms

Once something has been imagined as a commodity, it is still necessary for there to be some mechanism of exchange that enables the commodity to be bought and sold. When I speak of a mechanism of exchange, I am referring to a set of rules and practices through which an exchange of goods or services

---

20 Petter Holm, "Which Way Is Up on Callon?" in MacKenzie, Muniesa, and Siu, *Do Economists Make Markets*, 235–36.
21 Holm, "Which Way," 237.
22 Robert E. Litan, *Trillion Dollar Economists: How Economists and Their Ideas Have Transformed Business* (Hoboken, NJ: John Wiley and Sons, 2014), 55–56.

occurs. The numerous possible exchange mechanisms are especially evident in auctions theory. For example, auctions can be open, where bidders know the bids of others and can make multiple escalating bids, or they can be closed, where bidders make a single sealed bid without knowing other bids. In some auctions, the highest bid wins, while others go to the second-highest bid in an attempt to prevent overpaying.[23] To illustrate the significance of the selected exchange mechanism in an auction, Guillaume Haeringer gives the example of a Monet painting for sale. The highest valuation by a consumer might be $20 million and the second-highest $5 million. If the seller is willing to sell for over $1 million, an equilibrium price could be anywhere from $5,000,000.01 to $20 million, depending on how we determine equilibrium.[24] A closed bid, for example, might reach equilibrium closer to $20 million, while multiple escalating open bids would likely reach equilibrium of slightly over $5 million. Auctions are used in a wide range of markets, from the sale of fine art to the market for government contracts and even in some stock IPOs.

Economists have actively worked to expand the use of auctions in the economy, including the important role they play in the market for cellular phones. In the middle of the twentieth century in the United States, AT&T benefited from a natural monopoly in local telephone services, but AT&T argued that it also needed a monopoly in the telephone equipment and long-distance markets in order to be able to financially preserve the integrity of its network of local telephone lines. In the 1980s, lawyers and economists in the US Justice Department, unconvinced by these arguments, had been successful in their attempt to break up AT&T. During the time of antitrust disputes, AT&T had been granted a license by the Federal Communications Commission (FCC) to use a portion of the electromagnetic spectrum for cellular phones, and when the monopoly was broken up, so was the license between the resulting subsidiary companies.[25] Eventually, drawing on an idea from economist and Nobel laureate Ronald Coase to use auctions for the electromagnetic spectrum,[26] and authorized by an act of Congress,[27] the FCC ran auctions to determine the allocation of licenses for different portions of the spectrum. Knowing that different structures of auctions might change

---

23 Timothy P. Hubbard and Harry J. Paarsch, *Auctions* (Cambridge: MIT Press, 2015), 8–15.
24 Haeringer, *Market Design*, 2.
25 Litan, *Trillion Dollar Economists*, 232–44.
26 Litan, *Trillion Dollar Economists*, 253.
27 Litan, *Trillion Dollar Economists*, 246.

which firms won the rights for portions of the spectrum, various economists and corporations pushed for their preferred auction format.[28] The FCC settled on what is known as the "simultaneous-multiple round-independent (SMRI) auction."[29]

Similar auctions for 3G bandwidth in the United Kingdom required design decisions about how many permits to sell for different parts of the bandwidth, whether to restrict firms from holding more than one permit, and which bidding mechanism to use. Possible options included the "beauty contest," where officials would choose between single, closed bids; the English auction, where bids gradually ascended; and the Dutch auction, where the price gradually descended until firms made a bid, the first bid winning. Regulators also briefly considered a two-stage auction, first an English-style ascending auction until the number of bidding firms was one more than the number of available licenses, and then a second stage involving a final sealed bid by the remaining firms. Each style typically produces different outcomes in terms of price and number of bidders.[30] The final design involved a multistage English auction with simultaneous bids that permanently eliminated any firm that did not bid in a given round.[31] Such auctions may seem detached from moral considerations, but it is important to note that in the United States, the FCC pursued market design with efficiency in mind, not questions of distributive justice.[32] They designed an exchange mechanism appropriate to their goal.

---

28 Philip Mirowski and Edward Nik-Khah, "Markets Made Flesh: Performativity, and a Problem in Science Studies, Augmented with Consideration of the FCC Auctions," in MacKenzie, Muniesa, and Siu, *Do Economists Make Markets?*, 204–6.

29 Mirowski and Nik-Khah, "Markets Made Flesh," 207.

30 Roger E. Backhouse, *The Puzzle of Modern Economics: Science or Ideology?* (Cambridge: Cambridge University Press, 2010), 28–31. For example, English auctions communicate the value for a good that other firms hold. A bid higher than a firm expected might convince competing firms to increase their valuation of the good. This style of auction is also associated with the "winner's curse"—when bidding for items with an unclear valuation, the winning bid often overvalues the good. The two-stage auction was thought to be beneficial for new entrants into the market, who might otherwise fear bidding above current cell phone providers who had a head start on infrastructure.

31 Backhouse, *The Puzzle of Modern Economics*, 32.

32 "The FCC, however, would eventually take the position that all these complicated considerations involving industrial organization, macroeconomics, and distributional equity should be ultimately reduced to the narrower 'economic efficiency,' and that the most appropriate goal to pursue should be to award licenses to their highest users." Mirowski and Nik-Khah, "Markets Made Flesh," 203.

The variety of possible market exchange mechanisms is also evident in multisided platforms, companies like Uber, AirBnB, and Visa that "attract two or more types of customers by enabling them to interact *with each other* on attractive terms."[33] As David Evans and Richard Schmalensee explain, "All matchmakers . . . must construct the platform, whether from bricks or lines of code, and often develop tools that participants can use to find valuable matches."[34] Economists, computer programmers, and corporations have designed many unique mechanisms for multisided platforms. For example, school choice involves a matching algorithm, but there are competing algorithms. Using what is known as a deferred acceptance algorithm produces a stable matching assignment that is most preferable to students. An "immediate acceptance algorithm," however, may not produce a match that is preferable to students.[35] Economists would deny that this algorithm has reached equilibrium.[36] The match may also be unstable, meaning that it has not reached a state roughly equivalent to what economists called *equilibrium* in classic market theory. In other words, changes in matching could make everyone better off. Despite this, some school systems have used an immediate acceptance algorithm.

Thus far, I have focused on auctions and multisided platforms because markets of these types have garnered lots of attention from economists, but more traditional markets also have a range of possible exchange mechanisms. American restaurants typically involve a fixed price for food and a variable tip offered to the server, but European restaurants typically de-emphasize gratuity tipping, often affixing a standard service charge to the bill instead. In some markets and cultures, haggling is expected, while in other markets, customers are faced with fixed, take-it-or-leave-it prices. Because utility markets for electricity typically need monopolistic firms due to what is known as economies of scale, meaning that large firms can more efficiently

---

33 David S. Evans and Richard Schmalensee, *Matchmakers: The New Economics of Multisided Platforms* (Boston: Harvard Business Review Press, 2016), 15. In 2016, multisided platforms made up three of the five most valuable companies in the world—Google, Microsoft, and Apple—and seven of the ten startups with the highest market value. Evans and Schmalensee, *Matchmakers*, 8.
34 Evans and Schmalensee, *Matchmakers*, 122.
35 Evans and Schmalensee, *Matchmakers*, 246–50.
36 Evans and Schmalensee, *Matchmakers*, 154–55.

manage costs, they typically need to be designed.[37] Yet studies have shown that the regulations imposed on electricity markets can "have a substantial impact on the behavior of market-clearing prices."[38] Different exchange mechanisms are also possible in the world of finance. While high literacy rates and lack of collateral traditionally prohibited many of the poorest families from attaining loans, Muhhamad Yunus designed a new mechanism of exchange where microloans were granted without collateral and with alternative ways of tracking transactions.[39] Examples could continue to multiply, but the basic point is that markets can rely on a wide range of specific exchange mechanisms, each relying partly on price to facilitate an exchange but each with different actual processes and, potentially, different outcomes.

The Design of Information Flows

Since the publication of George Akerlof's seminal paper, "The Market for 'Lemons,'" economists have written extensively on the importance of the distribution of information in economic exchanges.[40] Akerlof pointed to the market for used cars, which is plagued by an information asymmetry: those who are selling a car they have owned for some time have a better idea about the quality of vehicle they are selling than do private or corporate buyers, a phenomenon that can drive down prices, which may in turn drive out of the market those who would sell a well-functioning vehicle worth more money. This is sometimes called *adverse selection*, a situation where market participants with additional information might engage in exchange in a manner financially harmful to other parties lacking the same information. Akerlof

---

37 On the need to design utilities markets, see Richard O'Neill and Udi Helman, "Regulatory Reform of the US Wholesale Electricity Markets," in Landy, Levin, and Shapiro, *Creating Competitive Markets*, 128–57.

38 Frank A. Wolak, "Market Design and Price Behavior in Restructured Electricity Markets: An International Comparison," in *Pricing in Competitive Electricity Markets*, ed. Ahmad Faruqui and Kelly Eakin (Boston: Kluwer Academic Publishers, 2000), 127.

39 Yunus provides a humorous account of these challenges in Yunus, *Banker to the Poor*, 52–54.

40 George A. Akerlof, "The Market for 'Lemons': Quality Uncertainty and the Market Mechanism," *Quarterly Journal of Economics* 84, no. 3 (August 1970): 488–500.

points to similar information asymmetries in insurance markets and "credit markets in undeveloped countries."[41]

Interestingly, market design has targeted the elimination of many of the information asymmetries discussed in Akerlof's article. In the United States, the Affordable Care Act (ACA) sought to overcome problems caused in the insurance market, where insurers often have difficulty discerning how many medical expenses a customer may have. As a result, insurers often charge more than the expected payout for healthy customers, which can cause them not to purchase insurance, further increasing average payouts and therefore average insurance prices, a phenomenon known as adverse selection. The ACA attempts to reduce adverse selection by establishing an insurance mandate, where employers of a certain size must offer insurance plans and where individuals who do not purchase insurance or receive Medicaid or Medicare are fined. This mandate is meant to establish a lower average risk rate, and despite the risk of noncompliance, it looked theoretically possible that it might succeed.[42] To ensure quality insurance for consumers brought into the market through the mandate, and for those with preexisting conditions or otherwise likely to be denied quality health insurance, the ACA also required minimum coverage and a minimum percentage of revenue that plans must pay out in medical expenses or else refund a portion of the revenue to the customer.[43] The ACA included a change in ethical framework away from actuarial fairness, which occurs when the cost of insurance equals the anticipated value of the insurance to customers.[44] In a system based on actuarial fairness, those likely to receive more payouts must pay higher prices, which often prevents those with the greatest medical need from being able to afford insurance. Under the ACA, fairness was framed in terms of equal access to healthcare, with all Americans having an implied—and sometimes stated—duty to contribute to

---

41 Akerlof, "The Market for 'Lemons,'" 492–94, 497. Akerlof makes a similar argument regarding the refusal to hire "minorities." I will address this morally problematic phenomenon in chapter 8.

42 Tom Baker, "Health Insurance, Risk, and Responsibility after the Patient Protection and Affordable Care Act," *University of Pennsylvania Law Review* 159, no. 6 (June 2011): 1619–21.

43 Baker, "Health Insurance," 1609–13.

44 Baker, "Health Insurance," 1598–601. Prices in a system of actuarial fairness also account for transaction costs and administrative costs, plus some degree of profit for insurers as a reward for taking on risks. The Affordable Care Act treats much billing based on actuarial analysis as discrimination, but it does not completely prohibit any influence from actuarial analysis.

insurance costs for the common good. One of the overarching goals of the ACA was to eliminate the economic problems established by information asymmetry between insurers and their customers.

Market design has also targeted credit in poor nations and the market for used automobiles, in this case largely through the effort of individual firms. In the market for credit in poor communities, microfinance typically engages in group lending, where loans are given to individuals only when they are in a group of borrowers and where each group is committed to help their other group members meet their obligations or else risk being ineligible for future loans.[45] This group-lending model helps overcome information asymmetry—while a lender may not know whether a borrower without a credit record or collateral will be likely to repay, members of the community with whom that borrower might partner have a better sense of his, or more often her,[46] level of responsibility, honesty, and diligence at work.[47] In the realm of car sales, since Akerlof's 1970 article, companies like CARFAX, founded in 1984, have sought to mitigate information asymmetry, while many online car markets have attempted to restrict participants to ensure high-quality vehicles, though typically commercial online markets sell far fewer vehicles than physical markets do.[48] In each instance, firms have intentionally designed information flows to improve the performance of markets.

The control of information is also important in the context of auctions, where information about the prices bid by other parties is important. For example, in FCC auctions for rights to run cell phone networks on part of the spectrum, Francesco Guala writes, "Computerized auctions are used extensively to create 'appropriate' market conditions, precisely because they allow controlling tightly the quality, amount, and flow of information between buyers and sellers."[49] With too little or ill-timed information, auction participants

---

45 The process is described in Yunus, *Banker to the Poor,* 62–65.

46 Many microfinance banks have especially targeted loans to women.

47 See Remko van Eijkel, Niels Hermes, and Robert Lensink, "Group Lending and the Role of the Group Leader," *Small Business Economics* 36, no. 3 (April 2011): 299–321.

48 Eric Overby and Sabyasachi Mitra, "Physical and Electronic Wholesale Markets: An Empirical Analysis of Product Sorting and Market Function," *Journal of Management Information Systems* 31, no. 2 (Fall 2014): 11–45.

49 Francesco Guala, "How to Do Things with Experimental Economics," in MacKenzie, Muniesa, and Siu, *Do Economists Make Markets?,* 148.

may not be able to act rationally, as defined by economists.[50] For example, an open auction with several bids may help auction participants to reach a better estimation of the value of the good being auctioned. Conversely, closed, single-bid auctions often result in the winner's curse, where the winning bid has actually overvalued the good being auctioned.[51] Meanwhile, many of the telecommunications firms participating in past FCC auctions relied on game theorists hired to help the firms determine when, whether, and how much they should bid.[52]

Market Design and Market Participants

In order for a market to function, there must be participants who are willing to buy and sell a given good using the specified exchange mechanism based on the available information. When designing markets, intentional efforts are often required to reach a critical mass of market participants. Reaching a healthy level of participants is often called establishing a thick market, and market designers must pursue thick markets among their other objectives. Regulators and business proprietors also are tasked with determining who can qualify as a market participant. For multisided platforms, this means that companies must perform platform screening, selecting the right participants for both sides of the matchmaking process.[53] For example, Google's Android platform was open-source and available to any technology company developing cell phones. This ensured the possibility of an adequately thick market. However, Google also developed a certification process for cell phone makers using its Android platform to ensure quality of customer experience and a degree of standardization.[54] This is an example of a corporation trying to regulate participants in a market it was helping design, but governments are the most likely to regulate participants in a market, as they do when requiring licensure for such varied professions as mental health counselors, truck drivers, and electricians.

---

50 Again, Guala notes, "Since it is partly by virtue of the structure of the situation that economic agents behave rationally, a great part of economic engineering is devoted to make sure that the structure is 'right.'" Guala, "How to Do Things," 149.

51 See the brief discussion in David J. Salant, *A Primer on Auction Design, Management, and Strategy* (Cambridge: MIT Press, 2014), 55–65.

52 Mirowski and Nik-Khah, "Markets Made Flesh," 201.

53 Evans and Schmalensee, *Matchmakers*, 124.

54 Evans and Schmalensee, *Matchmakers*, 116.

Regulation of participants is an important dimension of the ethical analysis of market design. For example, consider the market for mutual funds. Often, mutual funds composed of stocks picked by brokers fail to provide profits for investors that beat simple index funds that match the growth of indexes like the NASDAQ or S&P 500.[55] Yet the lure of potential high returns leads many firms to develop funds that are high in risk, volatility, and leverage relative to other possible funds, a situation resulting in higher income for fund managers but a higher possibility of lost savings for investors. Some mutual funds also charge substantial fees for their customers, which further increases the earnings of fund managers while reducing the returns for investors. In light of this, some managers began to push for low-fee mutual funds with long-term stability and added social value as chief goals. A sufficiently thick market for such firms emerged through the pioneering work of companies like Vanguard in the United States, but Japanese firms were initially reluctant to offer funds of this sort. Ultimately, a market for such products was established through the work of professionals in finance, like Haruhiro Nakano and Atsuto Sawakami, who helped push bank CEOs to pilot such funds, coupled with government involvement by the head of the Financial Services Agency, Nobuchika Mori, who established a policy allowing Japanese investors to invest up to ¥400,000 tax-free in funds meeting the criteria of such social-value funds.[56] Tax incentives supplied sufficient demand for low-fee, stable mutual funds, while personal advocacy ensured sufficient supply, establishing a thick market. Yet the market only exists because of intentional efforts by finance professionals and government regulators to ensure that it did.

The regulation of market participants is often the site of the most egregiously immoral aspects of market design. Consider the US housing market in the twentieth century, which intentionally excluded Black Americans from full participation through the joint efforts of the government, real estate professionals, and white homeowners. As Richard Rothstein explains, government officials and bureaucrats ensured segregated housing through a wide range of policies, from the design of segregated neighborhoods through the Public Works Administration to local governments' decisions to place

---

55 Here I remain convinced by the classic text by Burton G. Malkiel, *A Random Walk Down Wall Street: Including a Life-Cycle Guide to Personal Investing* (New York: Norton, 1990).

56 J. C. De Swaan, *Seeking Virtue in Finance: Contributing to Society in a Conflicted Industry* (Cambridge: Cambridge University Press, 2020), 48–49.

segregated Black schools in Black neighborhoods while refusing to bus Black students from other areas.[57] Meanwhile, the National Association of Real Estate Boards had "adopted an ethics rule prohibiting agents from selling homes to African Americans in white neighborhoods."[58] At the same time, many white-owned properties had deeds forbidding their sale to Black homeowners.[59] Here, a number of groups' coordinated efforts ensured *de jure* exclusion of Black participants in large segments of the housing market.

Unfortunately, rectifying such discriminatory policies requires more extensive market design than merely readmitting formerly excluded market participants, a point clearly made in Keeanga-Yamahtta Taylor's research. Taylor details how the Federal Housing Administration and the Veterans Administration had virtually excluded Black homeowners from their subsidized mortgage programs.[60] In 1968, the Housing and Urban Development (HUD) Act was signed into law, the main intent being to eliminate redlining and housing discrimination. The sad result of the HUD Act and similar policies was what Taylor labels "predatory inclusion," a term that "describes how African American homebuyers were granted access to conventional real estate practices and mortgage financing, but on more expensive and comparatively unequal terms."[61] Operation Breakthrough sought to increase mass production of affordable housing to meet HUD demand, but it did so through an auction going to the lowest bidder, an exchange mechanism that ensured houses were built cheaply and not up to code.[62] Meanwhile, the program relied on the same insurers, lenders, and government administrators to run the new program who had been involved in discriminatory practices

---

57 Richard Rothstein, *The Color of Law: A Forgotten History of How Our Government Segregated America* (New York: Liveright, 2017), 20–23, 132.

58 Rothstein, *The Color of Law*, 62.

59 Rothstein, *The Color of Law*, 78–81. Rothstein notes how such racial covenants required intentional design. If a racial covenant was linked only to the homeowner, neighbors had limited standing to sue if the homeowner violated the covenant and sold their house to a Black individual or family. However, developers designed community associations and required all residents to join to purchase property, and these associations could have racial covenants that were more easily enforceable.

60 For example, "ten years after the 1949 National Housing Act, less than 2 percent of FHA-insured properties went to nonwhites." Keeanga-Yamahtta Taylor, *Race for Profit: How Banks and the Real Estate Industry Undermined Black Homeownership* (Chapel Hill: University of North Carolina Press, 2019), 35.

61 Taylor, *Race for Profit*, 5.

62 Taylor, *Race for Profit*, 104–6.

the year prior.⁶³ As a result, Black home buyers often had no choices except between overpriced and poorly built new construction and overpriced and dilapidated homes. By 1974, six years after the passing of the HUD Act, 180 indictments, including three directors of urban FHA insurance offices, were passed down for fraud, profiteering, and housing speculation.⁶⁴ The St. Louis HUD foreclosed on 283 houses financed through HUD programs but found that 101 were unfit for repair, having been sold in such a poor state that the cost of needed repairs exceeded the market valuation of the properties. These homes were demolished.⁶⁵ Clearly, consideration of which market participants are excluded and included is an important step in moral analysis of market design, yet successful market design must consider many factors beyond this, including aspects like the mechanism of exchange discussed above and factors like the culture and wealth distribution underlying the markets in consideration. I will return to this example of market design in chapter 8.

Legal Regulation of Goods in the Market

Christian ethicists and theologians have been most prone to consider the design of the market when it comes to the matter of legal regulation of which goods can be sold in a market. When theologians object to the construction of a market for kidneys or express concern over the commodification of protest messages, they are arguing that certain things ought not to be exchanged within a market.⁶⁶ Daniel Finn presents a clear explanation of the regulation of goods available within a market, explaining markets with the metaphor of fences, where "sections of the fence represent laws, which restrict what is allowed to occur within the market.... In some cases, economic exchange of particular goods or services is forbidden altogether (e.g., buying and selling of body parts, children, the services of sexual partners or of thugs willing to murder your firm's competitors)."⁶⁷ Finn notes the metaphor properly applies to "the market," a form of economic organization rooted in freedom and

---

63 Taylor, *Race for Profit*, 67, 91.
64 Taylor, *Race for Profit*, 174.
65 Taylor, *Race for Profit*, 190.
66 Vincent Miller is concerned about the "commodification of dissent," in Miller, *Consuming Religion*, 18. Long's concern about kidney markets, discussed in chapter 1, is found in Long, Fox, and York, *Calculated Futures*, 61–62.
67 Daniel K. Finn, *The Moral Ecology of Markets: Assessing Claims about Markets and Justice* (Cambridge: Cambridge University Press, 2006), 114–15.

consisting of the aggregate of smaller markets of any given good.[68] However, the analogy also applies to individual markets as well. When eBay restricts the sale of alcohol other than wine, goods from embargoed countries, or human body parts, it is setting up fences within the market it has constructed to regulate which goods can be exchanged.[69] Market fences are also set up to prevent abusive behaviors within a market. As Finn notes, recognizing that there are numerous possible fence lines reminds us that a simplistic dichotomy between centralized planning and free markets is too reductionistic.[70]

TWO EXAMPLES OF MARKET DESIGN

Market design occurs through the imagining of goods as sellable, through the legal permission to sell such goods, through efforts to ensure sufficient and sufficiently regulated market participants for a thick market, through the selection of an appropriate mechanism of exchange, and through decisions about what information to share, when, and with whom. This chapter has provided numerous examples of governments, economists, and corporations engaging in these dimensions of market design, but it would be helpful to provide two brief examples of market design involving all five dimensions to fully illustrate the phenomenon under consideration. Two case studies should be particularly helpful illustrations: the development of amazon.com and the design of US markets for tradable pollution allowances.

Amazon and Corporate Market Design

Amazon is a complex corporation engaged in everything from web hosting through Amazon Web Services to the production and sale of software and hardware like Alexa and the Amazon Echo. However, one early and still important dimension of Amazon's business is the intentional design of a market, a website where Amazon could directly sell products to customers but also a multisided platform where vendors could sell through Amazon's

---

68 Finn, *Moral Ecology of Markets*, 115–16.
69 eBay's policies are available at https://www.ebay.com/help/policies/prohibited-restricted-items/prohibited-restricted-items?id=4207.
70 Finn, *Moral Ecology of Markets*, 120–21.

website to Amazon's customers.[71] Like any market design, the development of amazon.com required imagination, as individuals began to wonder about the possibility of the newly developed internet for retail sales. In this context, Jeff Bezos and his then-employer David Shaw of D. E. Shaw and Co. began to discuss an online marketplace for all products, called "the everything store."[72] Aiming to build such a market, Bezos recognized that he would need to begin with smaller aspirations, so Amazon began as an online bookstore, gradually expanding into other categories of merchandise.[73] As consumers across the world gradually began to imagine the internet as a space for selling and buying, Amazon was primed to become a major player in the market, provided it could navigate the other dimensions of market design.

Particularly important for an online market is the design of information flows and the effort to establish a sufficiently thick market. Markets need participants, but in online contexts, that raises the question of trust. How can you trust the person you are buying a product from if you never even see them face to face? Amazon's basic solution to this problem is known as the Amazon flywheel, a basic theory of how to foster growth by improving customer experience through things like "richness of product information" and "ease of use," which produce traffic, drawing sellers, which in turn leads to wider selection, thereby improving user experience *ad infinitum*.[74] Note that fundamental to Amazon's growth strategy is the design of information flows. Like other online marketplaces, Amazon relies on a public rating system for vendors on Amazon Marketplace to help build trust. Such systems also contribute a certain "stickiness" to vendors who don't want to move platforms and leave behind their visible reputations, building a thicker market.[75] Amazon also pioneered both "look inside the book" and "search inside the book" features, the former creating an experience similar to a physical bookstore and

---

71 This is a common combination for multisided platforms, which often mix their business model, providing some materials directly to consumers while providing space for other vendors to sell to consumers as well. See Evans and Schmalensee, *Matchmakers*, 106–9.

72 Brad Stone, *The Everything Store: Jeff Bezos and the Age of Amazon* (New York: Little, Brown and Company, 2013), 24.

73 Stone, *The Everything Store*, 25. Bezos chose books because they were "pure commodities," and books were the same regardless of where you bought them.

74 Colin Bryar and Bill Carr, *Working Backwards: Insights, Stories, and Secrets from inside Amazon* (New York: St. Martin's, 2021), 126.

75 Jennifer Brown and John Morgan, "Reputation in Online Auctions: The Market for Trust," *California Management Review* 49, no. 1 (Fall 2006): 63.

the latter providing something unavailable in one.[76] Such designed features provide customers with information that would increase the likelihood of their making a purchase, but previews of the book risked a loss of vendors, who worried they might be used to create illegal duplicates of books. Amazon got around this problem by restricting the search feature to customers with credit cards on file, reducing samples after a search to about two pages and using cookies to prevent repeat visits.[77] A thick market was preserved.

In an online market, design is clearly evident in the coding and algorithms of the website itself, which pairs market participants, presents relevant information, and even shapes the mechanism of exchange. Enabling efficient customer searches for products is a tremendously important dimension of web development since customers cannot simply browse aisles in a brick-and-mortar store. Amazon initially used Alta Vista to facilitate product searches before designing Botega, an internal search algorithm identifying items with the most clicks under a search term and then positioning those products higher in future searches.[78] With the rise of Google, customers were also finding Amazon products externally through Google searches; Amazon developed Urubamba, "one of the web's first automated search-and-buying systems," to give it a competitive advantage in Google searches.[79] Similarly, Clickriver allowed third-party vendors selling on Amazon to purchase higher search results on amazon.com.[80] Algorithms and purchased search results are a vital and designed means of connecting goods and vendors with consumers.

Deciding which mechanism of exchange to use is another important feature of designing an online market. Amazon could have chosen the route of eBay, using auctions for products, but instead has largely focused on pursuing frictionless transactions, where purchases can be immediate and easy. The transition to one-click purchasing, which Amazon had a patent on, ensured lower rates of shopping cart abandonment, proving to be a success for the company.[81] One-click therefore determines both how and whether a good

---

76 Stone, *The Everything Store*, 197.
77 Stone, *The Everything Store*, 197–98.
78 Stone, *The Everything Store*, 198–99. Eventually, Amazon had an entire office devoted to algorithms in Palo Alto, California.
79 Stone, *The Everything Store*, 195. The software is named after one of the tributaries of the Amazon River.
80 Stone, *The Everything Store*, 200.
81 Natalie Berg and Miya Knights, *Amazon: How the World's Most Relentless Retailer Will Continue to Revolutionize Commerce*, 2nd ed. (New York: Kogan Page, 2022), 184–87.

is purchased. Amazon offers an array of other exchange mechanisms, from "subscribe and save," which automatically purchases products on a schedule set by the consumer, to allowing purchases through the recently discontinued smile.amazon.com, where the terms of exchange include an automatic donation to a charity of the customer's choice. Of course, behind the scenes of such exchanges lies the physical infrastructure constituting the market, including the physical servers for Amazon (hosted by Amazon Web Services), an extensive network of warehouses for products,[82] and a delivery network including Amazon-owned trucks and drones.

Amazon clearly illustrates the full breadth of market design, beginning with a new way of imagining markets and extending into intentional construction of information flows and exchange mechanisms toward the pursuit of a thick market for goods. Even Amazon's goods themselves are subject to certain regulatory design. By 2018, Amazon led all technology companies in terms of size of lobbying offices in Washington, DC, and it also lobbied more federal agencies than any other tech firm. Lobbying efforts were focused on such areas as Amazon's exemption from assessing sales tax, its discounted rates for shipping with the US Postal Service, and protection from antitrust activity.[83] Conceivably, regulators could have prohibited the marketing of certain or all items through the internet, but instead, Amazon has enjoyed a competitive advantage via its ability to sell most products without sales tax and with reduced shipping. Nearly half a trillion dollars in products are sold on Amazon's carefully designed market each year.

Governments, Economists, and the Design of Markets for Pollution

One of the most heavily discussed examples of market design is in the market for pollution. Economists have frequently argued that markets should be established to efficiently allocate pollution allowances[84] within a cap-and-trade

---

One study put the rate of shopping cart abandonment at 69 percent for slower transactional systems.

82 After years of effort, forecasting and purchasing of Amazon products have been automated. Bryar and Carr, *Working Backwards*, 133.

83 Alec MacGillis, *Fulfillment: Winning and Losing in One-Click America* (New York: Farrar, Straus and Giroux, 2021), 86–87.

84 The term *allowance* is often preferred over *permit* given the former is more fungible/tradable; in the United States, this legally also allowed the country to take away some allowances without requiring compensation to their prior holders. Blas Luis Pérez

system. For example, the main sources of sulfur dioxide (SO_2), one of the primary causes of acid rain, are coal-burning power plants. There are two ways to reduce SO_2 emissions—scrubbers that clean emissions as they leave the smokestack and transitioning to low-sulfur coal, which is only available in some areas.[85] Some companies would therefore find it easier to reduce emissions than others, while environmental degradation made it necessary to reduce overall emissions. Economists argue that the most efficient outcome will occur if the government caps total allowable emissions of SO_2, distributing the pollution allowances to firms that can in turn buy and sell them. An equilibrium would be reached when those that valued the allowances most held them. The argument for tradable allowances illustrates the first step of market design—economists had to imagine the right to pollute as a sellable good. This perception was not as easily adopted in mainstream society as that of online retail, so there are many examples of articles where economists suggest ways to teach students to imagine pollution allowances as a fungible good.[86] In the end, enough people accepted the idea to construct a market.

Design of the Acid Rain Program for Emissions Trading (ARP) in the United States required a complex series of steps.[87] First, it was necessary to "create a homogenous unit" so that equivalent trade was possible. In this case, the selected unit was one ton of SO_2.[88] After setting a baseline of total allowances to be traded, the government had to decide how to establish initial allocations. Two main mechanisms are typically used when initiating a market for tradable pollution allowances: grandfathering distributes allowances based on some past or present pollution levels, or auctions distribute initial allowances using one of the many exchange mechanisms available

---

Henríquez, *Environmental Commodities Markets and Emissions Trading: Towards a Low-Carbon Future* (New York: Routledge, 2013), 86.

85 Backhouse, *The Puzzle of Modern Economics*, 23.

86 For example, see Amy W. Ando and Donna Ramirez Harrington, "Tradable Discharge Permits: A Student-Friendly Game," *Journal of Economic Education* 37, no. 2 (Spring 2006): 187–201; Mark S. Walbert and Thomas J. Bierma, "The Permits Game: Conveying the Logic of Marketable Pollution Permits," *Journal of Economic Education* 19, no. 4 (Fall 1988): 383–89.

87 I will only cover some details, but a full analysis is available in Henríquez, *Environmental Commodities Markets*, 84–99.

88 Henríquez, *Environmental Commodities Markets*, 87.

within various auction formats.⁸⁹ In the case of the ARP, grandfathering was the chosen method, adding an additional thirty adjustments to initial distributions that could apply to firms based on a wide range of reasons.⁹⁰ After the initial allocation, regulators needed to design a mechanism for future exchanges, which included analyzing a number of different trading rules. For example, would intertemporal trading be allowed or banking, where a firm might save allowances from one year in order to pollute more next year?⁹¹ The organized exchange was initially performed through the Chicago Board of Trade but later by the EPA itself.⁹² By 1998, 1.3 million allowances had been sold through EPA auctions, and 20.3 million permits had been traded privately.⁹³ To further complicate the exchange of allowances, some regions of the United States are affected by acid rain more than others. Depending on which polluters purchased allowances, the result could be regional hot spots. To prevent this, regulators established an exchange rate: in high-risk areas, two allowances were needed per ton of SO_2.⁹⁴

Besides designing the rules of exchange and the mechanism by which exchange would occur, economists, regulators, and participating energy firms needed to ensure that enough information was available to market participants. For example, facing concerns that the equilibrium value of allowances might not be evident to market participants, legislation required the EPA to offer an annual spot-sale of allowances—2.8 percent of which were initially owned by the EPA—to help establish price equilibrium in public knowledge.⁹⁵ It was also necessary to establish "information services" including trade publications and electronic bulletin boards to notify market participants of recent transactions, allowance values, and the cost and availability of technologies that could reduce pollution.⁹⁶ Such information ensured that the goals of the market might be met: a reduction in total pollution in a manner that was least costly for firms in the energy market.

---

89 See the discussion in Jacob K. Goeree et al., "An Experimental Study of Auctions versus Grandfathering to Assign Pollution Permits," *Journal of the European Economic Association* 8, no. 2–3 (April–May 2010): 514–15.

90 A. Danny Ellerman, "Designing a Tradable Permit System to Control SO_2 Emissions in China: Principles and Practice," *Energy Journal* 23, no. 2 (2002): 10–11.

91 Henríquez, *Environmental Commodities Markets*, 93–94.

92 Henríquez, *Environmental Commodities Markets*, 95. The Chicago Board handled trading from 1992 until 2006, when the EPA took over.

93 Backhouse, *The Puzzle of Modern Economics*, 25.

94 Henríquez, *Environmental Commodities Markets*, 88.

95 Henríquez, *Environmental Commodities Markets*, 93–94.

96 Henríquez, *Environmental Commodities Markets*, 95.

The design of pollution markets, which exist around the world for various pollutants, is another example illustrating the full array of market design features. After economists proposed the right to pollute as a tradable good, governments have to legally permit the exchange of pollution allowances—moving the market's fences, to use Finn's metaphor. This process is often quite complicated. Tradable permits in the European Union (EU), for example, involved consultants, working groups of stakeholders to provide feedback, and the coordinated work of the EU and national governments.[97] Often, several mechanisms of exchange must be designed—designers may develop initial and/or ongoing auctions for distribution of allowances, plus methods for allowance-holders to buy and sell allowances. Designing information flows is vital to this process. Whenever the government requires all polluters to participate in pollution markets, there will certainly be enough participants to establish a thick market. The example of the ARP and similar markets around the world illustrates what market design can look like through the coordinated efforts of economists and governments.

MARKET DESIGN AND ECONOMIC ETHICS

I have argued that a market is an imagined space where participants voluntarily buy and sell goods through a mechanism of exchange based on certain information, including price. I have also argued that markets are designed by governments, corporations, economists, and other stakeholders in at least five important areas: the collective imagination of something as a marketable good, the mechanism of exchange whereby a good is bought and sold, the information available to buyers and sellers, the recruitment and regulation of market participants, and the legal regulation of which goods may be sold under what conditions. As I wrap up this chapter and section, I should point out that the design of markets is significant for economic ethics and the theology of economics in at least three ways.

First, the fact that markets are designed and variable problematizes any comprehensive endorsement or critique of markets. For example, Michael Novak admits, "It is a mistake, I believe, to try to bind the cogency of Scripture

---

97 Jürgen Lefevre, "The EU Greenhouse Gas Emission Allowance Trading Scheme," in *Climate Change and Carbon Markets: A Handbook of Emission Reduction Mechanisms*, ed. Farhana Yamin (New York: Earthscan, 2005), 96–100.

to one system merely," criticizing liberation theologians for binding Scripture to socialism and adding that "Judaism and Christianity do not *require* democratic capitalism." Yet Novak does insist that capitalism is the best available current economic system.[98] It is wise to avoid identifying any system perfectly with Christianity, but even declaring an economic system as best is problematic insofar as capitalist markets can be designed in a staggering variety of ways with a wide range of goals in mind. Any claim that capitalism, socialism, or any other system is the best available must immediately meet resistance, for it is a far more important question to ask how specific markets are constructed.

Second, though the focus of this chapter has been on proving and analyzing the claim that markets are constructed, I have briefly noted throughout where market design can lead to more just or less just outcomes. For example, the attempt to design housing markets through HUD programs targeting increased participation by Black Americans shortly after the civil rights movement failed, causing the injustice that Keeanga-Yamahtta Taylor named "predatory inclusion."[99] Conversely, efforts by Muhammad Yunus to design credit markets that can be accessed by those poorest in the world successfully brought market participants into the credit market in a way that reduced poverty, eliminated one dimension of the social exclusion of poor people, and generally improved the quality of life of participants. Many more such examples could be provided, but the primary focus of this book is on moral formation in markets and not just outcomes through markets. Nevertheless, the outcome of markets is tremendously important and must take into account the varieties of market design available.

Third and finally, the phenomenon of market design raises theological questions that will lead into part II of the book, which establishes a theological framework suitable to engage experimental economics' discoveries regarding the morally formative nature of designed markets. If market design can shape the justice of the outcome of markets, we should not be surprised that market design can also shape the ways that markets morally form us—the subject of part III. Where some theological accounts argue that markets spontaneously emerge from human society as evidence of God's providence,[100] the phenomenon

---

98 Novak, *Spirit of Democratic Capitalism*, 335–36.
99 Taylor, *Race for Profit*, 5.
100 For example, see Richards, *Money, Greed, and God*, which links Adam Smith's idea of a providential invisible hand with F. A. Hayek's marvel at the "spontaneous order"

of market design requires a more robust theology of providence that can balance intentional human agency in market design with divine providence (chapter 4). A clear account of grace and sin (chapter 5) is needed as a foundation for our analysis, both to be able to name where and how God is active in market design and to ensure that market design consciously targeting positive moral formation does not become a Pelagian affair. Finally, since it is the triune God who providentially and graciously acts in creation, including markets, we need a trinitarian account of divine agency that will enable us to speak precisely of how Father, Son, and Spirit are encountered within the market (chapter 6). I turn now to theology proper to pursue these foundations.

---

of markets (75), arguing that God's providential work through markets results in "the miracles of free cooperation and interdependence" (81). He argues that "the market order is one of the things that God has made or that emerge when his image bearers interact in a certain way." It is "a stunning example of God's providence over a fallen world. As we've seen, the market order is beyond the ken of man. No mere human being or committee could have ever designed it" (214–15).

PART II

Theology

CHAPTER 4

Providence and Creaturely Agency

The Holy Spirit so worketh in us, as that he worketh by us; and what he does in us, is done by us.

—John Owen[1]

At the end of our survey of various emergent disciplines of economics, including experimental economics, behavioral economics, and market design, it is clear that markets do not automatically produce virtue or vice but can have varied outcomes based on many factors in market design. A theological account of the malleability of moral formation in the marketplace must explain how such human intentional design of markets relates to God's work in the moral transformation of Christians through regeneration and sanctification. This is but a precise application of the larger doctrine of divine providence, which describes God's ongoing causal work in creation. A robust doctrine of providence will account for genuine human causal powers and human freedom, while preserving the preeminence of God's work in applying grace. There is much at stake theologically. An account of providence that negates human freedom will eliminate the moral responsibility of humans within markets. Of course, at this juncture, freedom remains vaguely defined. A deterministic action—by which I mean one in which humans have no form of freedom whatsoever—would negate human moral responsibility. This is true in any context, including a market. The result would be to place complete

---

1 John Owen, *The Holy Spirit: His Gifts and Power* (Grand Rapids, MI: Kregel, 1954), 117.

responsibility for sin and evil on God, undermining divine goodness and holiness. On the other hand, an account that placed too much emphasis on human agency could undermine the gratuitous nature of salvation, which includes God's work in transforming Christians and conforming them to the perfect life of Christ.

Scripture consistently depicts the sovereignty of God in a manner that balances human agency and divine sovereignty. As Proverbs reminds us, "The human mind plans the way, but the Lord directs the steps" (Prov 16:9). Humans genuinely plan, and yet in another sense their acts remain determined by divine providence. To note a few famous examples from early in the Old Testament, Joseph's brothers sell him into slavery, intending harm, but God intended it for good (Gen 50:20). Similarly, Pharaoh hardens his own heart (Exod 8:15, 32; 9:34), yet God hardens Pharaoh's heart (e.g., Exod 7:22; 9:12; 10:1, etc.), while Pharaoh is consistently depicted as morally responsible for his own actions and justifiably condemned for resisting God's will. Particular passages could be multiplied, but the basic point is evident across the full scope of the biblical narrative, where the events of history are understood as the product of human actions that occur in accordance with God's sovereign plan.

Turning to the New Testament, the balance between divine and human agency is particularly evident in Philippians 2:12-13, from which I draw the title of this book: "Therefore, my beloved, just as you have always obeyed me, not only in my presence but much more now in my absence, work out your own salvation with fear and trembling; for it is God who is at work in you, enabling you both to will and to work for his good pleasure." In this brief passage, Paul affirms the priority of divine agency—God is working in the believer to cause their will and work without negating human agency, for we genuinely will and work.[2] There is a balance between the imperative—"work out your own salvation"—and the indicative—"it is God who is at work."[3] The work of God is the basis of our own work, which is why that

---

2 As G. Walter Hansen summarizes, "The priority of God's work does not vitiate our responsibility to work. We are not puppets on God's strings; we are fully responsible human beings obligated to continue to work out our salvation." G. Walter Hansen, *The Letter to the Philippians* (Grand Rapids, MI: Eerdmans, 2009), 178.

3 See Thomas R. Schreiner, *Paul, Apostle of God's Glory in Christ: A Pauline Theology* (Downers Grove, IL: IVP Academic, 2001), 253-55, 256-57. Schreiner shows that this balance between the imperative and indicative is characteristic of much of Paul's thoughts on the Christian life.

work proceeds in fear and trembling, which de-emphasize our human agency as insignificant compared with God's.[4] Broadly, such "fear and trembling" are an outworking of the humility that Christians adopt (Phil 2:3) in following Christ Jesus (Phil 2:6–11).[5] In Philippians again, like other passages mentioned above, divine providence and human freedom and responsibility are simultaneously affirmed.

Scripture places clear parameters around our analysis of providence and freedom, yet for the purposes of this study, it is beneficial to offer a conceptual framework to make sense of the Bible's teachings. The bulk of this chapter will therefore be spent developing an account of concurrent human and divine action that will equip us to understand moral formation in the marketplace to be the work of God without eliminating human freedom, responsibility, and causation. Along the way, I will briefly make connections between the doctrine of providence and the theology of economics, though the bulk of these connections will not occur until part III. I argue in this chapter that a noncontrastive account of transcendence combined with a robust doctrine of concurrence allow us to see God and creatures as causes of created effects in different ways, such that humans remain radically dependent on divine grace in all dimensions of salvation, including moral transformation in the marketplace, while remaining genuinely free agents who bear responsibility for the sins they commit, including those within markets. This theology of providence serves as the first of three theological foundations to be used in my analysis of market design and empirical economics.

A NONCONTRASTIVE ACCOUNT OF TRANSCENDENCE

Kathryn Tanner has developed what is, in my opinion, the most insightful account of divine transcendence and immanence among recent systematic theologians. Her account is rooted in the fact that "divinity is not a kind of thing at all, which might either be like some features of the world or simply opposed to them all, considered as a whole."[6] If God were part of a kind or

---

4 Karl Barth notes that the same phrase, "fear and trembling," is coupled with "weakness" in 1 Corinthians 2:3 and with the obedience of servants in Ephesians 6:5. Karl Barth, *The Epistle to the Philippians*, trans. James W. Leitch (Richmond, VA: John Knox, 1962), 71.

5 Barth, *The Epistle to the Philippians*, 71.

6 Kathryn Tanner, "Is God in Charge? Creation and Providence," in *Essentials of Christian Theology*, ed. William C. Placher (Louisville, KY: Westminster John Knox,

genus, then several things might follow. First, God would be reduced to one being "within a single order."[7] For example, if God were part of the kind *things in space*, space would serve as a determinant of divine existence, restricting or constricting God. However, God cannot be a member of the kind *things in space* because God is the Creator of space itself. Second, if God were part of a kind, transcendence and immanence might then be established on the basis of an opposition between two kinds of things within this single order. Thus, we might speak of God's transcendence in spatial terms as being up and God's immanence as being down. On this contrastive account, the more transcendent (up) God is, the less immanent (down). Of course, Scripture does speak of God in terms of elevation and in terms of spatial location, such that God is in the heavens or located within the temple. Yet God's presence in heaven was never understood to prevent God's being present in the temple (Ps 11:4) or acting for God's people wherever God pleased (Ps 135:6), nor did God's location in a specific spatial location indicate that God was restricted to that space (Isa 66:1).[8] All spatial language used of God is best understood as accommodation in service of communicating more substantive theological truths. The biblical account of God creating the heavens and the earth—shorthand for the entirety of the universe—suggests that God exceeds fundamental aspects of the universe that God has created, such as space and time. Second, if God is part of a kind of things, then it would follow that some created things would be more similar to God than others, establishing a hierarchy of divinity.[9] Conversely, a third conclusion might be that God would be limited by that which was opposed to God, as if divine agency were especially or only over other things of the same genus as God.[10]

Against such possible conclusions, Tanner argues for a noncontrastive view of transcendence where "God transcends the world as a whole in a manner that cannot properly be talked about in terms of a simple opposition within

---

2003), 120. Tanner sees this as typical of Hellenistic cosmologies, with limited exceptions found in figures like Plotinus who inconsistently attempt to affirm radical transcendence and immanence. Kathryn Tanner, *God and Creation in Christian Theology: Tyranny or Empowerment?* (Minneapolis: Fortress, 1988), 38–39, 42.

7 Tanner, *God and Creation*, 45.

8 On this point, see Walther Eichrodt, *Theology of the Old Testament*, vol. 2, trans. J. A. Baker (Philadelphia: Westminster, 1967), 186–94.

9 Tanner, "Is God in Charge?," 119.

10 Tanner, *God and Creation*, 46.

the same universe of discourse."[11] This account of transcendence is rooted in a clear rejection of univocal predication—at a basic metaphysical level, God and the world are not the same and so cannot be classified as members of a common kind.[12] An analogical account of theological language here requires rejecting any claims to God and creation, in part or in whole, being part of a common genus. Any attribute of creation that might seem to be shared by God—for example, God and creation both exist—cannot result in God and creation being members of a common genus, for the shared word for the divine and created attributes actually signify different things: God does not exist in the same way that creation does. Because God is not properly part of a kind, God's transcendence and immanence cannot be rooted in a contrast based on membership of a kind. God's immanence is not their being "down" in contrast to their transcendence in the realm "up there." God's transcendence is not rooted in any contrast between immanence and transcendence by virtue of God being a member of a genus.[13]

Tanner's noncontrastive account of transcendence is rooted in a robust doctrine of analogy, but it also has a strong Christological basis. She sees much modern Christology as rooted in a competitive or contrastive account of transcendence and immanence: "The more the humanity of Jesus is emphasized in modern Christologies the more the divinity of Jesus is downplayed."[14] A noncontrastive view of transcendence allows Tanner to argue that Christ can remain radically transcendent to creation in terms of the divine nature while also radically immanent within creation, even to the point of personal presence through the hypostatic union: "It is that very radical transcendence

---

11 Tanner, *God and Creation*, 42.

12 For example, see Tanner, *God and Creation*, 40, 42, 47.

13 Thomas Tracy objects to Tanner's position, arguing that God's transcendence cannot be defined in purely noncontrastive ways because at the very least there must be a contrast such as God being defined without contrast and creatures being defined through contrast. It would seem that Tracy misunderstands the object of noncontrastive claims about God. The claim is not that there is no contrast between God and creation. After all, Tracy's point is made far more simply by noting that God is God and creation is not God, a contrast. Rather, the proper claim is that transcendence is not defined in contrast to immanence, such that one must be sacrificed to obtain the other. God's being immanent in the world does not require that God sacrifice certain aspects of transcendence nor vice versa. Thomas F. Tracy, "Divine Action, Created Causes, and Human Freedom," in *The God Who Acts: Philosophical and Theological Explorations*, ed. Thomas F. Tracy (University Park: Pennsylvania State University Press, 1994), 85–87.

14 Kathryn Tanner, *Jesus, Humanity, and the Trinity: A Brief Systematic Theology* (Minneapolis: Fortress, 2001), 8.

that enables incarnation with what is other than God."[15] The fact that God can be radically different than creation and yet radically present is encoded within the Chalcedonian definition's claim that the human Jesus of Nazareth is the same one who is divine, yet "the distinction between the natures is not destroyed because of the union," for the absolute distinction between God and creation (i.e., transcendence) persists.

DIVINE TRANSCENDENCE, HUMAN CAUSATION, AND THE ECONOMY

For the purposes of this book, a noncontrastive account of transcendence is most significant for its implications for concurrent divine/human actions. The term *concurrence* traditionally refers to the manner in which something can be caused both by divine and creaturely efficacy. Concurrence can be understood to be mediate, in which case God conserves created causes that are the only needed cause of effects. Or it can be understood to be immediate, such that God is a direct cause of both the created cause and the created effect, without eliminating the efficacy of the created cause.[16] Tanner affirms an immediate concurrence, such that God is able to be radically immanent to human efficacy, which is "immediately and entirely grounded in the creative agency of God."[17] Created agency remains distinct from God's agency, but it does not cooperate with divine agency in the sense of conditioning God's agency.[18] Nor can we say that created agency and divine agency each contribute part of the causal power needed for an effect. Yet creaturely agency remains a genuine secondary cause of created events. In order to make sense of this, Tanner suggests that we "picture the plane of nondivine existence (which

---

15 Tanner, *Jesus, Humanity, and the Trinity*, 11.

16 Thomas Gornall, *A Philosophy of God: The Elements of Thomist Natural Theology* (London: Sheed and Ward, 1962), 103.

17 Tanner, *God and Creation*, 91. This claim can be linked to God's role in the immediate conservation of creation. As W. Matthews Grant notes, "It is hard to see what feature belongs to creaturely substances, but not to creaturely operations, such that the former, but not the latter, require that God directly cause them." W. Matthews Grant, *Free Will and God's Universal Causality: The Dual Sources Account* (London: Bloomsbury, 2019), 27.

18 See the discussions in Tanner, *God and Creation*, 96–97, and Tanner, "Is God in Charge?," 124; Kathryn Tanner, "Human Freedom, Human Sin, and God the Creator," in Tracy, *The God Who Acts*, 114.

is the whole of the world as we know it) suspended in existence at each and every one of its points, and therefore in its entirety, by God's creative action."[19]

We can work to develop a more robust account of human and divine cooperative agency through more extensive theological analysis. A starting point is recognizing that rejecting the idea of God being a member of any kind or genus requires that God and creatures are not causes in the same way. This is so in at least three cases. First, the word *cause* only applies to God in an analogical sense, not a univocal one. Created and divine causal agency are not the same, so the two do not compete in bringing an effect to be.[20] Second, created causality is dependent on the Creator, whose divine power is the basis of any created causality in terms of its "power, exercise, manner of activity and effect."[21] This means that created causes, in fact the entire causal structure of the universe, is dependent at all points on God's independent causal power. In this sense, God is wholly the cause of created effects without competitively eliminating the created cause. Third, we must insist that God is effective as a cause such that when God causes created causes, God ensures that they truly are causes. Thus, in concurrence, God causes in a manner distinct from human causation while establishing human causation as genuinely causal and efficacious.

Here, one might object to an account like Tanner's by arguing that it renders human agency superfluous and not actually causal in any meaningful sense.[22] Tanner replies to this concern by insisting that "it makes as much sense to deny there are created powers and efficacy because God brings about all that is, as to deny there is a creation because there is a creator."[23] W. Matthews Grant addresses the same objection to his account of concurrence, which is similar to Tanner's. He argues that the created cause would not be superfluous under the following conditions: "Necessarily, for any x and y, if any x causes the whole of y at a time t, then there is no other cause, z, of y, which brings about the whole of y at t and which would have done so even in the absence of x's bringing about the whole of y at t."[24] Suppose x refers to

---

19 Tanner, "Human Freedom," 113.
20 In Tanner's words, "God's transcendence prohibits talk of God's working with created causality in any way that implies the parity of divine agency and created causality within a common causal nexus or plane." Tanner, *God and Creation*, 93–94.
21 Tanner, *God and Creation*, 86.
22 For example, see Tracy, "Divine Action," 85–86.
23 Tanner, *God and Creation*, 86.
24 Grant, *God's Universal Causality*, 44.

a created cause, *y* is a created effect, and *z* is God's causal power. A created cause would remain an efficacious cause if God's causal power would not have brought about the created effect without that human cause. For example, consider a fire causing heat. If God (*z*) would not have caused the heat had not God also caused the fire (*x*), and if the fire (*x*) still causes the heat, then the fire is not superfluous.[25] Created causes remain truly efficacious, bringing about effects in a causal manner analogous to yet distinct from divine causation, which God has chosen to work in and through created causes, not without them.

The account of concurrence that I have been developing has significant implications for a theology of economics. God's use of secondary causes allows us to consider the possibility that social phenomena like markets may be a secondary cause of God's divine work in sanctifying Christians. Chapter 5 will develop a theology of grace that provides further reason to support this claim. Albino Barrera has already developed a helpful though general account of secondary causality in markets. Barrera explains that in secondary causation, "there are proper final effects imputed to both primary and secondary causes."[26] This means that secondary causes within the economic sphere—for example, certain acts of buying, selling, or producing—could contribute to our development of the virtues or even to the fulfillment of our supernatural end. In fact, Barrera argues that the economy is "unusually fertile ground for perfective human action because of the intrinsic difficulty of its requirements."[27] These difficulties include pursuit of "order among discordant wills, unceasing intelligent activity, and interpersonal resource transfers that are often sacrificial, especially in the case of scarcity."[28] Markets can thus contribute to the positive moral formation of market participants. At the same time, sanctification through the ordinary means of grace within the church should produce morally improved economic participation. As participants in the economy become increasingly renewed in the divine image, we can anticipate increasing excellence of secondary causes.[29] Though the ecclesial dimension of the moral formation of economic agents is vital to a complete

---

25 Grant, *God's Universal Causality*, 44.
26 Albino Barrera, *God and the Evil of Scarcity: Moral Foundations of Economic Agency* (Notre Dame, IN: University of Notre Dame Press, 2005), 30.
27 Barrera, *God and the Evil of Scarcity*, 30.
28 Barrera, *God and the Evil of Scarcity*, 31.
29 Barrera, *God and the Evil of Scarcity*, 32.

theological account of the economy, the scope of this study is more restricted, focusing on the formative role of markets.[30]

Tanner's and Barrera's insights provide a helpful theological starting point for the analysis of the findings of experimental economics. Economic agency can be perfective in the face of scarcity because it allows for the development of virtue through secondary causation in the market, if such causation is a participation in the divine perfections.[31] We cannot treat such perfection as an automatic outcome of market participation, as the *doux commerce* approach can sometimes seem to do, but we also cannot universally reject the possibility of divine agency in markets, as if God's immanence and causal agency were somehow restricted and limited in scope.[32] Because God is not part of a kind, he is equally and radically transcendent from all created realities, including markets, but this transcendence is also the basis for his absolute immanence to all of the created order, including markets. As a result, an ethic too heavily shaped by a realism rooted in human potential can ignore the divine aspect of concurrent market acts.[33] The universal causal efficacy of God does raise questions about human freedom and moral culpability within creation. Can secondary causes be free in a meaningful sense such that we can rightly speak of their sinning in the economic sphere? After all, terms like *sin* identify areas of human culpability and moral agency, which are widely held to require freedom. I turn now to consider this question.

---

30 Strong treatments of ecclesial moral formation of economic agents are found in Cavanaugh, *Being Consumed*, 47–58, 75–85; Kelly S. Johnson, "Praying: Poverty," in Hauerwas and Wells, *The Blackwell Companion to Christian Ethics*, 225–36. D. Stephen Long and Tripp York, "Remembering: Offering Our Gifts," in Hauerwas and Wells, *The Blackwell Companion to Christian Ethics*, 332–45.

31 Barrera, *God and the Evil of Scarcity*, 199–201.

32 This would run contrary to one of Tanner's main rules for speaking of divine agency: "Avoid in talk about God's creative agency all suggestion of limitation in scope or manner." Tanner, *God and Creation*, 47.

33 As Sean Doherty notes, the fact that the kingdom of God "*breaks in* to the present order" suggests that some gains in society are possible through God's work, even as a rejection of utopianism is valid. Sean Doherty, "The Kingdom of God and the Economic System: An Economics of Hope," in *Theology and Economics: A Christian Vision of the Common Good*, ed. Jeremy Kidwell and Sean Doherty (New York: Palgrave Macmillan, 2015), 151–52.

CONCURRENCE, HUMAN FREEDOM, AND MORAL RESPONSIBILITY

If the causes and effects of economic exchanges occurring within markets are rightly considered the effect of divine primary causality, one may suspect that the secondary causality of human beings is not free but, rather, determined. This is certainly a puzzle, but it must be made clear from the start that this is only a theological variety of a much larger philosophical question that extends into other religious, philosophical, and scientific perspectives. The existence of human freedom, though widely regarded as important and real, is notoriously difficult to substantiate.[34] Even within a naturalistic perspective, we are dealing with two levels of causation. What may appear to be a closed and determined causal chain of neurons in the body is also held to be the result of the free agency of the human mind. A blanket rejection of the supervenience of any primary cause on any secondary cause would therefore pose problems of a reductionist sort to human agency as well as to divine agency.[35] If we grant that a mind can act in a nondetermined fashion through the causal chain of the brain and nervous system, I see no *prima facie* reason to deny a similar account of dual causation in divine agency.

Affirmation of divine primary causation and creaturely freedom is found across the theological tradition. As surveyed in the introduction to this chapter, Scripture testifies to both human freedom and divine causation of human actions. This dual affirmation is found across a wide range of theological traditions and eras. Thus, Thomas Aquinas explains that God moves natural causes in such a manner that "he does not deprive their actions of being voluntary."[36] Similarly, John Calvin can write, "The Lord has furnished men with the arts of deliberation and causation, that they may employ them in subservience to his providence, in the preservation of their life."[37] In other words, humans do truly have choice and causal power, though such operations

---

[34] To defend human freedom, one must contend with a range of different kinds of determinism, including behavioral determinism, theological determinism, and various scientific determinisms that appeal to such things as the laws of physics, human neurology, and/or genetics.

[35] See Frank G. Kirkpatrick, *The Mystery and Agency of God: Divine Being and Acting in the World* (Minneapolis: Fortress, 2014), 110.

[36] Thomas Aquinas, *Summa Theologica*, trans. Fathers of the English Dominican province (Allen, TX: Christian Classics, 1981), I.I Q. 83 a. 1.

[37] John Calvin, *Institutes of the Christian Religion*, trans. Henry Beveridge (Peabody, MA: Hendrickson, 2008), I.17.4.

still occur within God's own causal agency. This basic position persists in Reformed circles for centuries, even if there is variety within some of the finer details of the doctrine of free will. For example, several centuries later, Herman Bavinck insists that "God—because he is God and the universe is his creation—by the infinitely majestic activity of his knowing and willing, does not destroy but instead creates and maintains the freedom and independence of his creatures."[38]

Nevertheless, more can be said about the relationship between human and divine agency. As I develop an account of providence and human freedom, I must be clear that I am restricting my analysis to the question of freedom and human causality generally speaking. I am not going to focus on the question of human freedom in conversion, belief, justification, or, more broadly, salvation. These theological disputes are particularly thorny, so attention to them at this juncture would merely distract us from the focus of this book.[39] The rest of this book will assume that humans are not saved by their economic actions. As a Protestant, I affirm that conversion and justification are *sola fide* and *sola gratia*, even as I will leave the finer details of these doctrines for another work. However, as will become especially clear in chapter 5, God's work of redemptive transformation can be aided or hindered by our concurrent work in markets, but we must still attribute our moral development to God's gracious working through markets—a grace I will call *common grace*, following the Reformed tradition. Insofar as God's work in all of creation, including markets, is oriented toward his work of salvation in the *ordo salutis*, then the more general question of freedom and human responsibility is related to, though not identical to, these complicated questions about freedom in conversion and salvation. Restricting discussion to the more general sense of concurrence leads to an emphasis on three dimensions of freedom: humans act in a voluntary manner, causally producing contingent effects.

---

38 Herman Bavinck, *God and Creation*, vol. 2 of *Reformed Dogmatics*, ed. John Bolt, trans. John Vriend (Grand Rapids, MI: Baker Academic, 2004), 377.

39 For a concise analysis of various perspectives on freedom and providence just within Catholic and Protestant circles during the time of the European reformations, see Justo L. González, *A History of Christian Thought: From the Protestant Reformation to the Twentieth Century*, rev. ed. (Nashville: Abingdon, 1987), 224–36; Matthew Barrett, "The Bondage and Liberation of the Will," in *Reformation Theology: A Systematic Summary*, ed. Matthew Barrett (Wheaton, IL: Crossway, 2017), 451–508.

Human Action as Voluntary

At a basic level, human actions are free in the sense that they are not completed under compulsion or coercion. In other words, providentially governed human actions do not happen contrary to our human willing but in accordance with our will and desires. As Anselm of Canterbury writes, "Every willing person wills his own willing."[40] Most definitions of free will include the dimension of human actions being taken voluntarily, but compatibilist definitions reduce free will to its voluntary dimension. Many theologians and philosophers are unconvinced that this voluntary dimension of freedom is enough to qualify something as freedom. Famously, Martin Luther defended a compatibilist position in what he called his "thunderbolt argument"—God knows everything necessarily, so everything happens necessarily.[41] Yet Luther dislikes the word *necessary*, "for neither the divine nor the human will does what it does, whether good or evil, under any compulsion, but from sheer pleasure or desire, as with true freedom; and yet the will of God is immutable and infallible."[42] Later Protestant authors would describe the voluntary dimension of freedom as the "spontaneity" of the will.[43] Erasmus argued that this view of freedom took away human culpability and merit, believing that choice was an important component of freedom.[44] While the voluntary nature of free human acts is important, an account of human freedom rooted in a noncontrastive view of transcendence permits us to say more.

The Reality of Human Causal Power

Some accounts of free will require that the will is ultimately moved by the human agent. In a minimal sense, this might mean that the causal power of the act includes something within the human agent. Thus, John Webster

---

40 Anselm of Canterbury, *On Free Will*, in *Anselm of Canterbury: The Major Works*, ed. Brian Davies and G. R. Evans (Oxford: Oxford University Press, 1998), §5.

41 Martin Luther, *On the Bondage of the Will*, in *Luther and Erasmus: Free Will and Salvation*, ed. E. Gordon Rupp and Philip S. Watson (Philadelphia: Westminster, 1964), 118–19.

42 Luther, *On the Bondage of the Will*, 120.

43 Willem J. Van Asselt, J. Martin Bac, and Roelf T. te Velde, *Reformed Thought on Freedom: The Concept of Free Choice in Early Modern Reformed Theology* (Grand Rapids, MI: Baker Academic, 2010), 84–85.

44 Desiderius Erasmus, *On the Freedom of the Will: A Diatribe or Discourse*, in Rupp and Watson, *Luther and Erasmus*, 84–85.

argues that "divine providential acts are not simple compulsion (the archer sending the arrow) but rather intrinsic to the creature whom God moves."[45] A stronger account of human causal powers is found in a definition considered by Eleanor Stump: "An agent acts with free will, or is morally responsible for an act, only if her own intellect and will are the sole ultimate source or first cause."[46] Historically, there was wide consensus that humans had genuine causal powers, but the extent to which such power should be treated as primary or derivative of God's power was debated.[47] To an extent, a noncontrastive account of divine transcendence evades some of these historical debates, especially if we restrict the scope of analysis to situations excluding conversion and saving faith. God and creatures are both complete causes of human acts of willing, but their causal powers are only analogically related. As such, they do not compete, nor is each a partial cause of the effect. Divine causal power is logically prior to human causal power, but given God's eternality, it is imprecise to consider this causal power temporally prior. One final matter remains: the question of whether human acts are contingent.

Human Acts as Contingent

There is a long tradition in Christian theology of speaking of three types of freedom: freedom from necessity, freedom from sin, and freedom from misery.[48] All humans are free from necessity; after the fall, none but Christ

---

45 John Webster, "Providence," in *Christian Dogmatics: Reformed Theology for the Church Catholic*, ed. Michael Allen and Scott R. Swain (Grand Rapids, MI: Baker, 2016), 162.

46 Eleanor Stump, "Augustine on Free Will," in *The Cambridge Companion to Augustine*, ed. Eleonore Stump and Norman Kretzmann (Cambridge: Cambridge University Press, 2001), 126.

47 Bac offers a distinction, historically common, between "previous concurrence" taught by the Reformed and "simultaneous concurrence" taught by the Jesuits and Remonstrants. The Reformed require "previous" because "simultaneous" does not effect the will itself but only the outcome, making the created will the cause of its own willing and thus, in some sense, of its salvation. There must be a dependence on God in becoming as well as in being: "Simultaneous concurrence subverts the order of causation, the creature determining the act of the Creator." J. Martin Bac, *Perfect Will Theology: Divine Agency in Reformed Scholasticism as against Suárez, Episcopius, Descartes, and Spinoza* (Leiden: Brill, 2010), 449–50.

48 This discussion is found across a wide range of sources, from Peter Lombard through the medieval period and into both Protestant and Catholic sources during the Reformation, including Zanchi, Bellarmine, Calvin, Arminius, and Molina. For further

is free from sin; and those who have died and gone to be with Christ are free from misery. The contingency of human acts must be considered from two angles: first, from that of God's causal power, and second, from the perspective of creaturely agency itself.

As noted above, Luther and some compatibilists have argued that human acts are necessary because God foreknows them. Given divine omnipotence and omniscience, what God has willed seems to be necessary. There is good reason, however, to argue that God's acts toward creation are in some respect contingent. After all, if it were necessary for God to create or redeem in an absolute sense, it would seem to jeopardize both the gratuity of grace and the aseity of God. This is why the necessity of created effects due to divine foreknowledge must be understood to be a consequent necessity, a necessity derived from and a consequence of God's logically—not temporally—prior free decisions to create, redeem, and more broadly govern the universe.[49] Even so, a consequent necessity might be seen to still eliminate the contingency of created actions, rendering them determined. Grant argues that such necessity would not be the same as having the effect be determined. According to classical understandings of the contingent divine actions, they require something within God but also a contingent created term.[50] Because God is free from causing the created effect, his willed reason for causing it is not logically sufficient for it; something in the created effect is required.[51] As Grant explains, "God is not logically sufficient for A, since there are [possible] worlds in which God exists and A does not. God is, however, logically necessary for A. For, A cannot exist unless caused by God, and A cannot be caused by God in any world where (*per impossibile*) God does not exist."[52]

---

information, see Eef Dekker, "An Ecumenical Debate between Reformation and Counter-Reformation? Bellarmine and Ames on *liberum arbitrium*," in *Reformation and Scholasticism: An Ecumenical Enterprise*, ed. Willem J. van Asselt and Eef Dekker (Grand Rapids, MI: Baker Academic, 2001), 145–46; Van Asselt, Bac, and te Velde, *Reformed Thought on Freedom*, 82–83; González, *History of Christian Thought*, 227.

49 See the discussion in Anselm of Canterbury, *Why God Became a Man*, in Davies and Evans, *Anselm of Canterbury*, II.17.

50 Robert M. Doran, *The Trinity in History: A Theology of the Divine Missions*, vol. 1 of *Missions and Processions* (Toronto: University of Toronto Press, 2012), 40–64. Contingent predication presupposes the created term so cannot be entirely logically prior, even though we can say that the created effect depends on God in a way that God does not depend on the effect. See Grant, *God's Universal Causality*, 62–63.

51 Grant, *God's Universal Causality*, 60–61.

52 Grant, *God's Universal Causality*, 63.

For some A to be determined by God, according to Grant, God must be both logically prior to A and logically sufficient for A. Since that is not the case here, human actions are not determined. Since God causes these events immutably, through consequent necessity, they are also not absolutely necessary, leaving space for some form of contingency.

Viewed from a human perspective, creaturely causes and effects are contingent as well, though the nature of this contingency is debated. The two leading proposals are those of diachronic contingency and synchronic contingency. As Richard Muller summarizes, "The diachronic definition appears to root contingency in past possibility, defining the contingent as something that, potentially, may either not exist or be false at a time other than when it exists or is true. The synchronic definition roots contingency in the existence of a present potency to the opposite, defining the contingent as something that, potentially, may either not exist or be false at the same time that it exists or is true."[53] Synchronic contingency points to a simultaneity of potency (*simultas potentiae*) where the will has the power to freely will two distinct effects in the same instant of time.[54] On this basis, the human act is thought to be contingent even at the time it was performed.[55] Diachronic contingency considers the act contingent prior to the time it was performed. Each approach decouples necessity and immutability in order to preserve a contingent creation, arguing that God may immutably will an outcome, but that outcome remains contingent in that it could be otherwise.[56]

Much more can be said about human freedom and divine providence, but I hope to have laid an adequate foundation for the purposes of this work. Humans act concurrently with God, including in market contexts, which

---

53 Richard A. Muller, *Divine Will and Human Choice: Freedom, Contingency, and Necessity in Early Modern Reformed Thought* (Grand Rapids, MI: Baker, 2017), 37.

54 Muller, *Divine Will and Human Choice*, 49. For analysis of specific theologians purported to accept the synchronic contingency perspective—many details of interpretation are contested—see Van Asselt, Bac, and te Velde, *Reformed Thought on Freedom*, 194–95; Andreas J. Beck, "Gisbertus Voetius (1589–1676): Basic Features of His Doctrine of God," in van Asselt and Dekker, *Reformation and Scholasticism*, 215–17.

55 Muller notes that the language of simultaneous potency is used rather than simultaneous contingency, suggesting that *contingency* may not be the right word to use here. Muller, *Divine Will and Human Choice*, 58–59.

56 Beck, "Gisbertus Voetius," 221.

establishes a basis for seeing market actions that contribute to positive moral formation as a divine action. Yet all concurrent human actions remain free insofar as they are willingly and spontaneously performed by creatures who are true causes of effects that are contingent, possibly being otherwise. Because human actions are free, immoral acts in the market are still rightly considered sin, for which human agents will ultimately be held responsible. One final puzzle remains concerning the concurrent acts of God and humans: is God culpable for the evils that creatures perform in the world?

CONCURRENCE AND THE PROBLEM OF EVIL

If creaturely agency is enabled by divine agency in such an exhaustive manner, we might be tempted to attribute evil and sin to God, contrary to the divine moral perfection and impeccability (e.g., Jas 1:13). This temptation explains the reasoning behind many modern contrastive accounts of transcendence that also restrict divine agency.[57] Tanner takes a different approach, advocating that we "simply admit the limits that this picture places on the intelligibility of sin." God does not cause sin and evil, but the mechanics here are not fully explicable. Tanner argues that this is exactly what we should expect, for if God is the explanation of all that exists and sin is an absence or diminishment of existence, then it would not be from God, nor would it be explainable.[58] I confess that I often vacillate between considering this response to sin brilliant and seeing it as a sleight of hand that evades the substantive issues at stake in the question. Admittedly, I am not sure that I have much more substantive to offer.

Despite the lack of an exhaustive explanation for sin given a noncontrastive account of divine transcendence and the resulting affirmation of exhaustive divine concurrence, some clear parameters for the culpability for sin and evil must be in place. Traditionally, numerous precise distinctions were posited within the simple divine will, distinctions meant in part to ensure that evil was not attributed to God. Francis Turretin, for example, distinguishes between the decretive and preceptive will. The latter refers to "what he wills that we should do," while the former refers to what actually occurs. There are goods

---

57 For example, see David Ray Griffin, *God, Power, and Evil: A Process Theodicy* (Philadelphia: Westminster, 1976).
58 Tanner, "Human Freedom," 132–33.

that God wills and commands that humans violate. When human creatures voluntarily cause contingent effects contrary to the preceptive will of God, God's decretive will is said to be negative or permissive. It is negative in the sense that it stops willing the good end declared in the preceptive will and wills rather to not interfere with creaturely action. The decretive will toward evil can also be described as permissive, a term suggesting that primary responsibility for the outcome lies on humans.[59] In my estimation, these distinctions assume a noncontrastive account of transcendence such that creaturely acts, including sinning, are radically dependent on God, without whose preserving work neither the sinner nor the effect of sin would exist. Nevertheless, this divine immanence to creaturely agency does not entail that God is not also transcendent of human sinful actions, such that God's preserving work here is a gracious restraint of judgment for an act that humans alone intend as a *telos* of their action. For God, sin is not the intent but rather the permitted result of human sinfulness. Yet I do not posit a consequent will here, such that God's will is seen as conditioned or determined by created decisions in a logically or temporally sequential manner.[60]

In terms of the theology of economics, God's innocence of sin and evil means that humans are at fault for the injustice and moral malformation of the marketplace. The account of concurrence I have offered here also precludes any fatalistic account of human agency; the real causal power available to humans enables them to make substantive improvements to unjust markets or to market processes prone to lead to moral malformation. If human freedom is in large part associated with the spontaneous and voluntary quality of human actions, then markets will also be an important part of Christian moral analysis insofar as markets have demonstrable effects on human desires. Such moral analysis will also require a conceptual framework for considering the social dimensions of sin and grace within markets. This is the subject of chapter 5.

---

59 Francis Turretin, *Institutes of Elenctic Theology*, trans. George Musgrave Giger, ed. James T. Dennison Jr. (Philipsburg, NJ: P and R, 1992), 3.15.1–6.

60 This is but an academically sophisticated way to say that humans are responsible for sin but God is not and that God remains immutable, simple, eternal, and absolute despite this human freedom and culpability.

CHAPTER 5

Sin and Grace

Common grace is united to special grace in the same way that redemption unites itself to creation. Thus, the fact of common grace includes the earthly, temporal calling.

—Cory Brock and Gray Sutanto[1]

Any theological attempt to understand the ways that markets shape market participants must rely on a theology of sin and grace. This is particularly the case as we wrestle with the thorny questions of how markets can contribute to the positive moral development of humans since the moral development of persons is typically the proper domain of the doctrine of grace in theology. Similarly, analysis of the problematic moral formations that result from markets intrudes on what was classically the domain of the doctrine of sin. With these overlapping domains in mind, this chapter will emphasize the more communal and collective aspects of sin and grace. In the doctrine of sin, this means that particular attention must be paid to the ideas of structural or systemic sin—How would impersonal markets play some role in harming our moral development? Who, if anyone, would have moral culpability for such malformation? By the end of this chapter, I hope to have laid the basic groundwork to allow for an answer to such questions. With the doctrine of grace, I will turn to the Reformed notion of common grace, which posits gifts of God bestowed on all humanity that restrain sin and allow for cultural and

---

1 Cory C. Brock and N. Gray Sutanto, *Neo-Calvinism: A Theological Introduction* (Bellingham, WA: Lexham, 2022), 234.

societal development. If such gifts are available to all, then presumably markets may be both a product of common grace and a means of transmitting that grace. Careful attention must be paid to the relationship between common and special grace in order to avoid a certain mechanistic soteriology rooted in social engineering. Risks notwithstanding, an analysis of these doctrines reveals the ways in which traditional concepts of sin and grace can serve as an analytic basis for turning again to consider the design of markets more in harmony with Christian visions of moral formation.

RELEVANT ASPECTS OF THE THEOLOGY OF SIN

Any theological analysis of markets must proceed within the framework of a sound hamartiology. Without such a framework, accusations against markets regarding the malformation they cause are imprecise at best and baseless at worst. This work will assume many classical Christian beliefs that are not controversial in the Western tradition, such as the fact that sin is universal and that the effects of sin extend into all dimensions of human nature, including mind, body, soul, and will.[2] I will also assume the doctrine of original sin, which suggests that all human beings are born under the effect of sin as a fundamental condition of human life for which human beings (i.e., Adam and Eve) are responsible, not God.[3] Given such basic Christian assumptions, it should be no surprise to find markets increasing particular sins or vices. Yet a theological understanding of how such moral formation occurs in a market context requires an analysis of a more recent development in hamartiology: the doctrine of social sin. Though widely discussed, the concept of social sin is still novel enough within the modern theological landscape that it can be used with a variety of meanings in mind. I turn now to the analysis of three common meanings: social sin as the sin of social groups, as structural sin, and as the social dimensions of the formation of personal moral subjects.

---

2 I will sidestep debates within theological anthropology over such subjects in the belief that many possible views could accept the basic ways that I appeal to these concepts.

3 I refer those seeking a more substantive explanation than I offer to the helpful introduction found in Tatha Wiley, *Original Sin: Origins, Developments, Contemporary Meanings* (New York: Paulist, 2002).

Social Sin and Collective Actions

In some instances, the term *social sin* is applied to what could be more precisely described as collective sin or as the sin of social groups.[4] There is a clear scriptural tendency to attribute sin and guilt to groups of peoples, for example, when a prophet might condemn entire nations of people (e.g., Zeph 2:4–15). In such condemnations, sinful actions and sin itself may be attributed to entire groups, as evident in Hosea's language of "the iniquity of Ephraim and the crimes of Samaria" (Hos 7:1) or in Amos's oracles of the punishment of Damascus, Gaza, Tyre, Edom, Moab, Judah, and Israel for their crimes (Amos 1:3, 6, 9, 11; 2:1, 4, 6). While such usage could be an example of synecdoche, where the whole of a nation is meant to stand for a part (i.e., those actually culpable), some parts of Scripture suggest a collective agency and responsibility. For example, God holds the entire people of Israel responsible for the sins of individuals (e.g., Num 21:4–6; Josh 7:1, 11–13), and the people are occasionally depicted as repenting of the sins of prior generations (Exod 20:5; Num 14:18; Deut 9:5; Neh 9:2; Dan 9:16).[5]

To my knowledge, a detailed moral analysis or theological explanation for such collective agency is not found in the biblical texts themselves. Biblical scholars and ethicists have long recognized that community is both (a) the primary context within which Scripture is read as an ethical text and (b) a major subject of the Bible's teaching on ethics.[6] For this reason, the prophets might address communities because communities are the primary locus of moral formation and deliberation. Yet this fact does little to clarify questions of guilt and culpability for such collective acts. It may be that groups are considered guilty where there is no active resistance to evil within the community.[7] Though I have briefly addressed the question of moral culpability

---

4 Maurizio Ragazzi considers this the "strict sense of the expression." This concept cannot be used to negate the personal dimension of sin. Maurizio Ragazzi, "The Concept of Social Sin in Its Thomistic Roots," *Journal of Markets and Morality* 7, no. 2 (Fall 2004): 372–73.

5 See a more detailed discussion in D. T. Everhart, "Communal Reconciliation: Corporate Responsibility and Opposition to Systemic Sin," *International Journal of Systematic Theology* 25, no. 1 (January 2023): 7–8.

6 For the former, see Brevard S. Childs, *Biblical Theology of the Old and New Testaments: Theological Reflection in the Christian Bible* (Minneapolis: Fortress, 1992), 661–68. The latter is evident in Richard B. Hays, *The Moral Vision of the New Testament: A Contemporary Introduction to New Testament Ethics* (New York: HarperCollins, 1996), 193–204.

7 Everhart, "Communal Reconciliation," 11. This would be a dire situation, for as Cornelius Plantinga notes, we are prone to condone evils in the name of groups in ways

for social sin elsewhere,[8] the bulk of this book will focus on the second two meanings of social sin. Before turning to these meanings, a final word on social sin as the sin of social groups is in order.

Regardless of how the sins of social groups are judged, we must be careful to ensure that one can participate in society without necessarily sinning or being guilty or culpable of sin. After all, as Daniel Lee Hill and Ty Kieser note, our theories of social sin must be compatible with our Christology. If a theory of social sin required us to accept the idea that participation in society necessarily resulted in guilt, we would be left with a choice between denying the full humanity of Christ by denying his true participation in society or else denying the sinlessness of Christ, contrary to clear biblical teaching (Heb 4:15; 1 John 3:5) and creedal orthodoxy.[9] Therefore, it is necessary to insist that fully human persons can transcend the sin of the societies within which they live, for Christological reasons, even if the doctrines of original sin and the universality of sin compel us to say that no one but Christ has done so.[10] Given the Christologically heterodox risks of viewing social sin primarily as collective actions with necessarily shared culpability, Hill and Kieser advise a focus on what they call the "sinful social structures" model, which does not ascribe moral guilt and culpability to all participants of a society marked by sin.[11] I turn now to consider this understanding of social sin.

---

we would be unlikely to act as individuals. Cornelius Plantinga Jr., *Not the Way It's Supposed to Be: A Breviary of Sin* (Grand Rapids, MI: Eerdmans, 1995), 76.

8 D. Glenn Butner Jr. *Jesus the Refugee: Ancient Injustice and Modern Solidarity* (Minneapolis: Fortress, 2023), 180–81.

9 Daniel Lee Hill and Ty Kieser, "Social Sin and the Sinless Savior: Delineating Supra-Personal Sin in Continuity with Conciliar Christology," *Modern Theology* 38, no. 3 (July 2022): 569.

10 Roger Haight puts it nicely: "Individuals and groups can react against various aspects of social sin; human freedom can transcend society at any given point and become countercultural. But no one can escape all the aspects of one's social existence and participation." Roger Haight, "Sin and Grace," in *Systematic Theology: Roman Catholic Perspectives*, vol. 2, ed. Francis Schüssler Fiorenza and John P. Galvin (Minneapolis: Fortress, 1991), 105. To this I would add one very important exception: no one but Christ can escape all the aspects of one's social existence. As Daniel Lee Hill and Ty Kieser remark, "If Jesus participates in a sinful society, then participation is not sufficient for culpability." Hill and Kieser, "Social Sin," 585.

11 Hill and Kieser, "Social Sin," 573, 576.

Social Sin and Structures of Sin

Derek Nelson argues that theories of social sin are strongest when they rely on analysis of social structures in relation to sin and of the social and relational aspects of human personhood.[12] I find his claims to be persuasive, so these two dimensions of social sin must now be considered. First, I will treat what is alternately called *structural sin* and *structures of sin*, terms denoting how institutions, laws, social norms, and cultures of given groups can perpetuate, amplify, or even cause harmful or unjust outcomes contrary to the common good.[13] Structures of sin perpetuate sin because, as Stephen Ray notes, "they no longer need their creator to proceed."[14] He points to the example of race, a "presumptive [category] that is assumed for our society to exist as it does."[15] The socially constructed category of race becomes a factor in how institutions classify human beings, how laws and policies work, and how culture shapes our perceptions of the world.[16] Yet it is beyond the power of any individual or group to eliminate the category of race from our culture—this idea now exceeds direct human control, a force seemingly beyond the sum of the individual policies, institutions, and ideas about race found within

---

12 Derek R. Nelson, *What's Wrong with Sin? Sin in Individual and Social Perspective from Schleiermacher to Theologies of Liberation* (London: T & T Clark, 2009), 4.

13 Here are two related definitions. For Conor Kelly, a structure of sin is "an institution or collective practice that either socially idealizes or economically incentivizes actions seeking exclusive self-interest(s) at the expense of the common good." Conor M. Kelly, "The Nature and Operation of Structural Sin: Additional Insights from Theology and Moral Psychology," *Theological Studies* 80, no. 2 (June 2019): 301. Ignacio Ellacuría argues that "structures manifest and actualize the power of sin, thereby causing sin, by making it exceedingly difficult for men and women to lead the life that is rightfully theirs as the daughters and sons of God." Ignacio Ellacuría, "Aporte de la teologia de la liberación a las religions abrahámicas en la superaction del individualismo y del positivism," quoted in Jon Sobrino, "Central Position of the Reign of God in Theology," in *Systematic Theology: Perspectives from Liberation Theology*, ed. Jon Sobrino and Ignacio Ellacuría, trans. Robert R. Barr (Maryknoll, NY: Orbis, 1996), 43.

14 Stephen Ray, "Structural Sin," in *T&T Clark Companion to the Doctrine of Sin*, ed. Keith L. Johnson and David Lauber (London: Bloomsbury T & T Clark, 2016), 417.

15 Ray, "Structural Sin," 420.

16 D. T. Everhart makes a similar point about how structures of sin can perpetuate injustice when he notes, "When a racist law is ratified, it does not disappear when the politicians who wrote, passed and enforced it retire; it continues to be upheld by the governing body and the individuals that replace its ratifiers." Everhart, "Communal Reconciliation," 4.

our culture.[17] In this sense, structures of sin can amplify the actual sins of individuals, which may be their causes—the individual actual sin may be resolved through that individual's repentance and any needed restitution, but that same individual may no longer be able to stop the effects of that sin as perpetuated in culture, institutions, laws, and policies.

Ray explains why such structures ought to be classified as sin by appealing to Paul's concept of "principalities" and "powers" that oppose us (Eph 6:2), illustrating a connection with the demonic structural sin frequently found among theologians and ethicists.[18] For example, Delores Williams decries the structural oppression of Black women as "demonarchy," which she defines as "the demonic governance of black women's lives by white male and white female ruled systems using racism, violence, violation, retardation, and death as instruments of social control."[19] Williams understands demonarchy to involve both "white-controlled American institutions"[20] and a culture that fosters "a state of consciousness that believes white women are superior to and more valuable than any woman of color and that white men are the most valuable and superior forms of life on earth."[21] Evangelical theologian Stanley Grenz develops a theology of structures in his treatment of angelology. Grenz explores religious, political, intellectual, and moral "structures of existence," which are "constructs that humanity has created" that "condition individual and corporate human life."[22] Grenz treats such structures as suprahuman because they are not consciously changeable by groups, yet they are not quite impersonal.[23] Rather, Grenz links such structures with *stoicheion* ("elemental principles"), which can be cosmological in the sense of fundamental elements

---

17 Conor Kelly appeals to the sociological idea of emergence to explain how social structures exceed the sum of their parts, to which they are not reducible. Kelly, "The Nature and Operation of Structural Sin," 297–98. See a similar point in José Ignacio González Faus, "Sin," in Sobrino and Ellacuría, *Systematic Theology*, 197–98.

18 Besides those discussed in this paragraph, see also Miguel A. De La Torre and Edwin David Aponte, *Introducing Latino/a Theologies* (Maryknoll, NY: Orbis, 2001), 81.

19 Delores S. Williams, "The Color of Feminism," in *Feminist Theological Ethics: A Reader*, ed. Lois K. Daly (Louisville, KY: Westminster John Knox, 1994), 50.

20 Williams, "The Color of Feminism," 53.

21 Williams, "The Color of Feminism," 51.

22 Stanley J. Grenz, *Theology for the Community of God* (Grand Rapids, MI: Eerdmans, 1994), 228, 230.

23 Grenz, *Theology for the Community of God*, 230.

(2 Pet 3:10, 12) but can also refer to human traditions (Col 2:20–22).[24] Though Grenz does not take *stoicheion* to be spiritual beings, he does consider them under the influence of such beings, who have an influence on various laws and governments throughout Scripture.[25] These examples are representative of broader patterns.

The commonly made connection between structures of sin and demons brings us to the challenging question of whether structures of sin cause sin. Derek Nelson represents a common concern when he writes, "In very loosely idiomatic English usage, structures are sometimes accorded agential status. However, closer semantic and analytical examination reveals the truth that action requires intention and consciousness, and that therefore impersonal structures cannot act."[26] Those who ascribe the demonic to structures of sin might counter that demonic personal agents do have agency and would work through such structures, though I suspect many who appeal to demonic language do so for more metaphorical purposes. Nevertheless, even if the powers and principalities that oppose us (Eph 6:2) are purely impersonal structures, it seems necessary to distinguish between agency and causal power. Surely, it would be improper to declare a law to be a sinner, if by such an accusation one meant that the law was obligated to repent because it had personal moral culpability for the injustice its agency produced. Yet the concept of sin in Scripture is not restricted to such usage. In the New Testament and in its larger cultural context, *hamartia* can refer to wrong acts—both intentional and accidental—to the defective nature of humanity, or to cosmic power.[27] Further, the doctrine of original sin includes notions like original pollution and original guilt, such that even before a particular human being commits an actual sin, they are considered to be in sin.[28] Thus, language of structures of sin can be taken to intend a defective institution or other social structure that can be characterized as having causal power that brings about unjust or

---

24 Grenz, *Theology for the Community of God*, 231.
25 Grenz, *Theology for the Community of God*, 232. Grenz points to the mediation of the law through angels in Galatians 3:19 and the association between evil spirits linked with different dynasties in Daniel 10:12–13, 20.
26 Nelson, *What's Wrong with Sin?*, 97. Compare with Grenz, *Theology for the Community of God*, 320.
27 Walter Grundmann, "ἁμαρτάνω, ἁμάρτημα, ἁμαρτία," in *Theological Dictionary of the New Testament*, vol. I, ed. Gerhard Kittel, trans. Geoffrey W. Bromiley (Grand Rapids, MI: Eerdmans, 1964), 294–96.
28 This point is well made by González Faus, "Sin," 199.

immoral outcomes. The positional dimension of sin may also be applied in a loose manner to structures that stand as judged before God.

What, then, might it mean to affirm a statement like the one made by José Ignacio González Faus when he says, "When human beings sin, they create structures of sin, which, in their turn, make human beings sin"?[29] Several answers could be in order. First, if such structures are linked with spiritual beings, then it could be a claim about such supernatural agency. Second, structures often include material components, such as written text (e.g., signs, literature, law codes, etc.) or geographic distributions of a given thing (e.g., urban and suburban development, ethnic groups within and across national borders, etc.). It is not difficult to imagine such material components having a causal effect on human moral agency, and such effects may extend beyond the intent or even awareness of those persons who originally produced the material components, if such components were even designed at all. My discussion of experimental economics already reveals several such examples. For example, the concept of framing (pp. 27–28) showed that something like a price affixed to a given action, such as being late to pick up a child from day care, may prompt a mental shift in those involved in the action from the realm of ethics to the realm of cost/benefit analysis, possibly resulting in immoral action. In such instances, the typed text of prices itself may have a causal effect on the human mind and resulting actions. More examples will be discussed later in this work. For now, it seems justified to claim that the material components of structures can function as causes yet not to the extent that the freedom and moral responsibility of human beings are eliminated.[30] Though this justifies speaking of structures of sin, we must grant the deeper point that, lacking intent, such components cannot rightly be labeled as sin in the sense of willful transgression of some standard of justice.[31] The claim that structures can cause sin cannot, however, veil the fact that the structures themselves are often caused and legitimated by individual sins.[32] Third,

---

29 González Faus, "Sin," 198. Similarly, Cornelius Plantinga argues, "Character forms culture, which then forms character." Plantinga Jr., *Not the Way It's Supposed to Be*, 70.

30 For a helpful initial survey of questions of moral responsibility in the context of behavioral economics, which often uncovers social sin and structures of sin, see McRorie, "Rethinking Moral Agency in Markets," 195–206.

31 Questions of the culpability of persons influenced by such material components of structures remain beyond the scope of this book.

32 As Antonio González Fernández reminds us, "The Adamic logic is always and at the same time the logic of Babylon." Our individual efforts at self-justification become the cause

moving beyond particular actions, it seems important to note that structures may have some influence on the formation of conscience. Yet such formation is more frequently interpersonal so will be treated in the next section as a distinct category.

Social Sins and the Social Dimensions of Moral Personhood

While the term *social sin* sometimes refers to the sins of social groups and sometimes references structures of sin, the term's third usage is rooted in the social dimensions of human personhood. This is the dimension of social sin most clearly attested to in Scripture, and it has played a significant role in some modern accounts of original sin. In the Bible, the reader is often warned of the ways in which other sinners drag us into their sinful ways (e.g., Prov 12:26; 16:29; 22:24–25; 1 Cor 15:33). Harmful social influences are likely also implied in the Johannine usage of "the world" as a force that is hostile to God and their people (John 7:7; 12:31; 15:19; 16:11; 1 John 2:16; 4:4–5, etc.).[33] These social influences of sin are understood by some modern theologians to explain the basis for the transmission of original sin. For example, Karl Rahner notes that humans "actualize" themselves as "free subject[s] in a situation which is always determined by history and by other persons." Rahner adds, "The guilt of others is a permanent factor in the situation and realm of the individual's freedom."[34] Human freedom is constrained by the sin of others insofar as that sin restricts the possible acts available to a given person[35] and insofar as a given person's subjectivity is influenced by others' sins.

---

of our exploitation and competitive relationships with others, and self-justification is then used to legitimize structures of sin, for the victim is blamed for their failings, while the oppressor is said to have earned their greater power. See González Fernández, *God's Reign*, 77.

33 González Faus begins his treatment of structural sin with this passage, which he interprets to be a socioreligious order hostile to God or an oppressive system based on money or power for the few." González Faus, "Sin," 198. I see the socioeconomic dimensions of sin more clearly in the prophets and Luke/Acts, though I grant the fact that the world is social and a force for evil and for moral malformation. See Craig S. Keener, *The Gospel of John: A Commentary* (Grand Rapids, MI: Baker Academic, 2003), I:329–30.

34 Karl Rahner, *Foundations of Christian Faith: An Introduction to the Idea of Christianity* (New York: Seabury, 1978), 107.

35 Thus, Mary Potter Engel can describe evil as "social, political, economic arrangements that distort our perceptions or restrain our abilities to such an extent that we find it difficult to choose or do good." Mary Potter Engel, "Evil, Sin, and Violation of the Vulnerable," in *Lift Every Voice: Constructing Christian Theologies from the Underside*,

We see the social dimensions of moral personhood clearly in the development of the conscience. Bénézet Bujo explains that the formation of conscience implies a "communicative community" that trains individuals in their knowledge of right and wrong.[36] Such training is manifest in the wisdom of intergenerational norms passed down within a community, and Bujo argues that many classic European treatments of conscience, such as those put forward by Søren Kierkegaard, John A. T. Robinson, and Joseph Fletcher, rely on individualist conceptions of love without factoring in how community shapes our conceptions of what love may be.[37] An ethic relying on the individual, personal sense of love could miss entirely how that sense could be misshapen through social influences. Similarly, Conor Kelly notes that the affective dimension of moral decision-making is also socially conditioned, as is evident in the emerging field of neuroethics.[38] Simply put, we learn how to feel in the face of a given moral dilemma partly through the emotional responses of others around us, which can partly explain the moral callousness that can arise within some groups toward particular moral evils. Yet, here again, we must qualify this dimension of social sin, as Hill and Kieser remind us, by recognizing that such social influences on conscience cannot be inescapable, lest we risk the genuine humanity or impeccability of Christ.

SIN AND MORAL FORMATION IN MARKETS

The foregoing analysis of social sin establishes a basis for thinking about the formative nature of markets and for the theological analysis of such markets. The first contribution of this analysis is that it provides a precise vocabulary

---

ed. Susan Brooks Thistlethwaite and Mary Potter Engel (San Francisco: Harper San Francisco, 1990), 155.

36 Bénézet Bujo, *Foundations of an African Ethic: Beyond the Universal Claims of Western Morality*, trans. Brian McNeil (New York: Herder and Herder, 2001), 109.

37 Bujo, *Foundations of an African Ethic*, 114–18, 125.

38 Kelly, "The Nature and Operation of Structural Sin," 317–21. Kelly points to the groundbreaking research of Joshua Greene, which found that the affective dimension of the brain was engaged during moral decisions. Two theories attempt to explain these findings: Jonathan Haidt's social intuition theory, which suggests all moral acts are merely affective with later rationalizations added, and Joshua Greene's dual-process theory, where both affective and rational parts of the brain are involved in moral decision-making. I am more inclined to accept a proposal like Greene's while still acknowledging the emotional dimensions of ethical decision-making.

for analyzing markets. For clarity's sake, since *social sin* is a term with so many possible meanings, I will use three distinct terms to analyze markets. On the rare occasion that I can speak of the collective sinful actions of groups, I will use the term *sins of social groups*, intending to reference sin broadly attributable to a group but leaving aside questions of whether all members of the group are guilty or whether the term is used only when a sufficient percentage of the group is culpable. I will use the term *structures of sin* to refer to those institutions, laws, policies, practices, or material components of a market that might cause sinful actions in the manner described above. Henceforth, when I use the term *social sin*, I will be referring to the social dimensions of moral persons, particularly in terms of how social influences may entice individuals to sin. In other words, language of *structures of sin* will highlight the influence of impersonal dimensions of markets,[39] while *social sin* will highlight the interpersonal dimensions of markets.

With these terms in hand, we have *prima facie* reason to expect the possibility of markets causing persons to sin in two manners. Here I assume the definition of markets established in chapter 3. Since markets involve a mechanism of exchange and require the provision of information, presumably the institutions, policies, and norms regulating such exchange and distribution of information could cause more people to sin. To use an example outside of economics, laws against rescue operations on behalf of imperiled migrants in the Mediterranean could cause callousness toward those same migrants among Europeans.[40] Since the imagined spaces of markets are often mapped onto material realities, these material components could also be a contributing cause to the sins of persons. It may be that the physical distribution of certain natural resources, for example, could tempt toward greed, selfishness, or envy. In such instances, we are dealing with structures of sin. However, market exchange is also between human participants, who may be influenced by other persons in a manner properly labeled as social sin. Further, given that markets are imagined, social sin may influence individuals' and groups' imaginations about what can be bought and sold, perhaps in a sinful manner. For example, the evil system of chattel slavery in the United States required participants to imagine human beings as property that could be bought and

---

39 Here I leave behind questions of demonic or angelic influence as a possibility that will not be explored within this work.

40 See the discussion in Danielle Vella, *Dying to Live: Stories from Refugees on the Road to Freedom* (Lanham, MD: Rowman and Littlefield, 2020), 62–65.

sold, a warped imagination facilitated in part through social influences on consciences. Similar dynamics are alive today in various degrees ranging from the commodification of sex-trafficking victims to the depersonalization and exploitation of labor.

My survey of social sin and structures of sin pushes back against one common theological defense of capitalism. Some have argued that capitalism is the best economic system from a Christian standpoint because it best accounts for sin. Decentralization is said to reduce the risks associated with giving too much power to an individual or group, who might sinfully abuse that power.[41] The point is well taken, and yet it may mask the ways that decentralized markets themselves can foster vice and perpetuate or amplify unjust social outcomes, as the above analysis of social sin suggests. If centralized economies risk the corrupting effects of the concentration of power, decentralized economies risk becoming inattentive to the amplifying effects of structures of sin. At a theoretical level, centralized and decentralized economies are also equally subject to the malformation of conscience through social sin, though actual economies may differ. A treatment of sin in markets must be carefully balanced: on the one hand, persons are the ultimate moral agents who cause structures of sin; on the other hand, structures of sin can so restrict agency so that some economic actions with unjust outcomes may not be genuinely free.[42]

Any theological economics that emphasizes the possibilities latent within market design must be wary of the risks of pursuing utopian projects that hope to establish on earth what can only be perfectly established with the return of Christ. As Jung Mo Sung warns, the pursuit of utopia often produces human sacrifices, those whose lives are expendable in the name of the higher good pursued within the economy.[43] This higher good often elusively remains on

---

41 The arguments is presented in a classic and sophisticated form by Michael Novak, who sees capitalism as a system designed for the reality of sinful human beings. While socialists "promise a new type of moral man," they tend to rely on the "coercive power of the state," while capitalism will "diffuse power broadly" to prevent dominance. Like Novak, I, too, reject the utopian idea that changes in structure can fully overcome sin. However, it seems reductionistic to deemphasize the malformation possible within markets. Novak, *Spirit of Democratic Capitalism*, 85–88. See also John E. Stapleford, *Bulls, Bears, and Golden Calves: Applying Christian Ethics in Economics* (Downers Grove, IL: InterVarsity, 2002), 85–86; Richards, *Money, Greed, and God*, 27–28.

42 For the former point, see Samuel Gregg, *For God and Profit: How Banking and Finance Can Serve the Common Good* (New York: Crossroad, 2016), 104–5. For the latter point, see Engel, "Evil, Sin, and Violation," 155.

43 Sung, *Desire, Market, Religion*, 90–91.

the horizon, while the suffering inflicted in pursuit of utopia is all too real. It is therefore important to pursue market design within a commitment to subsidiarity that recognizes how some needed market changes will occur at low institutional levels—within a particular small business or at the level of a change to local zoning laws. Yet larger issues will require state involvement. Sin is an important dimension of a theology of economics, but it must not be given too central a role in theological analysis of the economy. The universality of sin and our captivity to it demand such chastened goals. However, as D. Stephen Long warns, theologians often give "sin too important a role in theology. It becomes the rational basis for political and economic life rather than that against which Christianity is set."[44] An account of sin, especially social sin and structures of sin, can give precision in analyzing markets, but such concepts cannot be allowed to lead to a despair that avoids any hope of improvement of the economic situation or of beneficial moral formation in market contexts. Grace must play a role in the theology of economics too.

COMMON GRACE

My theological treatment of the economy will pay particular attention to the Reformed doctrine of common grace. This doctrine is especially associated with the Dutch neo-Calvinists Abraham Kuyper and Herman Bavinck, though it finds its roots in Reformed theology from the era of the sixteenth-century European reformations. In brief, the doctrine claims that God has extended certain blessings to the entirety of humanity, including God's gracious work to restrain sin, the delay of God's judgment, the provision of certain basic needs for life, and the latent potential to develop such fields as science, industry, and the arts for the glory of God. Though some Reformed theologians have raised concerns about naming such provisions "grace,"[45] it is fitting

---

44 Long, *Divine Economy*, 73.

45 For example, David Engelsma suggests that the notion of common grace confuses grace with providence. Providence, claims Engelsma, "works for the blessedness of the children of God.... Providence serves grace, but providence is not grace" (59). However, Engelsma draws too sharp of a distinction between providence and grace such that the world preserved by providence, which Englesma grants is a "continuation" of the work of creation (61), is cut off from the church as redeemed by grace. This is why Engelsma mistakenly believes common grace creates a purpose for creation apart from redemption: "the development of culture" (80). However, common grace allows us to understand such

to call such gifts grace because they are unmerited and are given freely by God. Particularly in Abraham Kuyper, the term *common grace* tends to focus more on the works of God rather than God's disposition.[46] They are common because they extend to all of humanity.[47] At the same time, it is important to distinguish common grace from special grace or saving grace as two different doctrines that are concerned with different theological questions.[48] Common grace enables Christians to understand markets as a mechanism for positive moral formation, but it does not explain whether or how individuals are saved, which is the proper domain of special grace. Even so, common grace is preparatory for and oriented to special grace.

The doctrine of common grace arises from several theological and experiential puzzles. First, as Abraham Kuyper explains, given the active sanctifying work of the Holy Spirit and the universality of sin, "the world turns out to be better than expected and the church worse than expected."[49] Common grace balances the weight of original sin and the observed moral and cultural achievements of those who do not know Christ by attributing all positive

---

cultural developments as ordered toward the salvation of the elect, and thus gracious, and yet distinct from the special grace present within the Church. Engelsma's mistake arises from the fact that he writes against a conception of common grace as the mere provision for the continuing existence of the world, the development of natural abilities, and Christian enjoyment of secular culture. Common grace is instead the proper means of connecting the divine work of creation with the divine work of redemption while preserving a distinction between the Church and the world and, further, between God's providential work on behalf of the elect through common grace and God's providential acts that may not directly contribute toward the sanctification of the Church but that rather allow for a temporary hindrance of such progress in holiness according to the permissive will of God. Without common grace, we are left with the inadequate binary of providence and grace. David J. Engelsma, *Common Grace Revisited: A Response to Richard J. Mouw's He Shines in All That's Fair* (Grandville, MI: Reformed Free Publishing Association, 2003).

46 See Jochem Douma, *Common Grace in Kuyper, Schilder, and Calvin: Exposition, Comparison, and Evaluation*, trans. Albert H. Oosterhoff, ed. William Helder (Hamilton: Lucerna, 2017), 26–27.

47 For a brief history of the Reformed use of the term *common grace*, see Louis Berkhof, *Systematic Theology*, 4th ed. (Grand Rapids, MI: Eerdmans, 1941), 434–35.

48 I will address the relationship between common and special grace in further detail below.

49 Abraham Kuyper, *Common Grace: God's Gifts for a Fallen World*, ed. Jordan J. Ballor and Stephen J. Grabill, trans. Nelson D. Kloosterman and Ed M. van der Maas (Bellingham, WA: Lexham Press, 2019), II.2.1.

cultural achievements to the beneficence of God, who is working to restrain sin among all human beings.[50] Second, common grace follows from the fact that the content of history is not exhausted with the history of Israel and the Church.[51] This reality raises the question of what work God is providentially bringing to pass throughout history beyond the Israelite and Christian worlds, a question that common grace answers by positing that the Holy Spirit works in all cultures to bring about works *soli Deo gloria*.[52]

Exegetically, a theologian might anchor the doctrine of common grace in scriptural teaching about the goodness of God extended to all creation (e.g., Ps 145:9; Matt 5:44–45) or in passages that describe God restraining sin and judgment (e.g., 2 Thess 2:6–7; 2 Pet 3:9). However, Reformed theologians often center their treatment in the Noahic covenant.[53] The Noahic covenant extends to all humanity (Gen 9:9, 10, 12, 17) and offers the grace of provision, protection, and preparation. God provides Noah the blessing of restoration to the role Adam had occupied in Eden when God reaffirms the mandate to be fruitful and multiply (9:1, 7) and when God restores dominion to humanity (9:2–3). In the Reformed tradition, such provision implies the institutions of family and of government, which is also understood canonically to be the enforcer of God's requirement of a life from those who take life (9:5–6; Rom 13:1–7).[54] God protects us from the hazards of a fallen creation, symbolized

---

50 Note that this does not undermine the doctrine of total depravity insofar as total depravity is not speaking of a "quantitative reduction" but rather of the contamination of all human faculties resulting in "the whole man [sic] before the face of God, man in the total orientation of his existence" facing condemnation and lacking merit apart from grace. See G. C. Berkouwer, *Man: The Image of God*, trans. Dirk W. Jellema (Grand Rapids, MI: Eerdmans, 1962), 150–51.

51 Herman Bavinck, "Calvin and Common Grace," in *Calvin and the Reformation*, ed. William Park Armstrong (Grand Rapids, MI: Baker, 1980), 99.

52 According to Bavinck, the Holy Spirit only sanctifies believers, but "as a spirit of life, of wisdom and of power He works also in those who do not believe." Bavinck, "Calvin and Common Grace," 119.

53 "The fixed historical starting point for the doctrine of common grace lies in God's establishment of a covenant with Noah after the flood." Kuyper, *Common Grace*, I.2.1. The Reformed notion of common grace finds one of its earliest expositions in Calvin's treatment of Genesis 9: "[God] addresses all the posterity of Noah and renders his gift common to all ages." John Calvin, *Commentaries on the First Book of Moses Called Genesis*, trans. John King (Grand Rapids, MI: Baker, 1979), 292. See also Herman Bavinck, "Common Grace," trans. Raymond C. Van Leeuwen, *Calvin Theological Journal* 24, no. 1 (April 1989): 40.

54 See Kuyper, *Common Grace*, I.8–9, 11; Berkhof, *Systematic Theology*, 441; Bruce Demarest, *The Cross and Salvation: The Doctrine of Salvation* (Wheaton, IL: Crossway,

in the fear that animals have toward Noah's progeny (9:2). God also protects us from ourselves by working to restrain our murderous desires (9:5–6), and God protects us from God's wrath by pledging to not destroy creation again (9:11, 15). Finally, God uses common grace to prepare for the gift of salvation in Christ—had judgment not been delayed, the rest of redemption history would have been impossible.[55]

Beyond direct biblical support, common grace is seen in the formation of the Bible itself, which draws on the accomplishments of non-Israelite peoples and cultures in a wide variety of ways. For example, the Bible itself was written down, relying on the invention of writing by the Sumerians around 4000 BCE.[56] Sumerian writing was initially pictographic, but eventually an unknown Sinaitic culture developed the alphabet, which, with Ugaritic and Phoenician influences, made its way into Old Hebrew.[57] Writing the Bible also depended on the invention and production of papyrus, likely in Egypt, or of parchment, the preferred writing material of Jews, which was invented by the Persians or Parthians.[58] Of course, the New Testament was written using the Greek alphabet and language. Some of the genres and styles used in the biblical narratives were first developed in other cultures, such as the treaty structure of Deuteronomy, which may reflect Hittite influence.[59] Occasionally, the actual content of the Old Testament reflects other Near Eastern laws and proverbs quite closely, showing that God was at work in other cultures through common grace, preparing bits of knowledge that would be incorporated into inspired Scripture.[60] In addition to these technologies and ideas that directly

---

1997), 93.

55 Kuyper, *Common Grace*, I.4.1.

56 Christopher A. Rollston, *Writing and Literacy in the World of Ancient Israel: Epigraphic Evidence from the Iron Age* (Atlanta: Society of Biblical Literature, 2010), 11.

57 Rollston, *Writing and Literacy*, 11–12, 42–44.

58 On the origin of parchment, see Richard R. Johnson, "Ancient and Medieval Accounts of the 'Invention' of Parchment," *California Studies in Classical Antiquity* 3 (1970): 115–22. For a description of the ingenuity required to make parchment and papyrus, see Harry Y. Gamble, *Books and Readers in the Early Church: A History of Early Christian Texts* (New Haven, CT: Yale University Press, 1995), 43–47.

59 Peter Enns, *Inspiration and Incarnation: Evangelicals and the Problem of the Old Testament* (Grand Rapids, MI: Baker Academic, 2005), 33–34. This structure may be drawn from Hittite culture.

60 See examples in Karen R. Keen, *The Word of a Humble God: The Origins, Inspiration, and Interpretation of Scripture* (Grand Rapids, MI: Eerdmans, 2022), 38–41; Enns, *Inspiration and Incarnation*, 27–32, 37–38. Enns makes too sharp of a distinction when he writes, "The moral standards by which Israel's first ancestors were expected to act seem

contributed to the development of Scripture, every biblical author wrote under the influence of their culture and society. Through common grace, God was working through the culture and industry of many peoples to bring about good things in a manner that contributed to and were incorporated within the writing of Scripture inspired through common grace.

COMMON GRACE WITHIN MARKETS

Common grace is used with some regularity in theological analyses of the economy, often as a basis for exploring values and ideas in the marketplace that are shared across religious traditions and political ideologies.[61] While the pursuit of common ground in a pluralistic society is an important area of research, common grace plays a different role in the analysis of this book. Here, common grace's dogmatic function is to balance and correlate the work of God in creation with God's redemptive work in the Church. Such balance is critical to a sound understanding of the moral formation occurring within markets, for too sharp of a divide between special and common grace could cause theological analyses of the market to emphasize only half of the full picture of God's grace. If common grace is the only grace recognized in a theology of economics, the risk is supplanting the church with markets as the primary place where God is transforming human beings. Such a theology might replace word and sacrament with the proper market mechanisms and institutions, a foolish substitution indeed. Whatever moral transformation or formation occurs in markets must be seen as a Christians fulfilling Paul's teaching to "work out [our] own salvation" (Phil 2:12) but not as the locus of that salvation itself. Such salvation is found only through union with Christ, the head of his body, the Church. On the other hand, if only special grace is recognized in a theology of sanctification, then the Church alone becomes the sole source of the mediation of Christ, as if God is not reconciling all things to Godself (Col 1:20) or working through all things for the good of those who believe (Rom 8:28). The bulk of this section on common grace will therefore

---

to come not so much by God's unique command but by expectations of the surrounding cultures" (Enns, *Inspiration and Incarnation*, 42). Common grace leads to the conclusion that God was in fact working through these surrounding cultures.

61 E.g., Barnes, *Redeeming Capitalism*, 116–18; Max L. Stackhouse, *Globalization and Grace: A Christian Public Theology for a Global Future* (New York: Continuum, 2007), 150–51, 189.

focus on the relationship between common and special grace before turning to one particularly sinful use of common grace in the past.

Common Grace and Special Grace

In part I of this work, I have shown how markets can function as spaces of either positive or negative moral formation. The doctrine of common grace allows for a more precise account of how this work of moral transformation relates to the sanctifying work of the Holy Spirit through special grace. An account of the relationship between moral formation in markets and the sanctification of Christians is but a specific application of the question of the broader relationship between common grace and special grace. Kuyper and Bavinck are both clear that common grace is oriented to special grace, though Kuyper is widely held to have an inferior exposition of how these graces relate. On the one hand, Kuyper can blur the distinction between these two graces. For example, Kuyper can read certain dimensions of grace that are Christologically determined, such as the Gospel of John's use of light as a reference to Christ, and treat them more generally as a reference to the light of reason among human beings through common grace.[62] At the same time, Kuyper can compartmentalize special and common grace, as when he explains that Christ is encountered in the church as an agent of salvation, but in the state and culture Christ is known as agent of creation.[63] This bifurcation ignores how the church contributes to the development of culture while also negating how culture feeds into the proclamation and life of the church—just remember the influences of common grace in the development of the canon of Scripture. Kuyper sees that common grace and special grace are related, but the nature of the relationship remains underdetermined in his thought.

Herman Bavinck, on the other hand, gives a clearer sense of how common grace is oriented toward special grace.[64] He puts the point quite nicely when he writes that "special grace is encircled by common grace ... the God of

---

62 See the discussion in Douma, *Common Grace*, 344–46.

63 Cornelis van der Kooi, "A Theology of Culture. A Critical Appraisal of Kuyper's Doctrine of Common Grace," in *Kuyper Reconsidered: Aspects of His Life and Work*, ed. Cornelis van der Kooi and Jan de Bruijn (Amsterdam: VU Uitgeverij, 1999), 99.

64 A helpful discussion of the supernatural orientation of Bavinck's account of common grace in comparison with Kuyper's is found in Jeffrey Skaff, "Common Grace and the Ends of Creation in Abraham Kuyper and Herman Bavinck," *Journal of Reformed Theology* 9, no. 1 (2015): 3–18.

creation and of regeneration is one." Common grace is, for Bavinck, the basis of relating nature and grace, a point he makes by caricaturing various other theological traditions. Socinians, he says, collapse the *ordo supernaturalis* by abandoning the notion of a special grace by which God redeems the elect, thereby retaining nothing but nature. Anabaptists abandon the *ordo naturalis* by denying the presence of any grace common to the world apart from the special grace of the church. Bavinck argues that Roman Catholics, on the other hand, maintain a stark distinction between nature and grace through the acceptance of a state of humanity in *puris naturalibus* completely divorced from grace. Against this wide range of mistakes, Bavinck argues that the content of history is not exhausted with the history of Israel and the Church as the recipients of special grace, but that through grace, God restrains sin in creation as a whole because this creation is part of the divine plan. Life and being itself are not "natural" but are dependent entirely on grace. Note here the echoes of Tanner's claim that every aspect of created being and existence is immediately dependent on the continued preserving work of God. Ultimately, Bavinck insists that we relate nature and grace, creation and re-creation, in the way that the Scriptures do. The first promises of grace are made to Adam and Eve and pertain to the entire human race, and special grace emerges from this common grace. The two forms of grace are fully united in Christ, who is the pinnacle of the old creation and the first fruits of the new creation.

While Bavinck's simplified treatment of other theological traditions may lead the reader to suspect that my own appeal to the doctrine of common grace is quite partisan, I actually see theological trends outside of the Reformed tradition that are comparable in their basic understanding of the relationship between nature and grace. For example, consider the Catholic *nouvelle theologie*. Like Bavinck, the theologians of the *nouvelle theologie* reject the idea of a "pure nature,"[65] instead pointing to a fundamental ordering of nature toward the supernatural.[66] In its fundamental structure, the *nouvelle theologie*

---

65 For example, Henri de Lubac, *Surnaturel: Études historiques* (Paris: Desclée de Brouwer, 1946), 105–6.

66 The structural similarities are ironic, given each group's penchant for demeaning the traditions of the other for similar reasons. Thus, Henri de Lubac describes Protestant theology as irreducibly a dualistic theology arising from a certain "bastard Augustinianism" that sees salvation only in a "complete severance between the natural and the supernatural." Henri de Lubac, *Catholicism: Christ and the Common Destiny of Man*, trans. Lancelot C. Sheppard and Sister Elizabeth Englund (San Francisco: Ignatius Press, 1988), 313. Bavinck, on the other hand, sees the entire theology of grace in the Roman

is quite similar to Bavinck's account of grace; grace / the supernatural cannot be collapsed into nature, but neither can nature be considered in pure form apart from grace and the supernatural. A Reformed account of common grace also has much to learn from the *nouvelle theologie*, which provides a clear articulation of the need to avoid reducing grace to something external to human beings; rather, humanity itself is fundamentally oriented to God, even as the grace enabling us to reach our *telos* remains gratuitous. Henri de Lubac's insistence on *supernatural* as an adjective rather than an opposition between two nouns, nature and supernature, serves as a helpful warning to the Reformed theology of common and special grace (two nouns!): what we are dealing with "is not a question of two substantial natures... one of which would override the other."[67] Rather, we are speaking of how creation itself, considered from the standpoint of nature itself or of God's common grace operative within that nature, finds fulfillment in the supernatural beatitude found through special grace.

Nevertheless, in the context of a theology of economics, the Reformed language of common grace and special grace yields several advantages in comparison with the *nouvelle theologie*'s terminology of nature and the supernatural. First, language of common and special grace is less prone to lead to debates around exclusivism, inclusivism, and universal salvation than are discussions of all of nature being oriented to the supernatural.[68] Such soteriological debates, though important, could distract from the development of a theology of markets.[69] Second, language of common and special grace, or more broadly of grace and sin, draws more attention to actions, while language of nature and the supernatural may tend toward a discussion of ontology and being. When considering markets, I find language with an emphasis on acts helpful since both *common grace* and *sin* are terms that

---

Catholic Church as dependent on a "sharp distinction between nature and grace." Bavinck, "Calvin and Common Grace," 107.

67 Henri de Lubac, *A Brief Catechesis on Nature and Grace*, trans. Richard Arnandez (San Francisco: Ignatius, 1984), 35.

68 As the basic themes of the *nouvelle theologie* spread beyond France, the implications of the supernatural for the theology of religions were raised among theologians such as Hans Urs von Balthasar, Hans Küng, and Karl Rahner. See especially Hans Urs von Balthasar, *Dare We Hope That All May be Saved?*, 2nd ed., trans. David Kipp and Lothar Krauth (San Francisco: Ignatius, 2014).

69 On the other hand, I suspect the perspective of the *nouvelle theologie* would be preferable in discussions of property, which would need to refute the sin of colonialism more extensively, which needs to directly develop a theology of other cultures.

are inescapably historical, whereas *nature* tends to connote ontology, which could be considered apart from history.⁷⁰ Reformed discussions of common grace tend to focus on culture, economy, art, science, and any number of other aspects of the historical development of human civilization. Such an emphasis on history and action is an easier starting point for a theology of economics. However, one could easily develop a similar approach drawing on the Catholic *nouvelle theologie*. Furthermore, while the theology of common grace offers some advantages, it also offers a number of risks, the most notable of which I must address before concluding the chapter.

Common Grace and the Risk of Racism

Common grace has sometimes been used to demean non-European peoples as less developed and less gifted with grace.⁷¹ For example, Kuyper writes that "common grace is undoubtedly at work even among the wild native African peoples, but how weak it is when we compare their life with the operation of common grace among the European nations."⁷² In such instances, common grace is used to hierarchically rank cultures and peoples as judged by a Eurocentric standard for what counts as development.⁷³ Those deemed more sophisticated to European eyes must be recipients of greater common grace. It should not be a surprise, then, that Kuyper's theology was used in

---

70 Though the posited underlying metaphysical relations between nature and the supernatural are quite similar between neo-Calvinism and the *nouvelle theologie*, in my estimation, the former is more likely to turn discussions of common grace to analysis of the historical realities of culture, economy, government, and society than is the latter in its discussions of the supernatural. Of course, I here reveal my own assumptions that ontology and history are sufficiently distinct.

71 For a brief survey of this problem, see James D. Bratt, *Abraham Kuyper: Modern Calvinist, Christian Democrat* (Grand Rapids, MI: Eerdmans, 2013), 200–201.

72 Kuyper, *Common Grace*, II.3.4. See also Kuyper, *Common Grace*, II.63.3–4.

73 Sometimes Kuyper presents European nations as the recipients of a greater common grace, but other times it is the special grace of the gospel that is used to argue for the superiority of Western civilization: "Factually only the Christian nations in Europe and America have attained that purer disclosure of nobler strength that has created human society as we know it, a society to which the former—and in part still present—heathen civilizations in China and British India can in no way be compared." Abraham Kuyper, *Our Program: A Christian Political Manifesto*, trans. and ed. Harry Van Dyke (Bellingham, WA: Lexham, 2015), 236.

defense of such unjust systems as apartheid in South Africa.[74] The fact that many preferred a secular justification for apartheid[75] or that some Black South Africans also developed Kuyperian challenges to apartheid[76] does not eliminate the concerning use of Kuyper's thought.

In order to prevent the risk of deploying the doctrine of common grace as a means to reinforce prejudiced ideologies or colonial ambitions, several protective measures must be in place. First, much as the doctrine of the invisible church insists that we are limited in our knowledge of which persons are the recipients of special grace,[77] it seems necessary to insist on the unknowability of the full workings of common grace. Deploying the doctrine of common grace in the context of a theology of economics provides a basis for expecting moral transformation in market contexts, not for exhaustively identifying where this change will occur, for the Spirit moves where it wishes (John 3:8). Second and related, it is important to remember that many rubrics can be used to measure the economic, social, political, and cultural strengths of a nation, so conclusions about which are advanced will always be shaped by the form of measurement used. Here again, positive and normative economics cannot be purely divided. For example, the United States currently ranks eleventh in GDP per capita, a measure of average total economic activity in a country per person.[78] However, it ranks one hundred and twenty-second on the Gini

---

74 On the use of Kuyper's thought in apartheid South Africa, see Saul Dubow, "Afrikaner Nationalism, Apartheid, and the Conceptualization of 'Race,'" *Journal of African History* 33, no. 2 (1992): 209–37. Emphasis was more heavily laid on Kuyper's notion of sphere sovereignty and the idea that God created and intends divisions.

75 On the limited influence of the neo-Calvinist justification of apartheid, see Andre du Toit, "Puritans in Africa? Afrikaner 'Calvinism' and Kuyperian Neo-Calvinism in Late Nineteenth-Century South Africa," *Comparative Studies in Society and History* 27, no. 9 (April 1985): 229–32.

76 See a cursory discussion of the anti- and pro-apartheid uses of Kuyper in Richard J. Mouw, "Calvin's Legacy for Public Theology," *Political Theology* 10, no. 3 (2009): 442–44. Though I am not as widely read in Kuyper as Mouw, I suspect Mouw overestimates the extent to which Kuyper considered interracial marriage as a solution to apartheid given his high esteem for the Boer system's avoidance of "mixed liaisons" elsewhere. See Abraham Kuyper, *The South-African Crisis*, 4th ed., trans. A. E. Fletcher (London: Stop the War Committee, 1900), 11, 24.

77 As Calvin notes, the invisible church is "manifest to the eye of God only." Calvin, *Institutes of the Christian Religion*, IV.1.7.

78 "GDP per capita (Current US$)," World Bank, accessed September 19, 2022, https://data.worldbank.org/indicator/NY.GDP.PCAP.CD?most_recent_value_desc=true.

coefficient, which measures economic inequality.[79] Even from an economic perspective, one can reach widely divergent interpretations about the health of a country, never mind other dimensions of culture and society that might be brought to bear. The wide variety of rubrics available points to the diversity of cultural strengths that may be brought about through common grace.

Third, it is important to link common grace to eschatology.[80] In an article addressing South African politics, Kuyper argued that "between blacks and whites there will never be lasting reconciliation,"[81] failing to predict the successes of Christian movements like the Truth and Reconciliation Commission, imperfect though those may be. If Kuyper's theology of society had deeper eschatological connection, he would recognize that among the benefits of a restrained sin nature is the common grace-enabled foretaste of a degree of peace and reconciliation that anticipates the true peace and reconciliation available at the eschaton. Many biblical motifs center this image of ethnic reconciliation. For example, the Isaianic image of all nations coming to Israel (e.g., Isa 2:2) certainly includes special grace insofar as it incorporates the sacrificial system (Isa 56:6–7) and eternal redemption (Isa 25:6–8), but the nations also bring the fruits of common grace to Mount Zion (Isa 60:1–16), including their economic prosperity, their industrial achievements like ships and architecture, and the leaders of their governments. If the fruits of common grace will be a component of the eschatological reconciliation, there is no reason to deny any possible reconciliation today, even as the doctrine of sin reminds us how truly challenging such reconciliation will be. It is unacceptable to settle for "cheap reconciliation" that ignores the very real and substantive challenges that must be resolved prior to genuine peace between ethnic groups; denying any hope of such peace results in an overly futuristic

---

79 "Gini Index," World Bank, accessed September 19, 2022, https://data.worldbank.org/indicator/SI.POV.GINI?most_recent_value_desc=false.

80 See the discussion in Craig G. Bartholomew, *Contours of the Kuyperian Tradition: A Systematic Introduction* (Downers Grove, IL: IVP Academic, 2017), 44–45.

81 Kuyper, *The South-African Crisis*, 27. Kuyper is ambiguous in his treatment of slavery, lauding the Boer system of slavery throughout *The South-African Crisis* and criticizing British advocacy for Indigenous rights in South Africa (Kuyper, *The South-African Crisis*, 19–21) yet also insisting in his "Lectures on Calvinism" that the life system of Calvinism condemns "slavery and systems of caste." Abraham Kuyper, *Calvinism: Six Stone Foundation Lectures* (Grand Rapids, MI: Eerdmans, 1943), 27.

eschatology and tempts us toward ethnocentrism.[82] These three qualifiers should hopefully prevent the racist abuse of the doctrine of common grace.

SIN, GRACE, AND MARKETS

With a theology of social sin and common grace in place, I am one step closer to being able to offer a theological analysis of moral formation through the marketplace. Markets may produce virtue as a secondary cause of God's work of common grace in restraining sin or as a secondary cause of God's work of special grace in sanctification. Markets may also cause or amplify sin through structures of sin and social sin. A theological analysis of experimental and empirical studies on moral formation in the marketplace should therefore be attentive to structural and social influences, being careful not to allow any account of moral formation in markets to supplant the role of the church in moral formation or to be completely severed from that role. A theology of common grace and of social sin reveals the economic data from part I to be unsurprising from a theological standpoint, but this theology will be used in part III to make analysis of markets more precise. Before turning to that task, one further theological framework needs to be established since the discussion of divine/human concurrent agency and of sin and grace has not yet been integrated with a theology of God as Father, Son, and Spirit. For this reason, chapter 6 turns to consider the doctrine of the Trinity.

---

82 Desmond Tutu clearly names the risks of the term *reconciliation* in South African context: it has been "thoroughly devalued by those who have used [it] to justify evil. Christ is our peace, who bought at a great price His own death on the Cross. That is what real reconciliation has cost." Desmond Tutu, "Spirituality: Christian and African," in *Resistance and Hope: South African Essays in Honour of Beyers Naudé*, ed. Charles Villa-Vicencio and John W. De Gruchy (Grand Rapids, MI: Eerdmans, 1985), 164. See also Allan Boesak, *Black and Reformed: Apartheid, Liberation, and the Calvinist Tradition* (Maryknoll, NY: Orbis, 1986), 29.

CHAPTER 6

The Trinity and the *Ordo Salutis*

The doctrine of the Trinity is not restricted to the religious sphere, for if what is said about God is true the same kind of implications must be spelled out for other spheres of life also.

—Colin Gunton[1]

There is no divinity that stands apart from or behind the three divine persons, so every divine act is in some sense an act of the Trinity. The triunity of all divine acts requires that any account of concurrence between God and humans in the market be explained in a trinitarian manner so that communion with the distinct trinitarian persons is recognizable. In other words, a sound theology of moral formation in the marketplace must necessarily be a trinitarian theology, a fact that has not gone unnoticed by many theologians addressing the theology of economics, political theology, and economic ethics. Nevertheless, as we shall see, many accounts of the connections between the Trinity and the market are theologically problematic, so much theological brush must be cleared in order to prepare a path forward. With this aim in mind, this chapter begins by surveying existing attempts to explain the connection between the doctrine of the Trinity and the economy, arguing that standard approaches are either overconfident due to downplaying the doctrine of analogy or else impractical—or both. Having explained why I am unwilling to follow existing theological trajectories, I will then lay the

---

1 Colin E. Gunton, *The Promise of Trinitarian Theology* (Edinburgh: T & T Clark, 1991), 12.

foundations for concurrent human/trinitarian action in the marketplace by briefly considering the doctrines of inseparable operations, divine missions, and appropriations. With this theological framework in place, I will identify three doctrines whose broad contours are natural conversation partners with existing research in behavioral and experimental economics. With a theology of the Father's providence, justification in Christ, and sanctification by the Holy Spirit in hand, we will be ready to turn to substantive analysis of moral formation in the marketplace.

A FLAWED WELL-TROD PATH IN TRINITARIAN THEOLOGY OF ECONOMICS

The twentieth century is characterized by what many would call a trinitarian renaissance.[2] One important dimension of this surge in trinitarian theology is a growing sense that the Trinity needed to be connected with the social concerns so prevalent in movements such as postliberal theology, ecclesial ethics, political theology, and various liberation theologies. Theological analyses of economics are no different, where the doctrine of the Trinity was frequently deployed to make the case for a wide variety of social programs.[3] I call such deployments of the Trinity the *exemplary approach* because they treat the Trinity as a model for the ideal human society. In contrast, my own use of the Trinity will focus on the economic acts of the Trinity, seeking a connection between theological accounts of divine action in redeeming

---

2 This characterization is not agreed on by all. For example, Stephen Holmes rightly notes that when it comes to modern retrievals of the doctrine of the Trinity, "methodologically and materially, they are generally thorough-going departures from the older tradition, rather than retrievals of it." Stephen R. Holmes, *The Quest for the Trinity: The Doctrine of God in Scripture, History, and Modernity* (Downers Grove, IL: IVP Academic, 2012), xvi.

3 I explore the connections between the doctrine of the Trinity and economics more extensively in D. Glenn Butner Jr., "The Trinity in the Theology of Economics," *Faith and Economics* 76 (Fall 2020): 29–42. In this article, I also address a second approach, which I name the *genealogical approach*. This less common approach, taken by theologians like John Millbank and philosophers like Giorgio Agamben, tends to explore where the theological ideas about God went astray, resulting in problematic forms of capitalism. Though also flawed as a method of transforming markets, I chose to avoid the extensive discussion necessary to explore this method in this volume to ensure that I avoided too weighty of a digression.

human beings and social-scientific accounts of the effects of markets on market participants, seeking a means of exploring the concurrent work of God through common grace.

Leonardo Boff is perhaps the most famous theologian to use the exemplary approach.[4] Boff argues that "human society is a pointer on the road to the mystery of the Trinity, while the mystery of the Trinity, as we know it from revelation, is a pointer toward social life and its archetype."[5] Defining the unity of the Trinity largely in terms of perichoresis, Boff explains that the triune persons are all different, irreducible, and eternally in reciprocal communion with one another.[6] The ideal set forward by trinitarian communion critiques the hierarchical domination of capitalism and the collectivism of socialism that enforces conformity through "bureaucratic imposition."[7] In Boff's understanding, "the trinitarian mystery invites us to adopt social forms that value *all* relations among persons and institutions and foster an egalitarian, family community in which differences will be positively welcomed."[8]

Boff's project illustrates the two common problems with the exemplary approach: our understanding of the Trinity is analogical in a manner that makes clear correlations impossible, and even once established, a correlation is insufficiently specific to provide any practical steps in designing a market. The analogical nature of human knowledge of God was clearly established at the fourth Lateran Council (1215), which states, "Between the Creator and the creature so great a likeness cannot be noted without the necessity of noting a greater dissimilarity between them."[9] The great difference between the

---

4 Though see also the classic presentations of this approach in M. Douglas Meeks, *God the Economist: The Doctrine of God and Political Economy* (Minneapolis: Fortress, 1989); Jürgen Moltmann, *The Trinity and the Kingdom*, trans. Margaret Kohl (San Francisco: Harper and Row Publishers, 1981), 192–200.

5 Leonardo Boff, *Trinity and Society*, trans. Paul Burns (Maryknoll, NY: Orbis, 1988), 119. Stanley Grenz notes that Boff is particularly influenced by his dissertation director Karl Rahner, whose *grundaxiom* leads to a close correlation between economic communion between the persons and a social immanent Trinity, and by Jürgen Moltmann, who had already seen in the Trinity a key to challenging problematic social structures. Stanley J. Grenz, *Rediscovering the Triune God: The Trinity in Contemporary Theology* (Minneapolis: Fortress, 2004), 125–26.

6 Boff, *Trinity and Society*, 137–40.

7 Boff, *Trinity and Society*, 150.

8 Leonardo Boff, "Trinity," in Ellacuría and Sobrino, *Mysterium Liberationis*, 400.

9 "Medieval Sourcebook: Twelfth Ecumenical Council: Lateran IV 1215," Fordham University, last updated October 6, 2023, https://sourcebooks.fordham.edu/basis/lateran4.asp.

Trinity and the world leads to a circularity, where the theologian confronted with a great deal of mystery about the Trinity but seeking a pattern for society fills in the analogical ambiguities with an already held social ethic. Then the newly modified Trinity is used to justify that same social ethic, completing the circle.[10]

This circular nature of modifying the Trinity is evident in how many disparate applications of the Trinity have been developed in recent decades. While Boff sees the Trinity as critical of capitalism, Michael Novak and Victor Claar see a clear support for capitalism in the cooperative missions and distinctive specializations of the triune persons.[11] It seems, when used as an exemplar for human society, the Trinity is a wax nose that can be bent in any direction. A quick survey of the literature can find exemplary appeals to the Trinity to justify everything from the submission of women in marriage to the queering of gender.[12] The problem is that each exemplary approach tends to rely on novel innovations to make its social application. For example, Boff's proposal relies on the novelty of rejecting causation, preferring "correlation and communion rather than production and procession," and equalizing the processions by proposing that "everything is *Patreque, Filioque,* and *Spirituque.*"[13] Through such modification and a reliance on the traditional idea of *perichoresis*—a doctrine that historically never bore the weight of explaining the unity of the three persons[14]—Boff describes a trinitarian society of perfect equitable communion.[15] I see no theological reason to accept Boff's modifications rather than those of trinitarian capitalism.

---

10 See the detailed analysis of this phenomenon in Karen Kilby, "Perichoresis and Projection: Problems with Social Doctrines of the Trinity," *New Blackfriars* 81, no. 956 (2000): 432–45.

11 Novak, *Spirit of Democratic Capitalism*, 337–40; Victor Claar, "What I Wish Theologians Understood about Markets and the Economists Who Study Them," *Faith and Economics* 60 (Fall 2012): 36.

12 For these three examples, respectively, see Bruce A. Ware, *Father, Son and Holy Spirit: Relationships, Roles, and Relevance* (Wheaton, IL: Crossway Books, 2005); Patrick S. Cheng, "A Three-Part Sinfonia: Queer Asian Reflections on the Trinity," *Journal of Race, Ethnicity, and Religion* 3, no. 2 (2012): 1–23.

13 Boff, *Trinity and Society*, 142, 146.

14 As Kathryn Tanner points out, perichoresis could not explain unity in the Trinity adequately since the concept is also deployed to describe the two natures of Christ, which must remain ontologically distinct. Tanner, *Jesus, Humanity, and the Trinity*, 23.

15 Admittedly, Boff might not mind the novelty, given his preference for socioanalytic mediation as the first step in liberationist methodology. On this account, theology is a "second moment" responding to a societal need presented to the theologian by the

A critic might respond that my appeal to analogy downplays the clear correlation between human beings and God. Thus, Miroslav Volf argues that it would be "anomalous" to insist on creation in the image of God (Gen 1:26–27) and renewal in the likeness of God (Eph 4:24) while denying that humans should "seek to be like God in their mutual relations." He also appeals to the Sermon on the Mount: "Be perfect, therefore, as your heavenly Father is perfect" (Matt 5:48).[16] Volf admits the necessity of analogous, not univocal, correlation between the triune relations and human beings,[17] and consequently he will not seek to derive "socio-economic structures" from the Trinity but only focus more broadly on a social vision.[18] Drawing on the perichoretic relationality of the trinitarian persons and the self-giving of God through the cross, Volf insists that Christians live in unconditional love for all, with a will to embrace that is prior to any distinction and difference.[19] Could such a trinitarian deployment in a theology of economics be viable?

Volf's theological vision illustrates the second major weakness of the exemplary approach: the limited applicability of any conclusions drawn from a comparison between the Trinity and society. Volf's trinitarianism is less innovative than Boff's,[20] but the end result is a lack of any specificity in terms of application. In fact, this vision offers little specific in terms of how to design markets, nor is it clear to me that the basic vision of unconditional love and egalitarian structures needed the doctrine of the Trinity at all. Even where Boff offers greater specificity by criticizing aspects of capitalism and socialism, the concrete application remains vague. Ivan Petrella notes that when theology merely mediates conclusions already drawn from the social

---

social sciences, to which theology seeks to respond. A novel treatment of the Trinity that responds to the inequality that liberation theology addresses might be seen as proper hermeneutic mediation, a second-moment theology. I am unconvinced, for it seems that such would reduce theology to a legitimizing tool for already existing social analysis, and, as we shall see, this legitimizing function for theology would add little of value to the social analysis. On liberation theology's methodology, see especially Clodovis Boff, *Theology and Praxis: Epistemological Foundations*, trans. Robert R. Barr (Maryknoll, NY: Orbis, 1978); Leonardo Boff, *Faith on the Edge: Religion and Marginalized Existence* (San Francisco: Harper and Row, 1989), 51.

16 Miroslav Volf, "'The Trinity Is Our Social Program': The Doctrine of the Trinity and the Shape of Social Engagement," *Modern Theology* 14, no. 3 (July 1998): 404.

17 Volf, "'The Trinity Is Our Social Program,'" 405.

18 Volf, "'The Trinity Is Our Social Program,'" 406–7.

19 Volf, "'The Trinity Is Our Social Program,'" 413, 415, 417.

20 Though I am convinced that social trinitarianism is still a novel understanding of the Trinity.

sciences, the end result is talk about change instead of an actual historical project.²¹ In this case, when the doctrine of the Trinity is used to illustrate a previously held critique of capitalism, appeal to the Trinity does not add anything to the critique and results in a theoretical discussion that may distract from specific historical acts of liberation. To offer the critique in different terms, the exemplary approach can at best only provide what Jung Mo Sung calls a "contestatory" theology, which offers a utopian critique of an economic system but typically cannot provide the insights necessary to manage an economy or even an NGO or cooperative seeking innovative and liberative economic practices.²² The exemplary model provides limited aid in guiding us to designing a market that produces more virtue, and it is equally vague in its recommendations for changes to produce markets that result in just outcomes.

A TRINITARIAN THEOLOGY OF DIVINE ACTION

If the Trinity cannot serve as an exemplar for ideal market structures, and if such an account of capitalism provides little specific guidance for market design, no matter what trinitarian assumptions are uncovered, then what connection is there between the Christian vision of God as Trinity and Christian moral formation in the marketplace? It seems to me that the clearest and most helpful connection between the Trinity and creation is found in the triune God's redemptive work in creation, often called the *divine economy,* or *oikonomia*. Simply put, when markets allow Christians to act in conformity with our identity in Christ in a manner that suits the sanctifying work of Spirit within the context in which the Father has providentially placed us, then Christians can work out their salvation in the context of a market that enables the development of virtue as hypothesized by the *doux commerce* thesis rather than develop vice as predicted by the ecclesial ethics movement. A brief presentation of the traditional theology of divine action will ensure that this proposal is not merely a historicized version of the exemplary approach, rooted in theological innovation that results in projection.

God's acts in the economy can broadly be sorted into three categories: inseparable operations, appropriated actions, and divine missions. Christians

---

21 Petrella, *Future of Liberation Theology,* 29, 38–40.
22 Sung, *Desire, Market, and Religion,* 106.

have traditionally held that the works of God in the economy are inseparable such that each act is indivisibly performed by Father, Son, and Holy Spirit in a manner that does not obliterate the personal distinctions of each. Because these personal distinctions persist, certain actions may allow us to see more clearly one divine person or another such that this action can be appropriated to one person, though it is technically performed by all three. Certain divine actions, called the *divine missions*, are unique to a single person because they are a byproduct of that person's unique procession carried into the created realm.[23]

Inseparable Operations

One of the distinctive beliefs of pro-Nicene theology is that the divine persons work inseparably in all divine acts *ad extra*.[24] The term *ad extra* restricts inseparable operations to those acts toward creation and not *ad intra* or immanent acts like the divine processions that are distinctive to each person. Several factors led to the widespread acceptance of inseparable operations. Within a philosophical context, the claim that Father, Son, and Spirit were of one being, substance, or nature led to affirmation of inseparable operations given the assumed meaning of such philosophical terms. The concept of nature in particular included within it the notion of a distinctive power (*dunamis*) that produced operations or acts that were unique to the kind of nature possessing that distinctive power.[25] Since Father, Son, and Holy Spirit are a single, infinite, and simple nature, pro-Nicene theologians recognized that the divine persons were not three distinct instantiations of the same nature performing three similar actions but rather a tri-hypostatic singular

---

23 I have written far more extensively on these doctrines elsewhere: D. Glenn Butner Jr., *Trinitarian Dogmatics: Exploring the Grammar of the Christian Doctrine of God* (Grand Rapids, MI: Baker Academic, 2022), 243–312; D. Glenn Butner Jr., *The Son Who Learned Obedience: A Theological Case against the Eternal Submission of the Son* (Eugene, OR: Pickwick, 2018), 13–16, 31–46, 49–61.

24 The centrality of inseparable operations is one of three defining aspects of pro-Nicene thought according to Lewis Ayres, *Nicaea and Its Legacy: An Approach to Fourth-Century Trinitarian Theology* (Oxford: Oxford University Press, 2004), 236. G. L. Prestige argues that the doctrine of inseparable operations was even "more widely held" than the homoousion. G. L. Prestige, *God in Patristic Thought*, 2nd ed. (London: SPCK, 1952), 260.

25 This point is most extensively explored in Michel René Barnes, *The Power of God: Δύναμις in Gregory of Nyssa's Trinitarian Theology* (Washington, DC: The Catholic University of America Press, 2001).

nature inseparably performing the same act in a threefold manner. As succinctly stated by Gregory of Nyssa, "The action of each [divine person] in any matter is not separate and individualized."[26]

Some contemporary theologians have criticized the doctrine of inseparable operations out of concern that it silences biblical testimony to unique acts performed by each divine person. A further concern is raised that inseparable operations may limit our ability to have communion with the distinct persons.[27] However, the doctrine of inseparable operations has deep biblical roots and was always articulated in a manner that ensured the possibility of distinctive communion with each divine person. Jesus claims in John 5:19 that "the Son can do nothing on his own, but only what he sees the Father doing; for whatever the Father does, the Son does likewise." This statement appears to directly support inseparable operations, for the Son does not act alone, nor does the Father, for whatever the Father does, so does the Son. Yet personal distinction remains, for the Son acts "likewise" as a distinguishable person.[28] Further biblical support of inseparable operations is found in the common trend of attributing divine agency in the Old Testament to Son or Spirit in the New Testament. For example, both Acts 28:25–27 and Hebrews 10:15–17 attribute words to the Holy Spirit that were attributed to the Lord in the Old Testament. Finally, we see clear patterns of divine action that are attributed to all three divine persons, such as the act of creating, which is done by Father, Son, and Holy Spirit (Gen 1:1–2; Ps 33:6; John 1:3). The doctrine of inseparable operations is rooted in Scripture, not an attempt to silence the Bible. Two further trinitarian categories must be introduced to explain how inseparable operations do not eliminate distinct relations with the divine persons.

---

26 Gregory of Nyssa, *An Answer to Ablabius: That We Should Not Think of Saying There Are Three Gods*, ed. and trans. Cyril C. Richardson, in *Christology of the Later Fathers*, ed. Edward R. Hardy (Louisville, KY: Westminster John Knox, 1954), 262.

27 For example, Catherine Mowry LaCugna is concerned that Augustine's theology of inseparable operations and appropriations deviates from the biblical emphasis on the economy and unique personal missions, ultimately rupturing *oikonomia* and *theologia*. Catherine Mowry LaCugna, *God for Us: The Trinity and Christian Life* (New York: HarperCollins, 1991), 97–101.

28 Modern interpreters have attempted to explain this passage in terms of the agency bestowed on an authorized messenger, but I find this interpretation uncompelling. For a brief summary of this perspective and response, see Adonis Vidu, *The Same God Who Works in All Things: Inseparable Operations in Trinitarian Theology* (Grand Rapids, MI: Eerdmans, 2021), 37–42.

Appropriations

Though the acts of the Trinity *ad extra* are inseparable, the actions do not mean that the persons of the Trinity are no longer distinguishable. Natures do not act anhypostatically (without hypostases/persons), for every divine action is personal, proceeding from the Father, through the Son, to the Spirit or else empowering Christians to act in the Spirit, through the Son, to the Father. This ordering, or *taxis*, ensures that the inseparable operations do not obliterate the divine persons in the economy.[29] The *taxis* of all divine acts also mean that the quality of a particular divine action may more clearly reveal one person over another, such that unique personal communion is not only possible but necessary through the inseparable divine actions.[30] When an action more clearly reveals one divine person, the act is said to be appropriated to that person.

To consider a few more technical definitions, appropriations are rooted in "a certain similarity between the appropriated attribute or activity and the special characteristic of the personality to whom it is appropriated,"[31] such that appropriated acts "better manifest the divine persons, in their distinctive properties, to the mind of believers."[32] In other words, to appropriate an action to a divine person is to make an epistemic claim—we know one divine person more clearly through the appropriations. Yet, as Adonis Vidu concisely states, "appropriation is not individuation."[33] Distinct actions do not distinguish the divine persons, but because the divine persons are eternally distinguished by the divine processions and the—logically but not temporally—resulting personal properties, when a particular action is similar to the

---

29 This point is especially clear in much Lutheran theology, on which see Carl L. Beckwith, *The Holy Trinity* (Fort Wayne, IN: The Luther Academy, 2016), 310–35.

30 I find T. F. Torrance's comments on appropriations curious in that he sees them as a response to an "unbalanced essentialist approach," which neglected the fact that in all triune acts "each Person who is himself whole God acts without any surrender of his distinctive hypostatic character." As I see it, appropriations are not a corrective to the neglect of the distinctive hypostatic character of each person but rather a necessary entailment of that character. See T. F. Torrance, *The Christian Doctrine of God: One Being, Three Persons* (London: T & T Clark, 1996), 200.

31 J. P. Arendzen, *The Holy Trinity: A Theological Treatise for Modern Laymen* (New York: Sheed and Ward, 1937), 122.

32 Giles Emery, *The Trinity: An Introduction to Catholic Doctrine on the Triune God*, trans. Matthew Levering (Washington, DC: Catholic University of America Press, 2011), 165.

33 Vidu, *The Same God*, 114.

personal property of one divine person, that divine person may be more clearly seen in the appropriated action. For example, since the Father alone is the unbegotten source of all that is, including the eternally begotten Son and eternally spirated Spirit, divine actions like creation and providence, the origination of all created being and created events, most clearly reveal the Father to us. For this reason, Scripture tends to speak of Father as Creator, though this inseparable act is technically shared by both Son (John 1:3; Col 1:16) and Spirit (Gen 1:2).[34] Appropriating divine actions to a particular person therefore helps us know that person in their hypostatic mode.

Missions

The divine missions are the proper work of the Son and the Holy Spirit. The missions can be described using various terminology, but several features are clear. First, the missions are unique to a particular divine person because they are rooted in the eternal processions by which the persons are distinguished. As Scott Swain helpfully clarifies:

> The relations of origin constitute the "whence" of the divine missions, the latter being the temporal embassy and extension of the former. The relations of origin also constitute the "whither" of the divine missions insofar as they provide the divine exemplars and goals of those missions: the goal of the Son's redemptive mission is to make *us* sons and daughters in order that *he* might be the firstborn among many brothers and sisters (Rom. 8:29; Gal. 4:5); the goal of the Spirit's sanctifying mission is to embrace *us* within the fellowship of the Father and the Son, pouring out the Father's love into our hearts (Rom. 5:5), and awakening within us the Son's filial cry of "Abba! Father!"[35]

Second, the mission is distinguished from the processions because of some connection with the created world. This, too, can be described in various ways: in the missions, a "created effect" is "attached" to a single divine person,[36] or there must be an "appropriate external term" that is contingent and constituted by the mission.[37] This is to say that in the missions, some-

---

34 Ideally, appropriations should be normed by the scriptural patterns in order to avoid becoming overly speculative.
35 Scott. R. Swain, "Divine Trinity," in Allen and Swain, *Christian Dogmatics*, 104.
36 Vidu, *The Same God*, 113.
37 Doran, *Trinity in History*, 47–48.

thing created is proper to a single divine person, as the human nature of Christ is proper to the Son only in the incarnation. The missions therefore are something proper only to a single divine person, though even here that person does not work in isolation in the divine mission. Rather, as Fred Sanders notes, the missions are "the foundation of our knowledge of the distinction of the persons."[38] We know the Son uniquely in the incarnation, but we inescapably know him as the one sent by the Father (e.g., Gal 4:4) and empowered by the Spirit (e.g., Luke 4:17–21, especially v. 18). The missions therefore deepen communion with each divine person, manifesting the eternal relational distinctions, without undermining the broader principle of inseparable operations.

COMMUNION WITH THE TRINITY IN THE *ORDO SALUTIS* AND THE MARKET

With a basic trinitarian account of divine action in hand, I can return to the question of how to interpret God's action in a market in such a manner that it might provide specific guidance for market design. Here, the temptation of many modern theologians has been to use the Trinity as a social model, which leads to problematic theological innovations and limited applicability. Yet if Christian transformation is rooted in communion with Father, Son, and Spirit, there must be some manner in which trinitarian action is a clear component of our account of moral formation in markets. We cannot simply neglect the Trinity altogether. What, then, is the path forward?

The trinitarian economy provides a much clearer point of contact with moral formation in markets than more common attempts to deploy trinitarian frameworks. The divine *oikonomia* already refers to the actions that God is doing in the created world, the same created world in which markets and economic interactions exist. Moreover, the economy especially focuses on redemption history, including the transformation of the faithful through special grace. At a deep theological level, whatever transformation occurs through common grace must therefore be correlated with these redemptive acts. For millennia, theologians have already undertaken the challenging work

---

38 Fred Sanders, *The Triune God* (Grand Rapids, MI: Zondervan, 2016), 124.

of logically analyzing different dimensions of God's transformative work, using the schema of the *ordo salutis* (the order of salvation). The theological pieces are all in place, and with a few precise summary theses, we can begin to assemble the puzzle:

- As a result of the fall, sin has permeated not only human nature but also human institutions such that we must assume that markets can and will lead to moral malformation, except where God graciously acts.
- Grace is both special grace, pertaining to God's redemptive work in the church, and common grace, which restrains sin and leads to positive moral, cultural, and social accomplishments in all peoples in contexts like markets.
- Common grace, as one subset of God's cosmic redemptive work in Christ, is oriented toward special grace, meaning that whatever positive moral transformation occurs in markets finds its perfection in the divine work of special grace.
- A noncontrastive account of transcendence allows us to conceptualize human actions carried out in the marketplace as concurrently divine actions.
- Because markets are constructed, it is possible that certain market formations better yield to God's work in common grace than others, thereby contributing to concurrent actions facilitating positive moral transformation.
- God's actions are inseparable operations that preserve the possibility of distinctive communion with each divine person through appropriations and missions.
- Accordingly, any action of God in the economy through common grace is a trinitarian action through which communion is possible, and this action will be oriented toward God's trinitarian work in special grace.
- The quest for a theological economics cognizant of market design must therefore identify aspects of God's appropriated and/or missional action in special grace—the *ordo salutis*—that correspond with market realities potentially shaped by common grace, using these correspondences to design markets that better yield to the concurrent action of God in producing moral transformation.

The duration of this chapter will therefore set forward three points of contact between the *ordo salutis* and a basic analysis of markets. Though at times it will seem I am belaboring the point, it is necessary to demonstrate that, unlike the exemplary approach, my connections between the economic works of the Trinity and the economy are not novelties driven by social commitments and then circularly used to justify those same commitments.

The Father's Providence, Culture, and Society

The Father, as the font of divinity, the unbegotten Generator of the Son and Spirator of the Spirit, is most clearly revealed in the divine providential governing of creation and history. This has been a consensus position of Orthodox, Catholic, and Protestant theologians from many generations. In tradition, the appropriation of providence to the Father is seen in the Apostles' Creed, in which the first article affirms faith in "God the Father almighty." This is especially true in the Greek, where *pantokrator*, which English translations render as "almighty," could also be translated as the "ruler and sustainer of all."[39] A specific theology of appropriating power to the Father was extensively developed in medieval Latin theology. For example, in Victorene theology, Hugh of St. Victor appropriated omnipotence to the Father,[40] and Richard of St. Victor explained that "the property of the Unbegotten is represented in power."[41] The typical pattern in Scripture is to attribute foreknowledge, providence, and predestination to the Father (e.g., in the sweeping summaries of redemption history in Rom 8:29–30 and Eph 1:4–5, 9–11), without denying the providential sovereignty of the other divine persons as seen in the title *Lord* being applied to all three, or in the Father sharing the throne with the Son (Rev 3:21; 7:17; 22:3), or in Son and Spirit being involved in election (John 6:70; 13:18; 1 Cor 2:7–14). Care is also consistently taken to distinguish the directing of the faithful through the inner guidance of the Holy Spirit as part of the Spirit's mission and the inseparable operation of divine providence,

---

39 Olivier Boulnois, "From Divine Omnipotence to Operative Power," *Divus Thomas* 115, no. 2 (May/August 2012): 83–84.

40 Hugh of St. Victor, *On the Three Days*, in *Trinity and Creation: A Selection of Works from Hugh, Richard and Adam of St. Victor*, ed. Boyd Taylor Coolman and Dale M. Coulter (Hyde Park, NY: New City Press, 2011), III.27.

41 Richard of St. Victor, *On the Trinity*, in Coolman and Coulter, *Trinity and Creation*, VI.15.

which is appropriated to the Father. For example, nineteenth-century American Reformed theologian Charles Hodge clearly distinguished between the mission of the Holy Spirit, which involved the operation of grace, and the providential guidance of God over "ordinary acts of men,"[42] which included acts like preservation and election that can be appropriated to the Father.[43] Providence can reasonably be appropriated to the Father.

Justification in the Son and Identity

The justification of the Christian is properly associated with the Son. Justification is linked with the divine mission of the Son in two ways. Due to the human nature assumed in the incarnation, the Son is ground for our justification both in the sense that the God-man accomplished the atonement required for justification to be possible and in the sense that our unity with Christ's humanity is a central component of justification. Moreover, though God's act of justifying us is an inseparable operation—the Father justifies (e.g., Rom 8:30), as does the Spirit—justification is most typically appropriated to the Son, especially among Protestants who emphasize justification *solus Christus*. In justification, which is accomplished by Christ and through which we share in the status and righteousness of Christ, we most clearly see the mode of existence of the second person of the Trinity as the eternally beloved and righteous Son.

A growing body of literature in behavioral and experimental economics explores markets and identity. As we shall see, this concept of identity is quite complex, but in its broad contours, it functions similarly to certain aspects of the doctrine of justification. Both concepts are fundamentally relational, determining status and opening certain possibilities of acting and/or being. There is a wide range of theories about identity in psychology, sociology, and philosophy—disciplines on which economics might draw for its understanding—but we see these three basic components in many of them. Similarly, justification is a controversial doctrine that famously plays a key part in the historical divisions between Protestantism and Roman Catholicism. Yet we see these

---

42 Charles Hodge, *Systematic Theology* (Grand Rapids, MI: Eerdmans, 1940), I. 614–15.

43 Hodge, *Systematic Theology*, I.445. Hodge divides providence into preservation and government, technically treating the election as a distinct locus.

same three features in theologies as diverse as John Owen's and the modern Joint Declaration on the Doctrine of Justification.

The treatments of identity by social constructionists Peter Berger and Thomas Luckmann and in the philosophy of Charles Taylor provide sociological and philosophical examples of the three basic features of identity outlined above. Berger and Luckmann explain that identity is established through a process of internalization, whereby individuals "'tak[e] over' the world in which others already live," accepting the social realities of those with whom one relates—parents or other caregivers are especially important to this process.[44] Through this relational process, one is "assigned a specific place in the world," which results in the determination of what internalized roles will guide proper behavior in society.[45] Charles Taylor explains that identity provides "the frame or horizon within which I can try to determine from case to case what is good, or valuable, or what ought to be done, or what I endorse or oppose. In other words, it is the horizon within which I am capable of taking a stand."[46] Identity thus determines certain morally possible courses of action, but it does so only in relation: "A self can never be described without reference to those who surround it."[47] Furthermore, it requires that we understand our status or position within a certain narrative.[48] More examples could be provided, but this illustrates broadly accepted basic contours of the concept of identity.[49]

Justification overlaps with the concept of identity because of the way that the biblical materials connect justification with our relation to God, our status as those who trust in Christ, and the resulting ways of being and doing available to us. Justification is a predominant theme in Paul, so we can especially see the link between identity and justification in Paul. Of course, the interpretation of Pauline theology has been a source of contention in

---

44 Peter L. Berger and Thomas Luckmann, *The Social Construction of Reality: A Treatise in the Sociology of Knowledge* (New York: Anchor, 1966), 129–32.

45 Berger and Luckmann, *The Social Construction of Reality*, 132–33.

46 Charles Taylor, *Sources of the Self: The Making of Modern Identity* (Cambridge: Harvard University Press, 1989), 27.

47 Taylor, *Sources of the Self*, 35.

48 Taylor, *Sources of the Self*, 47, 51.

49 One caveat is that Christian notions of identity must be rooted in some ontic core, insofar as Christ himself becomes constitutive of Christian identity, and there is a real union between Christ and the believer that serves as the basis of this aspect of identity. See the discussion in Edward Rommen, *Get Real: On Evangelism in the Late Modern World* (Pasadena, CA: William Carey, 2010), 57–82.

recent decades, but there is general consensus across different perspectives that justification relates to identity. Among the New Perspective on Paul, for example, the displacement of "works of the law" (Rom 3:20; Gal 2:16, etc.)[50] is often taken to mean that belonging to the covenant community (status) is no longer determined by works of the law but by faith. To put it in James D. G. Dunn's terms, faith in Jesus becomes "a primary identity marker that renders the others superfluous."[51] The "Lutheran" perspective is less prone to using the terminology of *identity*, likely due to its prevalence among advocates of the New Perspective. Yet we see the basic dimensions of identity present in this perspective too. For example, Thomas Schreiner claims that forensic justification bestows a "new status before God," a forensic status out of which grows any righteousness of the believer.[52] Among those who emphasize union as the central theme in Paul, subordinating justification under this theme, there is still some sense that this central image of union with Christ includes within it our sharing in the identity of Christ.[53]

While many details of the Bible's teaching on justification are disputed—What is the role of faith and works? Is justification progressive or positional? Is it individualistic or communal?—it is also clear among important historical and contemporary Protestant and Catholic theologians that justification serves similar functions to what psychologists, sociologists, and philosophers often mean by identity. Puritan John Owen, to name one historical example, defends justification by imputation. For Owen, the imputation *ex gratia* (of mere grace and favor)[54] must have just grounds.[55] In fact, it is based on our

---

50 Here I deviate from the NRSV's translation, following the more common phrasing found in the NASB, NIV, ESV, and other translations.

51 James D. G. Dunn, *The New Perspective on Paul: Collected Essays* (Tübingen: Mohr Siebeck, 2005), 103. N. T. Wright links new identity to new behavior patterns. Tom Wright, *Justification: God's Plan and Paul's Vision* (London: SPCK, 2009), 95.

52 Schreiner, *Paul, Apostle of God's Glory in Christ*, 205, 209.

53 Constantine Campbell calls this aspect of union "identification," by which he means "believers' identity is shaped by their belonging to Christ . . . and this is to shape believers' sense of who they are and to whom they owe allegiance." Constantine R. Campbell, *Paul and Union with Christ: An Exegetical and Theological Study* (Grand Rapids, MI: Zondervan, 2012), 408.

54 John Owen, *The Doctrine of Justification by Faith*, in *The Works of John Owen*, vol. V, ed. William H. Goold (Philadelphia: Leighton Publications, 1862), 171.

55 "To impute unto us that which is not our own antecedently unto that imputation, includes also in it two things: (1) A grant or donation of the thing itself unto us, to be ours, on some just ground and foundations; for a thing must be made ours before we can justly be dealt with according unto what is required on the account of it. (2) A will

union with Christ, for imputation is not contrary to truth even if it is contrary to our nature.[56] Those who are united with Christ, receiving justification, have a new status associated with new possible ways of acting and being: the justified live acquitted from guilt and freed from the curse,[57] and having received the righteousness of Christ, they bear "right and title" to eternal life and a blessed inheritance.[58] All of this occurs as a result of the right relationship with God through faith, which involves among other things assent to God and trust in God's provision in Christ.[59]

The Joint Declaration on the Doctrine of Justification (JDDJ) is one final example of theological consensus that justification relates to identity. This joint statement between Lutherans and Roman Catholics is the fruit of years of ecumenical efforts, to the result that signatories agree on basic consensus with respect to the doctrine of justification and do not consider lingering differences church-dividing.[60] The Lutheran and Catholic signatories of the JDDJ agree that justification puts an end to imputed sin and imparts a new life (§22). As a result, justification must be seen as "the basis for the whole Christian life" (§25) in several senses, including that justification obligates certain actions and brings forth good works in the face of ongoing wrestling with sin (§37).[61] Like identity, justification clearly determines status and which possible sets of actions are proper to an individual in a given context. Despite the many disagreements over the doctrine of justification, this basic point

---

of dealing with us, or an actual dealing with us, according unto that which is so made ours." Owen, *The Doctrine of Justification by Faith*, 167.

56 Owen follows a typically Reformed approach here. There is a tendency for Lutherans to say forensic declaration/imputation makes union possible, while the Reformed see union as basis of imputation/justification. George Hunsinger, "Justification and Mystical Union with Christ: Where Does Owen Stand?" in *The Ashgate Research Companion to John Owen's Theology*, ed. Kelly M. Kapic and Mark Jones (New York: Routledge, 2016), 199–200.

57 Owen, *The Doctrine of Justification by Faith*, 8.

58 The phrase "right and title" is a regular one for Owen. See Owen, *The Doctrine of Justification by Faith*, 7, 8, 173, etc.

59 Owen, *The Doctrine of Justification by Faith*, 100–101.

60 See Susan K. Wood, "Catholic Reception of the Joint Declaration on the Doctrine of Justification," in *Rereading Paul Together: Protestant and Catholic Perspectives on Justification*, ed. David E. Aune (Grand Rapids, MI: Baker Academic, 2006), 43–59.

61 "The Joint Declaration on the Doctrine of Justification," accessed August 29, 2023, https://www.lutheranworld.org/sites/default/files/2022-02/joint_declaration_2019_en.pdf.

is evident from various perspectives in biblical studies, historical theology, and systematic theology.

Sanctification in the Holy Spirit and Norms of Behavior

When seeking a created feature of the economy that correlates with the person and work of the Holy Spirit, the most obvious point of connection is that of norms of behavior. As with identity, many possible detailed theories of social norms are possible, but at a basic level, many theories would overlap conceptually with what Christians speak of when referring to such terms as *infused virtues, regeneration, holiness,* and *sanctification*. As James D. Wallace states, "Practical knowledge, know-how, is knowledge of how things are properly done. What we know, items of practical knowledge, are properly called norms."[62] Such norms are generalizable and normative—they express what generally ought to be done in a certain kind of situation. They are also open to reformulation and require the ability to sort among various norms to determine which takes precedent in a given situation.[63] Definitions like Wallace's fit the prescriptive meaning of social norms, but Nicole Dubois reminds us that some attempt to use the term descriptively to name what most people in a given group do. Even in such contexts, Dubois argues that there is an implicit prescriptive dimension, at least from the standpoint of the group who acts according to a norm.[64] Moreover, such descriptive appeals to frequency do not work, for some norms must be "activated" to produce "norm-consistent behavior."[65] Dubois argues that norms are "observable events (behaviors and judgments) which are socially valued as such in a given collectivity."[66] Such treatments of norms show that norms pertain to the ability to act a certain way in a certain context, which requires the activation of certain norms with respect to other norms and values. There is thus considerable conceptual

---

62 James D. Wallace, *Norms and Practices* (Ithaca, NY: Cornell University Press, 2009), 94.

63 Wallace, *Norms and Practices*, 95–97.

64 Nicole Dubois, "Introduction: The Concept of a Norm," in *A Sociocognitive Approach to Social Norms*, ed. Nicole Dubois (London: Routledge, 2002), 1–2. "This facet shows up in the fact that whoever does not do what the majority of the people do is considered at best odd or original, and at worst, a deviant or a misfit." Dubois, "Introduction," 2.

65 Dubois, "Introduction," 6–7.

66 Dubois, "Introduction," 10.

overlap between norms and traditional ways of speaking of the work of the Holy Spirit.

Consider the theology of Thomas Aquinas. In Aquinas, the invisible mission of the Holy Spirit is to indwell Christians in the gift of sanctifying grace.[67] As Brian Davies summarizes, "Aquinas thinks that grace is at work when people come to be virtuous [by possessing the infused theological virtues of faith, hope, and love]. That is what he means by 'grace' primarily."[68] Aquinas explains that virtues are a kind of habit, and habits are certain dispositions or qualities of a human nature.[69] Charity, for example, is a disposition resulting from the grace-enabled transformation of the will toward a supernatural end.[70] The Holy Spirit's mission must therefore be seen as a theological description similar to what is described in sociology as norms, which result in predispositions toward certain acts and behaviors. A Thomist account of the mission of the Holy Spirit also connects with concrete acts themselves, for the Spirit also provides the fruits, which are "any virtuous deeds in which one delights."[71] In a sense, we could say the Spirit is the one that, by infusion, activates a given virtuous habit or norm. A clear association is made here between the mission of the Holy Spirit and the patterns of behavior seen in a Christian's life.

A similar position is found in the seventeenth century by Reformed Puritan theologian Thomas Goodwin, who disagreed with the Roman Catholic view of habitual grace because of the way it was connected with merit and justification but whose pneumatology retained a connection to human action parallel to that of Aquinas.[72] Goodwin argues that "the Holy Ghost doth not only move and stir us up to all good actions which we do, but that in the work of conversion, he produceth in us living and lasting principles of a constant holy life."[73] He explains how these principles are analogous to natural powers of human nature, which is why we can speak of being given eyes to see and ears to hear (e.g., Deut 19:4) or of having a new spiritual body (1 Cor 15:44–45;

---

67 Aquinas, *Summa Theologica*, I.I Q. 43 a. 3.

68 Brian Davies, *The Thought of Thomas Aquinas* (Oxford: Oxford University Press, 1992), 264.

69 Aquinas, *Summa Theologica*, I.II Q. 55 a. 1; I.II Q. 49 a. 1.

70 Aquinas, *Summa Theologica*, I.II Q. 62 a. 3.

71 Aquinas, *Summa Theologica*, I.II Q. 70 a. 2.

72 For Goodwin's criticism of the Roman Catholic perspective, which he cites from Bellarmine and Suarez, see Thomas Goodwin, *The Work of the Holy Ghost in Our Salvation*, in *The Works of Thomas Goodwin*, vol. VI, ed. Thomas Smith (Edinburgh: James Nichol, 1863), 187–88.

73 Goodwin, *The Work of the Holy Ghost*, 191.

Phil 3:21).[74] In other words, regeneration by the Spirit infuses a habit whereby we perform patterns of moral action, yet nonmeritorious ones. To put this in another way, regeneration by the Holy Spirit involves mortification of "an inherent corruption," the destruction of what Paul calls the "body of death" (Rom 6:6), which is replaced through vivification with a "habitual principle of grace."[75] Again, there is considerable conceptual overlap between Goodwin's notion of regeneration producing lasting principles of a holy life and norms that produce consistent patterns of human behavior.

Let us turn to one more figure: Phoebe Palmer. Palmer is quite distinct in her theology from both Goodwin and Aquinas. Rather than *regeneration* or *virtue*, Palmer prefers the terminology of *holiness*, which she defines as "that state which is attained by the believer when, through faith in the infinite merit of the Saviour, body and soul, with every ransomed faculty, are ceaselessly presented, a living sacrifice to God."[76] Palmer's emphasis on holiness as a state of ceaseless offering functions similarly to Aquinas's discussion of theological virtues as infused habits and to Goodwin's theology of regeneration as mortification and vivification. She insists that holiness is a gift of the Spirit as a result of our faith, not works.[77] Holiness is given through "the purifying, consuming energies of the Holy Spirit."[78] When exploring biblical patterns of speaking about sanctification, Palmer notes that the Father sanctifies (Exod 31:13; 1 Thess 5:23), the Son sanctifies (Eph 5:25–26), and the Spirit is the one who gives the washing of rebirth and renewal (Titus 3:5).[79] Though not drawing on the term itself, Palmer also attests to concurrence in sanctification, for God sanctifies, but the people of Israel also sanctify themselves (Lev 20:7).[80] Within a Thomistic, Reformed, and Second Blessing Wesleyan perspective, we see consensus that the Holy Spirit works to bring about patterns, "habits," or "ceaseless" behaviors that shape human actions, much as economists and social scientists might speak about norms. The difference is that theologians

---

74 Goodwin, *The Work of the Holy Ghost*, 194–95.
75 Goodwin, *The Work of the Holy Ghost*, 201.
76 Phoebe Palmer, *Entire Devotion to God*, in *Phoebe Palmer: Selected Writings*, ed. Thomas C. Oden (New York: Paulist, 1988), 187.
77 Palmer insists that sanctification is by faith and by the power of God, and this is the reason we can expect immediate, entire sanctification. If it depended on our works, we could excuse ourselves because we might need time to sufficiently work out our sanctification. Palmer, *Entire Devotion to God*, 195–96.
78 Palmer, *Entire Devotion to God*, 199.
79 Palmer, *Entire Devotion to God*, 188–89.
80 Palmer, *Entire Devotion to God*, 188.

speak of the Holy Spirit as the one activating good behavior, while social scientists would consider social factors that might lead to activating norm-consistent behavior. Drawing on a theology of concurrence and common grace, we can easily see how sociological factors might lead to norms and norm-consistent behaviors that are less consistent or more consistent with virtuous works brought about by the Holy Spirit.

POINTS OF INTERSECTION BETWEEN THEOLOGY AND ECONOMICS

Part I revealed that markets neither automatically produce positive moral formation nor automatically result in vicious formation. Rather, the particular ways that markets are constructed in terms of their borders, mechanisms for exchange, and context yield differing results in terms of moral formation. The variability of possible outcomes in terms of moral formation led to a number of theological questions for one committed to assess markets from a consciously theological standpoint. Part II, therefore, argued that we must understand God's grace to extend to all parts of creation, speaking of common grace as a means whereby God potentially even works through markets in a manner that is oriented toward God's redemptive work in the *ordo salutis*, though as a result of original sin, such positive moral formation is never guaranteed. A theology of concurrence allows us to assume that human efforts in the marketplace may also be used by God as secondary causes for the divine work of salvation. This chapter has clarified these theological claims by situating them within the context of trinitarian theology. While the Trinity is not an exemplar for our social program, the appropriated works of God as well as the divine missions are the basis of our transformation in the *ordo salutis*. For this reason, whatever concurrent works of common grace are occurring in markets must also be correlated with divine actions.

While there are many such possibilities for exploring such connections, I will now turn to part III to expand on the connections established here. Chapter 7 will explore how providentially given factors of an economy like culture and wealth distribution may affect moral formation, chapter 8 will focus on empirical and experimental studies of identity in terms of their relevance for moral formation, and chapter 9 will explore norms in economics, particularly in relation to motivation, connecting these features of markets to God's redemptive work through providence and in justification and sanctification, respectively.

PART III

Theology and Economics

CHAPTER 7

The Father's Providence and the Context of Markets

The economy is not a natural fact, a phenomenon that we find; rather it is a reality that we make, and how we conceptualize the economy will greatly shape how we make it.

—Charles M. A. Clark[1]

In 2010, a group of psychologists decided to test the hypothesis that "lower class individuals are more concerned with the needs of others relative to upper class individuals, and, guided by this concern, will act in a more prosocial fashion to improve others' welfare."[2] To test this hypothesis, they ran four experiments, attempting to falsify or verify their hypothesis. The first experiment was a dictator game, the experimental game discussed in chapter 1 (p. 29) where participants are given money and allowed to distribute it between themselves and another participant, who was forced to take the amount given. The study found that individuals who were of a lower socioeconomic standing were likely to give more to their participants in the

---

1 Charles M. A. Clark, foreword to Luigino Bruni, *The Wound and the Blessing: Economics, Relationships, and Happiness*, trans. N. Michael Brennen (Hyde Park, NY: New City Press, 2012), xi.

2 Paul K. Piff et al., "Having Less, Giving More: The Influence of Social Class on Prosocial Behavior," *Journal of Personality and Social Psychology* 99, no. 5 (2010): 772.

game.[3] In a second study, participants were primed to think of themselves as relatively high or relatively low in social class by reflecting and writing on how they compared with individuals on the lowest or on the highest rung of a ten-rung ladder representing different US social classes. After this time of reflection, participants were asked to answer what percentage of annual income families should spend on various categories, including charitable giving. Those who compared themselves with members of the top social rank and saw themselves in a relatively lower social class were more likely to propose high charitable giving levels in the survey than those who compared themselves with members of the lowest social rank.[4] The first two studies seemed to validate the hypothesis, suggesting those lower in socioeconomic class were more generous and favored charitable giving more.

Wanting to ensure that they had sound results, the researchers conducted another study, with similar results. In this third study, the same psychologists used the trust game. In this experiment, an initial participant would receive thirty points and could choose to give a fraction of their points to a fellow participant. Whatever amount they gave would be tripled, and the partner could return whatever share they wished to the original participant. If both participants trust one another, both can earn a far larger share of points, which were said to have a potential monetary value.[5] Participants had already disclosed extensive personal information, including data identifying socioeconomic class. Given the results of the first two studies, it is unsurprising that participants of a lower socioeconomic class chose more egalitarian strategies in the trust game, giving more to their partners.[6] Their willingness

---

3 Piff et al., "Having Less, Giving More," 774. Socioeconomic class was measured both in an objective sense based on a questionnaire and in a subjective sense based on where participants self-identified in a social hierarchy. Other factors like gender, race/ethnicity, and religiosity were not found to be statistically significant.

4 Piff et al., "Having Less, Giving More," 775–76. This study also collected objective data about family income, finding that participants with higher objective income were also likely to propose giving less.

5 In point of fact, this game was a computer simulation, and the second partner did not exist.

6 Piff et al., "Having Less, Giving More," 777–78. Participants in this study also filled out a questionnaire exploring how egalitarian their values were, with lower-socioeconomic-class participants answering more favorably toward egalitarian answers. A fourth and final study considered the effect of social class, finding that inducing a compassionate mindset before an opportunity to help mitigate the effects of socioeconomic class to a

to give more suggests that they trusted their partners more than members of higher socioeconomic classes.

The cumulative results of these experiments strongly suggest that socioeconomic class shapes how generous and trusting individuals are. The distribution of socioeconomic classes in a market economy is related to markets themselves in a dialectical manner. On the one hand, any given market participant is born into a particular socioeconomic class, a condition that is given prior to any market participation they undertake. Markets are constructed by individuals already shaped by economic class. On the other hand, various structural features of markets, which I will discuss later in the chapter, can be changed to affect which market participants are in which socioeconomic classes and to shape how significant of a distance there is between the lowest and highest classes. Markets design substantially influences the nature and distribution of classes. In this chapter, I will examine factors like economic inequality and culture that shape human beings from childhood, prior to their active participation in markets. I will interpret such factors theologically as the result of divine providence, drawing on the doctrine of concurrence to suggest a spiritual response to these situational factors that enables active human efforts to shape markets through market design in order to ensure that moral formation in markets better aligns with God's redemptive work in the church. But first, I must survey the role of economic inequality and culture in experimental economics, Christian ethics, and Christian theology.

THE CONTEXT OF MARKETS AND MORAL FORMATION

The question of whether markets contribute positively or negatively to moral formation depends in part on the social, cultural, and economic contexts within which markets occur. I have already shown some evidence of this fact, but there are extensive examples across the social sciences since experiments in economics, psychology, and sociology have explored the relationship among inequality, culture, and moral formation. In this section, I will survey a selection of the relevant literature, connecting it with the ideas of Christian ethicists and theologians where appropriate.

---

large extent. I have not focused on this study because of its complexity, which renders it challenging to describe in an introduction.

Wealth, Poverty, and Moral Formation

Kate Ward's *Wealth, Virtue, and Moral Luck* offers the most extensive Christian analysis of the formative role of wealth inequality of which I am aware. Ward defines wealth broadly as "having more than we need" and poverty as "lacking the basic goods of life."[7] She uses the concept of "moral luck," especially as developed by feminist ethicists, to explain the role of wealth and poverty in virtue formation. Moral luck refers to factors beyond the control of a moral agent that affect one's ability to make moral choices or develop virtue. In this case, we are dealing with "constitutive moral luck," which impacts the sort of person that a person can become.[8] In many respects, Ward's category of moral luck functions like my appeal to the Father's providence, and, much like my account of concurrence, Ward is clear that a Christian account of moral luck is more optimistic about moral development through God's grace despite moral (bad) luck.[9] Yet both wealth and poverty play a significant role in moral formation, and Ward is one of the few Christian ethicists who appeal to economic data and experiments to make her case.

Jesus warns that it is easier for a camel to pass through the eye of a needle than for a rich man to enter the kingdom (Mark 10:25 and pars.), so we should not be surprised to find that wealth is associated with greater vice. For example, Ian Harper and Eric Jones note that "a survey of 10,000 school children in North West England shows that those with surplus pocket money are the ones who buy alcohol at the youngest ages and grow up to be binge drinkers."[10] Ward notes that those who are wealthy also give a lower proportion of their wealth, suggesting that they are less generous and more subject to avarice.[11] As Ward explains, "Someone who walks around every day, able to save precious human lives through her freely available surplus, and chooses not to do so,

---

7 Kate Ward, *Wealth, Virtue, and Moral Luck: Christian Ethics in an Age of Inequality* (Washington, DC: Georgetown University Press, 2021), 7, 118.

8 Ward, *Wealth, Virtue, and Moral Luck*, 90–91. Ward is particularly indebted to M. Shawn Copeland and Cheryl Townsend Gilkes.

9 Ward, *Wealth, Virtue, and Moral Luck*, 99.

10 Ian R. Harper and Eric L. Jones, "Treating 'Affluenze': The Moral Challenge of Affluence," in *Christian Theology and Market Economics*, ed. Ian R. Harper and Samuel Gregg (Northampton, MA: Edward Elgar, 2008), 148. Ward points to similar data in Ward, *Wealth, Virtue, and Moral Luck*, 158.

11 Ward, *Wealth, Virtue, and Moral Luck*, 146–47.

is deformed morally both by the system she inhabits, which distributes the basic goods of life so unequally, and by her own choices within that system."[12]

Economic experiments have provided further evidence that wealth can decrease virtue.[13] Several of the psychologists who ran the experiments in this chapter's introduction contributed to another series of studies exploring the role of wealth in moral formation. Their second series of experiments confirmed the results of their earlier publication. For example, after a psychological experiment, participants were offered candy but were told the leftover candy would be given to children in another experiment. Upper-class participants in the experiment were more likely to take candy from children than were lower-class participants.[14] In another experiment, participants were asked to play a game of chance on a computer, where they had five separate rolls of a digital die. The participants were asked to self-report their score after five roles, with a higher score purportedly increasing the chances of winning a cash prize. What participants did not know is that the game was rigged to always produce a score of 12, so any reported scores above 12 were direct evidence of dishonesty and cheating. Participants were also asked to complete a survey, which included questions identifying their attitude toward greed. Social class and favorable attitudes toward greed both predicted cheating, but a further regression analysis suggests that the favorable attitude toward greed was predictive both of being in a higher social class and of being likely to cheat.[15] Again, there is evidence that "the love of money is a root of all kinds of evil" (1 Tim 6:10).

Though wealth seems to have mostly negative effects on virtue, there are some positive aspects of wealth for moral development. As Ward notes, "Middle- and upper-class people are more likely to marry, less likely to divorce, and more likely to say they are 'very happy' in their marriage than those with fewer resources."[16] The data can be interpreted in several ways. It might suggest that members of higher socioeconomic classes are more likely to manifest the virtue of fidelity, or it could indicate the results of long-term stress of

---

12 Ward, *Wealth, Virtue, and Moral Luck*, 136.

13 Though I will appeal to the primary sources for these experiments, I first learned of their existence through Ward, *Wealth, Virtue, and Moral Luck*, 145–46.

14 Paul K. Piff et al., "Higher Social Class Predicts Increased Unethical Behavior," *Proceedings of the National Academy of Sciences of the United States of America* 109, no. 11 (March 13, 2012): 4087.

15 Piff et al., "Higher Social Class," 4088.

16 Ward, *Wealth, Virtue, and Moral Luck*, 150.

financial strain on marriages, or it could attest to the fact that the financial benefits of marriage for the wealthy incentivize them to remain married.[17] Wealth also allows parents to spend more time caring for children, and while most studies suggest that adults in lower socioeconomic classes are more generous than wealthy participants, one experiment running the dictator game among children found that children of parents with low educational levels are less likely to be altruistic than children of more educated parents.[18] This study hints at the possibility that the emotional strain of poverty-induced anxiety in family contexts especially affects children. Similarly, data shows that children from families on food stamps are more prone to discipline problems near the end of the month, when parents are likely facing extra stress.[19] Those who are impoverished face their own challenges in moral formation, even as they are more likely to act in prosocial and altruistic ways. Given that all human beings are born into situations of poverty or wealth that are independent of their control—the debate over the extent to which social mobility is possible is best left for a different time—we have good reason to identify factors like socioeconomic status to be a byproduct of the Father's will. Yet the clear biblical condemnations of oppression, wealth, and injustice discussed below prohibit us from seeing such conditions as a result of God's preceptive will. Rather, poverty is something inexplicably permitted by providence, an opportunity for Christians to act justly now and a reminder of the imminent justice of the day of the Lord.

The considerable evidence that wealth can contribute to moral malformation challenges the arguments made by some Christian ethicists and theologians that affluence is beneficial for moral development. For example, Brent Waters argues, "Affluence is a good that should be pursued."[20] Waters

---

17 Ward is helpfully cautious in her assessment: "It is hardly necessary to observe that a couple can remain married even while their daily actions belie the values of a loving commitment, or that a never-married couple could pursue the virtue of fidelity in their lives together. This caveat stated, resources of money and time have the potential to enable acts of fidelity in partnerships . . . those with hyperagency, with money and time to dispose of, can pursue fidelity by using their resources to connect with loved ones and to meet their needs." Ward, *Wealth, Virtue, and Moral Luck*, 150.

18 See Michal Bauer, Julie Chytilová, and Barbara Pertold-Gebicka, "Parental Background and Other-Regarding Preferences in Children," *Experimental Economics* 17, no. 1 (2014): 24–46.

19 Ward, *Wealth, Virtue, and Moral Luck*, 189.

20 Waters, *Just Capitalism*, 80.

distinguishes affluence and wealth; the former is just having surplus economic resources available, while the latter refers to "an order of magnitude of surplus resources that few attain."[21] Affluence is a proximate good, neither a virtue nor a vice and yet something that promotes responsibility and enables generosity, argues Waters.[22] The problem with such an argument, as this chapter has shown, is that the moral malformation of wealth extends beyond a few multimillionaires into average participants in social psychology studies or members of the middle class. Yet Waters raises an important point when he advocates that affluence is a proximate good, for some degree of economic accumulation is necessary to escape absolute poverty, lacking the basic resources needed for life. However, some who qualify as lower socioeconomic classes in the above studies are better explained as those who are relatively poor, those who have less than other members of their own society. The issue may be reframed, then, as one of economic inequality.

Economic Inequality and Moral Formation

While it is certainly the case that the accumulation of economic resources has benefits, including, for example, health benefits, many countries with market economies have risen above the levels of absolute poverty where the most immediate health benefits for increases in wealth are found.[23] In a situation of absolute poverty (i.e., poverty below a standard necessary for life), increased earnings can increase nutrition, decrease infant mortality, and extend lifespan. Waters is correct to point to the benefits of money in this respect, and rightly designed markets can contribute to such increases in wealth. However, in many countries where theological debates about markets occur, absolute poverty is infrequently a problem.[24] In fact, as Richard Wilkinson summarizes, "Rich countries have reached a level of development

---

21 Waters, *Just Capitalism*, 81.
22 Waters, *Just Capitalism*, 83, 87.
23 "Above a national income of $10,000 there is very little relation between national income and life expectancy." Michael Marmot, *The Health Gap: The Challenge of an Unequal World* (New York: Bloomsbury, 2015), 39–40.
24 This is not to deny the existence of homeless populations, for example, though such situations are different in many respects from situations of absolute poverty that affect majorities of the population. For example, medical and mental health needs, addictions, and criminal records are often factors within homeless populations to a higher extent than for those living in absolute poverty around the world. Both groups are deserving of urgent attention, but specific solutions will vary between the groups.

beyond which further rises in absolute living standards do not help reduce social problems nor add to well-being or happiness."[25] Affluence may help the basic health and flourishing in many poorer countries of the world, but such gains are not clearly available today in many wealthier nations.

The wealthiness of a nation as a whole may not be indicative of the health of that nation. The very wealthy United States still ranks fiftieth in terms of "adult mortality"—the likelihood of fifteen-year-old boys to reach sixty (13 percent do not).[26] Michael Marmot has spent much of his career studying the effects of economic inequality on health, documenting clear health gaps within wealthy nations, where both low and high socioeconomic classes make more per year than the average worker in a poor nation. Despite this, he notes, "On average people at the top [of wealth distribution] live twelve years of their lives with disability, people at the bottom twenty years."[27] Obviously, such health discrepancies are a matter of great moral concern because they suggest a violation of justice, sacrificing the right of members of the lower socioeconomic classes to life and health for the sake of the wealthier socioeconomic class's ability to pursue ever greater levels of wealth. However, these discrepancies are also important in terms of our moral formation.

Divergences in health among socioeconomic classes may be a reflection of different levels of stress, a hypothesis that bears directly on moral formation. Surveying experiments on cognitive development, Marmot has found that when children of two socioeconomic classes are comparable in cognitive development at twenty-two months in age, there is a significant divergence over time. Cognitive scores are diminished for lower socioeconomic classes relative to higher socioeconomic classes as time progresses.[28] In part, such divergences in cognitive scores can be traced to stress found in mothers, which has a demonstrable effect on the developing structure of a child's brain.[29] A survey of two hundred experiments determining what prompted rises in cortisol, "a central stress hormone," found that the most substantial influences were those that "included social-evaluative threat (such as threats to self-esteem or social status)."[30] In other words, the lower one's social sta-

---

25 Richard Wilkinson, "The Impact of Inequality: Empirical Evidence," in *Social Inequality and Public Health*, ed. Salvatore J. Babones (Chicago: Policy Press, 2009), 160.
26 Marmot, *The Health Gap*, 32–33.
27 Marmot, *The Health Gap*, 27.
28 Marmot, *The Health Gap*, 122.
29 Marmot, *The Health Gap*, 135.
30 Wilkinson, "Impact of Inequality," 164.

tus, the more likely one is to experience stress, which can impede cognitive development of children from lower socioeconomic classes. Combining the effects of stress on childhood development with the way that stress for adults can limit our cognitive functioning—Kate Ward calls this the "bandwidth tax"—we can expect that more unequal societies may result in members of lower socioeconomic classes facing challenges in developing prudence and moral reasoning.[31]

Inequality in itself has also been shown to be a more direct factor in moral formation. Some social scientists have suggested that the studies attempting to measure ethical divergences based on socioeconomic class may actually be revealing the implications of economic inequality. Experiments in unequal societies have found upper-class status associated with less generosity, whereas studies performed in societies with less inequality (e.g., Germany, Japan) have found a smaller correlation between socioeconomic class and generosity.[32] This may indicate that the above studies suggesting that upper socioeconomic classes are less prosocial are actually demonstrating that wealthier members of unequal societies are less prosocial. Some experiments validate this hypothesis. For example, one study used a dictator game to distribute tickets to enter a raffle to win $10 or $500. There was no correlation between economic class and generosity nationwide. However, when data were then filtered based on the economic inequality in the different regions where the game was played, a clear correlation between the inequitable distribution of tickets and relative wealth was found in regions with high inequality between socioeconomic classes. Where significant inequality was present, people were neither fair nor generous.[33]

Multiple studies have found a clear correlation between increases in economic inequality and violence, including homicide. Data shows a similar correlation between increases in inequality and prison populations.[34] Societies with high degrees of economic inequality are also more likely to adopt

---

31 See Ward, *Wealth, Virtue, and Moral Luck*, 176–80, 188. While neither prudence nor moral reasoning is identical to cognitive bandwidth, it is reasonable to infer at least some degree of overlap among these faculties.

32 Stéphane Côté, Julian House, and Robb Willer, "High Economic Inequality Leads Higher-Income Individuals to be Less Generous," *Proceedings of the National Academy of Sciences of the United States of America* 112, no. 52 (December 29, 2015): 15838–39.

33 Côté, House, and Willer, "High Economic Inequality," 15839.

34 Wilkinson, "Impact of Inequality," 159. Wilkinson notes that at least forty studies have found this correlation.

harsher punitive measures for crime.[35] Economic inequality contributes to both criminal violence and state-sanctioned violence, likely resulting in an escalating cycle of violence. Amy Chua has even argued that in situations where an ethnic minority has predominated in a higher socioeconomic class in situations of great economic inequality, a shift to democracy can often lead to war or ethnic cleansing.[36] Chua's argument reminds us of the intersectionality of moral formation in markets—poverty and economic inequality will, in most markets, also connect with categories like race, ethnicity, nationality, and gender. These subjects will be discussed in greater detail in the next chapter.

The data on economic inequality suggests that the overall features of the economy and society within which a market participant buys, sells, invests, and produces goods will influence the likelihood of developing given virtues in that society. Economic inequality is clearly an example of social sin, where the social-psychological consequences of inequality produce sin. This data could be interpreted in a semi-Pelagian manner, suggesting that the moral transformation occurring through God's saving work is merely the product of social factors, which humans have the ability to change. However, such an interpretation would be wanting from a Christian standpoint for two reasons. First, these experiments and datasets show probabilistic averages, but individuals can break outside of these averages, and such statistical deviations could be appropriately identified as a product of common grace. Second, most market participants will lack the agency to change the social and economic conditions within which they live and work in a manner sufficient enough to change the way that basic features like economic inequality shape their moral formation. This need not lead to despair—some change is possible, as I will argue below. Humans have moral responsibility and genuine causal agency. But our somewhat limited abilities should prevent a Promethean view of human potential here. Instead, it is better to treat such economic factors as inequality and wealth distribution as factors that are givens in the short term—unlikely to change in the next several years yet also subject to human control and influence over the long run. Switching to theological idiom, they can be interpreted as the work of divine providence and yet subject to human control through a robust notion of concurrence. I am getting ahead of myself,

---

35 Ward, *Wealth, Virtue, and Moral Luck*, 28.
36 See Amy Chua, *World on Fire: How Exporting Free Market Democracy Breeds Ethnic Hatred and Global Instability* (New York: Anchor, 2003).

though, for one more situational factor behind the moral development of agents within markets must be considered: culture.

Culture and Moral Formation

Culture has been shown to have an effect on moral formation in markets. For present purposes, I can simply define culture as socially derived and historically contingent ways of seeing the world and oneself in it, resulting in particular customs, actions, symbols, values, and artifacts comprehensible within such a way of seeing the world. Because culture shapes our expectations and resulting actions, it is no surprise that culture influences markets. For example, some studies have found cultural differences in terms of the ultimatum game, "suggesting that cultural differences may play a role in the formation of other-regarding preferences."[37] In one series of cross-cultural experiments, economists found differences in altruism that correlated with the extent of economic and social interactions participants faced in daily life. In societies where interaction with others through a market is frequent and culturally reinforced by standards of fairness, distribution was likely to be fair. In cultures where there is limited economic exchange and/or few cultural norms enforcing fairness in such exchanges, distribution was far less equitable. The economists concluded that "economic choices ... are shaped by the economic and social interactions of everyday life."[38] Such studies challenge those critics of markets that treat them as always problematic for moral formation, even as they remind us that the extent of positive moral formation in markets is dependent on cultural factors. However, we must be careful not to reduce the formative nature of markets to the influence of culture.[39]

Cultural differences may influence how markets work even within a single country. Economist John MacMillan explores how different understandings of the labor market between Silicon Valley in California and Route 128 in Boston allowed Silicon Valley to be more effective in software design. No-compete contracts were strongly enforced in Boston but not in Silicon Valley. As a result, a "culture of sharing" and "job hopping" emerged in Silicon Valley, where software engineers would openly share ideas from their firm with

---

37 Michelle Baddeley, *Behavioural Economics and Finance* (London: Routledge, 2013), 83.
38 Henrich et al., "In Search of *Homo Economicus*," 73–78.
39 See the discussion in Finn, *Moral Ecology of Markets*, 51–52, 68–70.

competing firms collaboratively, partly because if they had a good reputation, they might get a better job at the competitor's firm and partly because they may have once worked with engineers in the competing firm: "The spreading of ideas through job-hopping is not in the interest of the firm that does the innovating, for it dilutes the firm's returns. But the industry as a whole advances, on the strength of every firm's ideas."[40] Here, economic success is attributable to a different imaginary that eschews competition between technology firms and encourages collaboration.

Culture is also shown to influence corruption in two ways. First, the definition of corruption may be culturally determined. For example, one study (Wade 1982) found that Indian villagers considered officials corrupt if they asked for a bribe above market rates, while Americans could consider all bribes corrupt.[41] Second, however, empirical studies suggest that corruption is more likely to occur in societies with a history of corruption, in societies with a significant power difference between members, and in more collectivist societies.[42] Experimental studies have also provided some support for this data, though evidence is somewhat mixed. Bribery experiments often involve three parties. One, the "firm" can offer a bribe from their money to an "official," who can take or reject the bribe. The third participant, the "citizen," can then financially punish the official and/or firm if the bribe is accepted. Numerous studies have used participants from different cultures to explore whether cultures deemed more corrupt based on the Corruption Perceptions Index (CPI) would accept bribes more regularly or punish bribes less frequently. Studies have had mixed results; for some countries, the CPI appears to predict well the acceptance of a bribe, but in others, this is not the case. At a minimal level, there does appear to be a difference across cultures, but the results could undermine the validity of the CPI, which is based only on perceptions, or of the experiments themselves.[43]

---

40 John McMillan, *Reinventing the Bazaar* (New York: Norton, 2002), 114.

41 See Robert Wade, "The System of Administrative and Political Corruption: Canal Irrigation in South India," *Journal of Development Studies* 18 (1982): 287–328.

42 Sheheryar Banuri and Catherine Eckel, "Experiments in Culture and Corruption: A Review," in *New Advances in Experimental Research on Corruption*, ed. Danilla Serra and Leonard Wantchekon (Bingley, UK: Emerald Group, 2012), 57–58. Collectivist societies in this sense are those that are less individualistic. In societies especially concerned with social obligations, laws that violate moral standards are more likely to be broken or ignored.

43 Banuri and Eckel, "Experiments in Culture and Corruption," 60–66.

Many Christian ethicists and social commentators, Christian and otherwise, have pointed to the role of culture in the formation of virtue in markets.[44] Sometimes ethicists' appeals to the role of culture can too confidently rank cultures hierarchically, much like the tendency we saw in Kuyper's deployment of common grace. For example, Michael Novak rightly recognizes that culture can play a role in the ways in which markets serve as a helpful context for developing virtue.[45] However, when Novak asks, "Why, then, didn't Latin America become the richer of the two continents of the New World?" he claims that the "decisive" difference between Latin American and North American rates of success is the difference between their "moral-cultural system."[46] Novak is too confident in his ability to discern the extent of strengths and weaknesses in a particular culture, where the doctrines of original sin and common grace should make us more apt to see sins and fruits of common grace in both North and Latin America. For example, while critiquing corruption in Latin America, Novak turns a blind eye to the imperialism that helped weaken many Latin American economies and political systems. It is quite likely that the sins of Latin American social groups can hinder economic growth, but it is quite unreasonable to ignore the way that the sins of North American and Europeans have also played a role through imbalanced trade agreements and military interventionism, to name only two factors.[47] A more sophisticated theological response to culture and other situational factors like wealth and inequality is needed for analyzing the results of experimental economics introduced in this chapter. "Culture" cannot be used as a cypher for condemnation of a different people group, and hierarchical appeals to culture like Novak's often come across as mere prejudice.

---

44 See, for example, Thomas L. Friedman, *The World Is Flat: A Brief History of the Twenty-First Century*, 3rd ed. (New York: Picador, 2007), 420–26; Barnes, *Redeeming Capitalism*, 132; Richards, *Money, Greed, and God*, 165.

45 Novak, *Spirit of Democratic Capitalism*, 57–58.

46 Novak, *Spirit of Democratic Capitalism*, 275. See also Novak, *Spirit of Democratic Capitalism*, 300.

47 Such intervention and trade imbalances are well documented. See, for example, Max Boot, *The Savage Wars of Peace: Small Wars and the Rise of American Power* (New York: Basic Books, 2002). Corporations were also involved in such imperialism. For example, see Peter Chapman, *Bananas: How the United Fruit Company Shaped the World* (Edinburgh: Canongate, 2007).

SPIRITUALITY AND DIVINE PROVIDENCE

A theological response to the situational factors like culture and economic inequality that may shape our moral formation in markets must go as deep as our fundamental spiritual posture to the divine providence appropriated to the Father. Here, I find a helpful starting point in Jean-Pierre de Caussade's spiritual theology of abandonment to divine providence. De Caussade begins with Mary's response to the angel in Luke 1:38 as an example of surrender to God's will, a pattern for all Christians to emulate.[48] If we recognize our present circumstances as a result of divine providence—de Caussade speaks of God's providence penetrating every atom and running through the entire universe[49]—we can interpret them as an appointed opportunity to fulfill our moral duty and vocational call as Christians. As explored in part II, a noncontrastive account of transcendence opens up the possibility of seeing situational factors such as culture and economic inequality that arose through historical human actions as concurrently the result of God's providential work. Recognizing these situational factors as a result of God's work does not allow us to sanction them as necessarily good—after all, the decretive will of God is not the same as the preceptive will, and we can easily find aspects of any economy that fall short of biblical standards. De Caussade is quite clear that a faithful response to divine providence does not lead to quietism but rather calls us to action.[50] Rather, a Christian is called to recognize that they have been providentially placed in such circumstances to respond to the duties God's preceptive will would place upon them, which requires faith, hope, and love.[51]

---

48 Jean-Pierre de Caussade, *Abandonment to Divine Providence*, trans. John Beevers (New York: Doubleday, 1975), I.1. De Caussade also points to the Lord's Prayer—"your will be done, on earth as it is in heaven" (Matt 6:10)—and to Paul's question, "Lord, what do you want me to do?" (Acts 9:6). De Caussade, *Abandonment to Divine Providence*, I.1., I.6.

49 De Caussade, *Abandonment to Divine Providence*, II.11, I.3.

50 In one place, de Caussade writes, "I shall not, as the Quietists do, believe that true religion means doing nothing, for we become holy by the law of God, and he always makes all he chooses useful to us." In another, he adds, "It is a waste of time to try to picture any kind of self-abandonment which excludes all personal activity and seeks only quiescence, for if God wishes us to act for ourselves, then action makes us holy. For some, God wills only that they should attend to the duties of their everyday life and to what other matters he confronts them with." De Caussade, *Abandonment to Divine Providence*, IV.5, I.8.

51 De Caussade, *Abandonment to Divine Providence*, III.3.

Let me make this discussion a bit more concrete. To interpret economic inequality in the context of providence, for example, is not to say that it is morally justifiable.[52] Nor can we assume without moral analysis that such situational factors are automatically morally condemnable, though in many cases I believe they are. Instead, de Caussade allows us to see such situational factors as a providentially appointed opportunity for moral action. A robust doctrine of concurrence cannot permit a utopianism that would believe a full resolution to structures of sin contributing to economic inequality can be attained by human effort alone. Pelagianism must be rejected. So, too, must an entirely realized eschatology that leaves no room for hope for a coming kingdom nor a futurist eschatology that rests in an inactive spirituality.[53] The doctrine of concurrence requires that we leave space for human agency in the economy while placing ultimate hope in Christ's kingdom.

De Caussade does not take us quite far enough in a spiritual response to providence adequate for the economy. Primarily, this is because he tends to have too otherworldly of an emphasis to his spiritual theology. For example, he notes that "although we have been warned time and time again that all the affairs of the world are but shadows and mysteries to be understood only by faith, we still persist in looking at them as if they had intrinsic value and reality."[54] A denial of any value and reality to the affairs of the world would certainly make markets insignificant for moral analysis, neglecting both the goodness of creation (Gen 1) and the contributions that the realities of the world can make toward moral development thanks to common grace. It is no surprise, therefore, to find de Caussade argue that, since each present moment "is like an ambassador who declares the will of God," we can say "nor do poverty or riches, sickness or health, life or death matter in the least."[55] It seems to me that de Caussade has emphasized several important themes of

---

52 One can wrongly identify providence with the "invisible hand" such that the output of markets may seem to be purely a divine blessing. However, it is important to remember that God's decretive will includes some sinful and unjust outcomes that he permits humans to bring about by their own agency.

53 For a helpful analysis of utopianism in the theology of economics, see Jung Mo Sung, *The Subject, Capitalism, and Religion: Horizons of Hope in Complex Societies* (New York: Palgrave Macmillan, 2011), 40–41. Sung argues that we cannot seek to establish a utopia but rather must have a utopian horizon toward which our efforts are oriented.

54 De Caussade, *Abandonment to Divine Providence*, II.1.

55 De Caussade, *Abandonment to Divine Providence*, II.10. De Caussade does reopen the potential significance of creation later in his work when he suggests that we deal with the created things of the world when God wills it, but this seems both too vague and

Scripture at the expense of others.[56] His discussion of abandonment to divine providence fits biblical tropes of a faithful perseverance and long-suffering in the face of suffering (e.g., Matt 5:12; Rom 5:3; Jas 1:2; 1 Pet 1:6–7), but it neglects biblical imperatives to be engaged in economic, social, and political concerns. For that reason, his thought must be supplemented.

Jon Sobrino's liberation spiritual theology provides a helpful corrective to our starting point in de Caussade. In its basic contours, Sobrino's treatment of the presuppositions of a spirituality of liberation is quite similar to de Caussade's yet with a sharper emphasis on the significance of history. Sobrino argues, "Any genuine spirituality will demand, in the concrete: (1) honesty about the real, (2) fidelity to the real, and (3) a certain 'correspondence' by which we permit ourselves to be carried along by the 'more' of reality."[57] Sobrino understands "honesty to the real" to involve a willingness to see reality as it is, which requires an awareness of creation as a "sacrament of transcendence." However, it also requires us to see the economic and historical dimensions of reality for what they are. Honesty is for the sake of the reality, not for the sake of the subject.[58] Because honesty sees the world as it is for the benefit of the world, honesty about the needs of the world prompts the Christian to acts of love and solidarity.[59]

If honesty about the real prompts love, fidelity to the real and being carried along by the "more" of reality prompts faith and hope, respectively. We respond to reality in love, but we often meet resistance. In the face of this, we have to be faithful to our initial response to the real. Here, Sobrino points to the example of the suffering servant in Isaiah, who had a loving response to the historical problems and injustices of his day and who remained unwaveringly hopeful and steadfast in this initial response despite opposition: "Fidelity to the real . . . is simply and solely perseverance in our original honesty, however we may be burdened with, yes engulfed in, the negative element in history."[60] If we see the real for what it is—suffering, injustice, and all—but if we continue to

---

too late in the development of his spiritual program. See de Caussade, *Abandonment to Divine Providence*, IV.2.

56 On the importance of balancing the tensions in Scripture within our ethics, see Hays, *The Moral Vision of the New Testament*, 187–92.

57 Jon Sobrino, *Spirituality of Liberation: Toward Political Holiness*, trans. Robert R. Barr (Maryknoll, NY: Orbis, 1988), 14.

58 Sobrino, *Spirituality of Liberation*, 15–16.

59 Sobrino, *Spirituality of Liberation*, 16–17.

60 Sobrino, *Spirituality of Liberation*, 18.

act in love, then we are swept along by the "more" of reality, and here I think Sobrino has in mind something akin to what I have been calling *providence*, using traditional terminology. In such circumstances, our honesty to the real is hopeful, but an active hope manifests in love.[61]

The spiritual theologies of Sobrino and de Caussade provide a framework within which the Christian can recognize both the structures of sin that contribute to inequality and the social sins latent within a culture as opportunities to act in faith, hope, and love providentially provided by the Father. De Caussade fosters a mentality that balances human action and divine providence, much in line with the account of concurrence I offered in chapter 4. Sobrino brings the historical and economic dimensions of our providentially determined situation to the center, which helps us recognize the possibility of improvement in the economy through common grace while also emphasizing the need to stand in solidarity against structures of sin, social sin, and the sins of social groups. Turning again to the ways in which situational factors like culture and inequality influence the moral formation of Christians in markets, this spirituality enabled activism prompts the question, How do we design markets that better enable us to work out our salvation in the economy? The duration of the chapter will explore a range of possible options, drawing on the principles of market design introduced in chapter 3.

MARKET DESIGN AS A FAITHFUL, HOPEFUL, LOVING RESPONSE TO THE FATHER'S PROVIDENCE

The context in which markets exist modifies the ways in which markets influence the moral formation of economic agents. I have argued that a proper theological interpretation of such situational factors as the economic inequality of a society, the socioeconomic class of an individual, and the cultural shaping of an economy is to interpret them as the work of the Father's providence providing an opportunity for Christians to act according to their duty in the context in which they find themselves. Here, we are called to honesty and fidelity about the real. Part of this honesty to the real is admitting (a) many markets are unjust and increase vice, (b) full planning of markets will generally exceed our abilities, yet (c) some degree of market design always remains

---

61 Sobrino, *Spirituality of Liberation*, 19.

possible. Recall from chapter 3 that I explained that markets are designed in four dimensions: the ways in which we imagine markets themselves, selection of various exchange mechanisms and information flows used in markets, regulation of market participants, and the legal regulation of goods. Drawing especially on Old Testament economic ethics, I will show some methods of market design that can be used to reduce the structures of sin in markets and make market participants more receptive to common grace.

Scripture's Critique of Wealth and Economic Inequality

Scripture is clear and consistent in its critique of economic inequality, and it links this critique to its theology of faithfulness to God and love of neighbor. Old Testament laws concerning tithes to the poor (Deut 14:29), the Sabbath release of debts (Deut 15:1–3), and the year of Jubilee (Lev 25:8–13) are designed to ensure that economic inequality does not become too excessive. Though the Sabbath law is sometimes interpreted as a delay in payments, this is unlikely given the fact that the law addresses the risk of loans not being given close to the Sabbath (see Deut 15:9).[62] The fact that there was a legal device (the *prosbul*) that allowed lenders and borrowers to agree to repay loans and ignore the remission of debts suggests that the Sabbath debt remissions were actually followed.[63] During the monarchic period, there was an increase in trade, raising land prices and allowing for more profits for those who grew tradable goods like olives or grapes. People wanted more land than was needed for subsistence farming, and this was apparently acquired through loans, which could result in seizing land as collateral when payments were missed as a result of crops failing due to weather, for example, which prompted the later critiques of the prophets against the exploitation of impoverished people by the rich.[64]

---

62 Craig Blomberg, *Neither Poverty nor Riches: A Biblical Theology of Possessions* (Downers Grove, IL: InterVarsity, 1999), 44.

63 Barrera, *God and the Evil of Scarcity*, 76–77. Scholars are not convinced, on the other hand, that the year of Jubilee was actually practiced, though it arguably still dates from an early stage of Israel's history when the institutions of the Israelite family and government were still strong. See Christopher J. H. Wright, *God's People in God's Land: Family, Land, and Property in the Old Testament* (Grand Rapids, MI: Eerdmans, 1990), 126; Barrera, *God and the Evil of Scarcity*, 90; Blomberg, *Poverty nor Riches*, 44–45.

64 Edith Rasell, *The Way of Abundance: Economic Justice in Scripture and Society* (Minneapolis: Fortress, 2022), 28–31. Rasell also identifies this as the context for laws

Old Testament commands intended to reduce inequality were given directly to the people of Israel as a part of their covenant identity with God, so one might challenge my appeal to them as an example of ignoring the original context of the laws. Perhaps the promised land had to be kept in the hands of all Israelite families as part of their covenant inheritance, but non-Israelite peoples today have no equivalent land-based covenant and thus might be thought to have no equivalent basis for a critique of inequality. I find this possibility uncompelling for at least four reasons. First, Israel is paradigmatic for the nations, so Israel's equitable sharing of land must be considered paradigmatic in some ways for the nations.[65] Second, a Christian ethic of the redistribution of wealth begins before the Mosaic covenants. A theological understanding of property finds its earliest basis in the biblical narrative in the garden of Eden, where Adam and Eve are given the land and its produce for their benefit (Gen 1:29–30; 2:16).[66] Because Adam and Eve represent all of humanity, there is a robust theological tradition—often named the *universal destination of goods*—that understands God's gift to be given to all of humanity, which prohibits any individuals from claiming so much that others are excluded from the property they need for life.[67] Third, in the New Testament, Jesus's ministry partly consisted of proclamation of Jubilee (Luke 4:17–21), which was then extended into early Christian practices of wealth redistribution through communal ownership (Acts 2:44–45; 4:32–37), tithes and offerings, and restitution of ill-gotten wealth (e.g., Luke 19:1–10). This extension of Old Testament laws into New Testament practice suggests that Christians today ought to continue to fight economic inequality. It is not surprising, therefore, to find various contemporary Christian

---

pertaining to gleaning and tithing that were added in the later books of Leviticus and Deuteronomy. Rasell, *The Way of Abundance*, 32–39.

65 Christopher J. H. Wright, *Old Testament Ethics for the People of God* (Downers Grove, IL: IVP Academic, 2004), 155–56.

66 This gift is expanded when Noah and his descendants are given every animal to eat in Genesis 9:3.

67 This perspective has been particularly influential in Catholic social teaching. See, for example, *Centesimus Annus* §31. Kathryn Tanner explores John Locke's political thought, which overlaps to some extent with Catholic social teaching in terms of its view of property, though she raises substantial concerns with Locke, including especially his idea that we own our persons and our work, which means we can become alienated from them. Tanner, *Economy of Grace*, 40–46.

movements appealing to Old Testament laws regarding wealth redistribution.[68] However, the fourth and most compelling reason to believe that Old Testament principles regarding wealth redistribution apply today is that they are fundamental to Christian faith, love, and hope.

It is clear that biblical teaching against wealth inequality is rooted in the love of neighbor and is the appropriate response to faith in God. Consider the Decalogue, which is rooted in God's identity as the deliverer of Israel from Egypt (Exod 20:2). To have faith in the God of Israel is to follow the Ten Commandments. However, much of the Decalogue is concerned with economic justice. This is obvious in the case of the prohibitions against stealing (20:15) and coveting (20:17). Somewhat less obvious is the fact that the command to honor your father and mother would include economic provision after parents are too old to work.[69] It is also easy to forget that Sabbath observation is both religious and economic—it is a rest from labor (20:9–10).[70] Such economic emphases explain how the law can be summarized by the commands to love God and neighbor (Matt 22:36–40). Looking particularly at the laws about land redistribution and Sabbath years, we see a similar pattern. The implications for loving one's neighbor are clear, but the Bible is also careful to show that these are sabbath years *to the Lord* (Lev 25:2–7).[71] In other words, de Caussade and Sobrino's spirituality of faithful and loving response to God's providence / the real fits easily with the contours of Old Testament economic ethics.

A point of clarification is needed before ending this section: Scripture's critique of inequality does not seek to undermine the possibility of private property or free exchange, so it ought not be seen as a complete rejection of markets as much as it is a clear framework for how markets ought to be structured. The fact that the Old Testament also has laws against moving

---

68 For example, Martin Dent and Bill Peters, *The Crisis of Poverty and Debt in the Third World* (Brookfield, VT: Ashgate, 1999). Dent and Peters founded the Jubilee 2000 campaign to forgive the national debts of impoverished countries.

69 Brevard Childs follows Abrecht Alt and others in hypothesizing that the commandment originally had a negative form—"You shall not curse your father and your mother." He adds, "Lying at the heart of the original prohibition was a command which protected parents from being driven out of the home or abused after they could no longer work." Brevard S. Childs, *The Book of Exodus* (Philadelphia: Westminster, 1974), 418.

70 "Sabbath is not only a religious symbol (rest and worship) but also an economic one. . . . Sabbath and shalom are correlated to one another." Hak Joon Lee, *Christian Ethics: A New Covenant Model* (Grand Rapids, MI: Eerdmans, 2021), 307.

71 See Wright, *God's People*, 146–48.

boundary markers, for example, shows that private property is to be affirmed, and violating property rights is an act against God (see especially Deut 19:14; Prov 23:10–11).[72] As Christopher Wright explains, the fact that theft is included in the Decalogue suggests it is "fundamentally incompatible with personal loyalty to Yahweh and membership of the community of his people."[73] Nevertheless, we must remember that property rights can be construed in a variety of ways. In Scripture, these rights are consistently subordinate to the claim that God has on land for God's purposes. To name only one example, the Deuteronomic covenant is clear that wealth is ultimately from God and for the purposes of God's covenant (Deut 8:17–18).[74] Insofar as God's preceptive will expressed in the covenant demands provision for those who are poor, property ought to be disposed toward such ends. This requires market design.

Market Design and Inequality

The aspects of market design that I explored in chapter 3 can be deployed as part of a Christian response to economic inequality today. For example, economic inequality might be addressed through a change in the mechanism of exchange. Here, we must be careful to avoid reducing possible mechanisms of exchange to the macroeconomic debates around the relative merits and weaknesses of capitalism, socialism, and communism. A more practical and easily implemented approach can center the role of labor unions and collective ownership. Often, transactions in the labor market involve an exchange mechanism where one employee negotiates with one representative of the employing company, whether that be a representative from human resources, a direct supervisor, or someone from upper management. However, it is also possible to negotiate through labor unions, in which case union members first collaborate with representatives to establish goals in terms of salary, benefits, and working conditions.[75] As Edith Rasell explains, "A worker covered by a union contract earns an average of 13 percent more than a similar nonunion

---

72 Wright, *God's People*, 128–31.
73 Wright, *God's People*, 135.
74 Wright, *Old Testament Ethics for the People of God*, 166. Wright contrasts such claims in Deuteronomy with God's absolute ownership of creation expressed in such passages as Psalm 95:4–5.
75 For example, Rosemarie Henkel-Rieger advocates a "deep solidarity" that emphasizes the benefits of unions, collective bargaining, and strikes. Rosemarie Henkel-Rieger, "Deep Solidarity: A Pre-requisite to Resisting Capitalism and Building Economic

worker and has better benefits."[76] Unions are an example of market design of the mechanism of exchange in labor markets by union members and by the lawmakers who pass legislation governing unions.[77]

Similar design of mechanisms of exchange occurs in the establishment of cooperatives. Jamin Hübner defines cooperatives as firms in which employees have greater than 50 percent ownership and manage the distribution of profits.[78] Cooperatives often establish rules governing the exchange of labor between an employer and an employee. For example, cooperatives often have a maximum ratio of wages of top earners in comparison with wages at the bottom of the income distribution. They often also rely on democratic processes rather than hierarchical ones in the distribution of profits and setting of wages. Hübner argues that changes focusing on wages or tax law fight the symptoms and not the root of the problem, the matter of who owns the factors of production.[79] Cooperatives more equitably distribute ownership, which reduces economic inequality, which in turn diminishes violence and is a factor in improving prosocial behavior in society. In fact, higher levels of profit-sharing correspond with higher levels of trust between management and employees.[80] Cooperatives assume a range of forms from employee stock ownership plans (ESOPs) to the small business cooperatives of Emilia-Romagna in Italy to the massive Mondragon Corporation in Spain, founded under the guidance of a priest and holding tens of billions of dollars in assets today.[81] Cooperatives are another example of reducing economic inequality

---

Democracy," in *Faith, Class, and Labor: Intersectional Approaches in a Global Context*, ed. Jin Young Choi and Joerg Rieger (Eugene, OR: Pickwick, 2020), 191, 196–98.

76 Rasell, *Way of Abundance*, 141.

77 Right-to-work laws are one example of government regulations. In some states, nonunion employees who benefit from union negotiations are required to pay union dues, but in right-to-work states, no such dues can be imposed.

78 Jamin Hübner, "Owning Up to It: Why Cooperatives Create the Humane Economy Our World Needs," *Faith and Economics* 76, no. 2 (Fall 2020): 134. Cooperatives were a major emphasis of distributism, one Christian attempt at a "third way" beyond capitalism and communism. See Allan C. Carlson, *Third Ways: How Bulgarian Greens, Swedish Housewives, and Beer-Swilling Englishmen Created Family-Centered Economies—and Why They Disappeared* (Wilmington, DE: ISI, 2007), 1–34.

79 Hübner, "Owning Up," 145–46.

80 Hübner, "Owning Up," 158. Hübner appeals to the Trust Index, a measurement of trust in corporate culture, to prove this point.

81 These examples are helpfully explained in detail in John C. Médaille, *Toward a Truly Free Market: A Distributist Perspective on the Role of Government, Taxes, Health Care, Deficits, and More* (Wilmington, DE: ISI Books, 2010), 246–47, 249–50, 254.

through modifications in the exchange mechanism, all while remaining financially successful.[82]

Market design can also affect economic inequality through regulation of market participants and through legal regulation of goods sold within markets. One way to regulate market participants is through antitrust interventions, which have a long history of support in Christian thought and prevent trusts from participating in markets, reducing inequality.[83] I have previously discussed the regulation of goods in terms of what is legally permissible to sell and what is illegal to sell, but legal regulation of goods bought and sold in markets also occurs when governments intervene in consumer decisions by providing incentives for making certain choices; see chapter 9 for a full discussion of incentives. Edith Rasell argues that one contributing factor to economic inequality is tax expenditures, "special provisions . . . that reduce a taxpayer's liability (and reduce government revenue) in return for what are deemed to be socially desirable activities."[84] In the United States, tax expenditures cost the government more than social welfare programs—in 2019, the former cost $1.6 trillion and the latter only $810 billion.[85] Rasell argues that when tax expenditures apply to income put into retirement plans, or when capital gains taxes are not assessed for sales of principal residences valued up to $750,000, it is members of higher socioeconomic classes who benefit at the expense of members of the poorer socioeconomic classes.[86] Here, it is the government's design of the market that influences economic inequality.

Médaille notes that some ESOPs are really just used as a tax-evasion scheme and are not implemented in any substantive way.

82 See Hübner, "Owning Up," 152–54. Hübner shows evidence that co-ops can be competitive in the market, experience lower employee turnover, and have better worker/manager relations.

83 Kenneth G. Elzinga and Daniel A. Crane, "Christianity and Antitrust: A Nexus," in *Christianity and Market Regulation: An Introduction*, ed. Daniel A. Crane and Samuel Gregg (Cambridge: Cambridge University Press, 2001), 76–80. Elzinga and Crane conclude that antitrust regulation "generally serves to help those at the low end of the income distribution range without decreasing economic efficiency." Elzinga and Crane, "Christianity and Antitrust," 91.

84 Rasell, *Way of Abundance*, 176.

85 Rasell, *Way of Abundance*, 177–78.

86 "Nearly 60 percent of this benefit" from retirement plan investments "went to the 20 percent of households with the highest incomes," and "over 60 percent of the benefit" from capital gains exemptions on the sale of primary residences "went to the highest-income 20 percent of taxpayers." Rasell, *Way of Abundance*, 179–80.

My purpose in this section is not to resolve debates about the proper policy means for addressing economic inequality, nor will I focus on the question of what specific market equilibrium reflects the just distribution of wealth. As important as those questions are, I am making another point more relevant to the purposes of this book. When we ask whether markets contribute in positive or negative ways to moral formation, clearly the answer to that question depends in part on the extent to which economic inequality is found in each society. Further, economic inequality is based in part on market design through such factors as the presence and legal regulation of unions, the extent to which cooperatives exist, government decisions regarding antitrust regulation and tax expenditures, and many other factors not treated here. Viewing the situation with a theological lens, we can conclude that moral formation in markets relies in part on providentially determined situational factors like inequality. Christians can respond in faith to the Father's providence by fulfilling their duties as outlined in the preceptive will of God, pursuing economic justice by designing markets that result in better outcomes for those who are poor. Such efforts can be understood as the secondary causes of God's primary agency, a conduit of his common grace that supports moral formation oriented toward the ultimate sanctification found in the church.

Christian Challenges to a Culture of Commodification

I am aware that human abilities to consciously design markets will always be limited, but I am even more pessimistic about the human ability to intentionally direct culture.[87] Nevertheless, Christians can have some influence over cultural factors shaping markets. Perhaps one of the most significant areas of influence is in fighting to restrict the commodification of reality, or, to put it another way, resisting imagining certain spaces as markets. Margaret Radin offers a more technical definition of commodification: (1) exchanges of things in the world (2) for money, (3) in the social context of markets, and (4) in conjunction with four indicia of commodification and conceptualization. Those four conceptual indicia characterize complete commodification

---

87 For a compelling argument against our ability to direct culture, see James Davison Hunter, *To Change the World: The Irony, Tragedy, and Possibility of Christianity in the Late Modern World* (Oxford: Oxford University Press, 2010).

in rhetoric. They are (i) objectification, (ii) fungibility, (iii) commensurability, and (iv) money equivalence.[88]

Since the apostles rebuked Simon the magician's request to buy the ability to dispense the Holy Spirit (Acts 8:18–23), Christian theologians have been regularly concerned with the commodification of certain things that are theologically better understood as gifts or as inalienable aspects of personal identity. While some things become commodified through hidden and unpredictable cultural forces, others are made so more intentionally. For example, flour is today treated as a commodity that can be traded in commodities markets much like stock markets, but this sort of commodification of flour was only made possible when the Chicago Board of Trade established a physical space in which grains could be sold plus a metric of wheat categories, allowing wheat to be easily deemed identical and fungible—identical and replaceable with other wheat.[89] When we recall chapter 2's discussion of facts and values, such intentional efforts at commodification should remind us that when we change the description of something, its "conceptualization" and the "rhetoric" surrounding it, to use Radin's language, there may be significant moral consequences. Thus, it is no surprise that Christian theologians often critique reducing value to money equivalence in markets.[90]

Christians might have cause to fight commodification in several of the dimensions of Radin's definition. Through legal regulation of goods, they might prohibit the exchange of certain things in the world, as has been the case in movements to abolish slavery or the nuclear arms trade, for example. Christians might also teach a vision of something, for example, human sexual relationships, that does not have money equivalence—you cannot put a dollar value on it—or fungibility—sex with one person is not fundamentally the same as sex with another, particularly when one of the two possible partners is your spouse and the other is not. Alternatively, Christians might refuse to place a dollar value on certain goods, such as human life.[91] Radin notes that some commodification can be incomplete, as when someone works, receiving

---

88 Margaret Jane Radin, *Contested Commodities: The Trouble with Trade in Sex, Children, Body Parts, and Other Things* (Cambridge: Harvard University Press, 1996), 118.

89 I draw this example from Haeringer, *Market Design*, 5. Haeringer notes that the Ethiopian Commodities Exchange was just opened in 2008.

90 For example, Long, Fox, and York, *Calculated Futures*, 51–54.

91 See Bell, *The Economy of Desire*, 105.

a salary that they need, while also working in a particular field out of interest, conviction, or a sense of calling.[92]

I am convinced that the church's proclamation can play some role in producing incomplete commodification where it would otherwise be absolute, so much of a theological response to commodification will occur in the context of a theology of special grace and in ecclesiology.[93] Surprisingly, experimental economics provides some support for this claim. For example, higher levels of consumerism were observed after consumers were primed with images of death, guilt, or meaninglessness, suggesting consumption is a strategy for existential security.[94] The proclamation of the church offers a truer source of existential security, which could mitigate the consumerism that drives commodification. Radin suggests that regulated markets can also have some effect in fighting complete commodification, for instance, "where regulation expresses and fosters an important nonmarket aspect of the interactions between persons who buy and sell things."[95] This may happen through certain social welfare programs, where basic necessities are seen as a right and not purely a tradable good. Certainly much more can be said about commodification, but my purpose for now is mainly to show that market design has some small role even in the direction that cultures take.

PROVIDENCE AND MORAL FORMATION IN MARKETS

In this chapter, I have argued that moral formation in markets depends in part on the context of markets, a context that is largely given at any time and that is typically beyond the ability of any individual to change in a rapid manner. Experimental economics has provided strong evidence that socioeconomic class, economic inequality within a society, and culture all influence the ways that the character of individuals develops in a market context. I have argued that such situation factors are best interpreted by Christians to be permitted by divine providence, which I appropriate to the Father. These factors are a providentially appointed opportunity for Christians to respond in faith, hope, and love. Communion with the Father, then, involves a spiritual recognition

---

92 Radin, *Contested Commodities*, 104–5.
93 See, for example, Cavanaugh, *Being Consumed*, 33–58.
94 See the discussion in Rittenhouse, *Shopping for Meaningful Lives*, 147.
95 Radin, *Contested Commodities*, 116.

of inequality, for example, as a providentially appointed opportunity for moral action. When we work to reduce inequality, as guided by the Father's preceptive will in the Old Testament law, we respond in faith to God and in love to our neighbors. Such responses also require hope that our action is not in vain. Therefore, market design can serve as a faithful response to Scripture's economic teachings. The key factor here is not the rejection of markets but their proper design. The arguments of this chapter provide an initial framework for analyzing moral formation in markets, but more is needed. For this reason, chapters 8 and 9 advance the argument by looking at the identity and agency of market participants, respectively.

CHAPTER 8

Markets, Discrimination, and Identity in Christ

Like all social arrangements that organize consumption and production, market economics has an identity-moulding *function. Any economic system can potentially provide us with the table, chairs, and coffee to be with our friends. But it will also influence how we think and talk about ourselves—our identity—when we are with our friends.*

—Gordon Menzies[1]

Theologians and economists studying the market have become increasingly focused on identity in capitalism. For example, Kathryn Tanner has argued that capitalism works when members of the working class come to understand their desires, values, and self-realization in ways that align with their employers. When motivated by fear—of layoffs, for example—employees will only work as hard as is necessary to avoid being fired, but this level of work cannot support the continued improvements in productivity, efficiency, and profits required by late capitalism.[2] She adds, "Corporations have such an interest in fostering employees' sense of self-realization through work, not simply because it makes them more efficient and lowers costs, but because it cements their commitment to their work."[3] I will analyze such self-realization

---

1 Gordon Menzies, "Economics as Identity," in Harper and Gregg, *Christian Theology and Market Economics*, 94.

2 Kathryn Tanner, *Christianity and the New Spirit of Capitalism* (New Haven, CT: Yale University Press, 2019), 26–27.

3 Tanner, *Christianity and the New Spirit*, 78.

as one dimension of the concept of identity. Considered more extensively, I will use the term *identity* to analyze (1) personal continuity over time, particularly in terms of the progress one has toward realizing goals or a *telos*; (2) the self-understanding and experience of belonging to a particular group; and (3) constructed aspects of group membership that take on an objective dimension in society.[4] These three dimensions of identity include the basic aspects of identity discussed in chapter 6: they are relational, confer status, and shape possibilities for action. These dimensions also can converge to create the sorts of situations that Tanner discusses. For example, fieldwork in Indian call centers collecting qualitative, narrative data indicates that the identity of being a call center "professional" establishes group membership distinct from "support staff" (aspects 2 and 3) while also tending to commit the "professional" to sacrificing personal wellbeing for the purpose or goal of the welfare of the company.[5] In particular, such identity undermined efforts to establish a union of call center employees, pointing to substantive intersections of identity with one possible market design solution to wealth inequality discussed in the previous chapter.

Tanner is not alone in her theological analysis of identity formation in capitalist markets. Many theologians have diagnosed problems of identity as fundamental to the flaws inherent in capitalism, late modernity, and/or markets in general.[6] For example, Edward Rommen argues that late modernity is characterized by what he calls "expeditious associations," which are "transitory commitments in which what is important is some semblance of utility within a given arena of action."[7] In part, this is due to the way that technology in a globalized economy has fostered undue reliance on "abstract systems" where identification of self and others is trivialized.[8] With such a

---

[4] I will explore these dimensions of identity in greater detail later in the chapter.

[5] Ernesto Noronha and Premilla D'Cruz, *Employee Identity in Indian Call Centers: The Notion of Professionalism* (Los Angeles: Response, 2009), 74–75, 122–23. "Employer organizations cultivated the notion of professionalism in their agents in order to gain the latter's compliance and commitment to the realization of organizational goals." Noronha and D'Cruz, *Employee Identity*, 75.

[6] The conceptual overlap among capitalism, late modernity, and markets is considerable.

[7] Rommen, *Get Real*, 60. Rommen admits he is indebted in his thought here to Anthony Giddens, *The Consequences of Modernity* (Stanford, CA: Stanford University Press, 1990), 88. Giddens speaks of a "trust in systems" that is prevalent in modern society and that depends on "faceless commitments."

[8] Rommen, *Get Real*, 61–62, 73.

weakened network of meaningful relationships, and with a loss of any sense of the *imago Dei* as providing a core to identity, late moderns are left with a radically reflexive notion of identity where human subjects are left trying to define themselves.[9] Similarly, Antonio González Fernández interprets the primeval history in Genesis as a depiction of the dangers of self-justification. Noting that God did not request Cain and Abel's sacrifices (Gen 4:3–5), González suggests these sacrifices are a means of self-justification by the brothers.[10] He summarizes, "The logic of the fundamental sin of humanity requires that human work be always a fretful race to produce results that will inevitably turn out to be inferior to what is desired."[11] This logic results in Babylon, the characteristic ideology of empire found in capitalism, among other systems.[12] Gawain de Leeuw argues that markets can foster a competitiveness rooted in rivalry that undermines community. However, faith in Christ "begins a liberation from what accompanies a status anxiety that justifies acquisitiveness," allowing for the possibility of markets that contribute to the development of virtue, provided participants share a vision of the common good.[13] These three examples among many show a common trend: wrongly designed markets contribute to moral malformation.

Economists are also increasingly focused on the question of identity, sometimes in a philosophical sense concerning, for example, an economic model's ability to trace the identity of an individual over time (aspect 1 of identity).[14] Behavioral economists have focused on group membership (especially aspect 3 of identity) and its implications for the outcomes of market transactions. Such analysis often aims to develop more accurate models of economic choices that incorporate factors like identity.[15] Adjacent fields like sociology also often address identity, particularly with an eye to how identity may be shaped by participation in the economy. For example, fluid labor markets facilitating

---

9 Rommen, *Get Real*, 59.

10 Fernández, *God's Reign*, 67.

11 Fernández, *God's Reign*, 72.

12 Fernández, *God's Reign*, 63. González Fernández claims that Babylon extends through all of history so is not coterminous with capitalism.

13 Gawain de Leeuw, *The Body of Christ in a Market Economy: An Anglican Inquiry into Economic Thinking* (New York: Peter Lang, 2019), 146–47, 141.

14 For example, see John B. Davis, *Individuals and Identity in Economics* (New York: Cambridge University Press, 2011).

15 For example, see George A. Akerlof and Rachel E. Kranton, *Identity Economics: How Our Identities Shape Our Work, Wages, and Well-Being* (Princeton: Princeton University Press, 2010).

changes in jobs, place of residence, and so forth hinder the development of stable identity markers, a problem enhanced by increasingly prevalent corporate mergers and restructurings.[16] Thus, it is no surprise that experimental economics has also explored the question of identity in fruitful ways, making it a helpful point of contact in our analysis of moral formation in markets.

This chapter will narrow the potentially vast scope of discussion on identity in markets by focusing on identity as a factor resulting in discrimination in markets. In particular, I will explore economic experiments that have demonstrated the presence of discrimination in labor and housing markets, among others. The analysis will include two theories for the discrimination, bigotry, and profit maximization. I will argue that such discrimination is contrary to our identity in Christ regardless of the reason and that the logic of profit maximization, if it even applies in this context, does not justify the outcome of the experimental studies. Participating in discriminatory markets can hinder proper moral formation, resisting the common grace available in markets and instead perpetuating social sin. As a solution, I will explore several aspects of market design that might resist both discrimination and the vices that such discrimination fosters.

DISCRIMINATION IN MARKETS

Given the long history of racism in the United States and elsewhere in the world, it is no surprise that economists have studied racism extensively. However, the term *racism* can refer to many things, so it is important to be precise regarding what this chapter will address. One dimension of racism includes what I have called structures of sin, for example, laws or policies that exclude members of a particular race or ethnicity from market participation. This dimension of racism is tremendously important, but I will not address it except briefly at the end of the chapter. Racism also includes at a more basic level bigotry, the animosity that a person or group feels toward a particular race or ethnicity. When bigotry is found in high levels among a particular social group, we are dealing with the sins of social groups. Bigotry appears throughout this chapter but not as the central focus. The bulk of this chapter

---

16 Richard Sennett, "Street and Office: Two Sources of Identity," in *On the Edge: Living with Global Capitalism*, ed. Will Hutton and Anthony Giddens (London: Jonathan Cape, 2000), 176–84.

will be dealing with discrimination, the exclusion of a person or group on the basis of their identity. Though I will focus on racial discrimination, I will also briefly mention discrimination based on categories like gender, sexuality, or immigration status. As we will see, two theories explain the discrimination found in markets. One appeals to bigotry as a basis for discrimination, but the other suggests that discrimination is a result of the logic of profit maximization, a purportedly "rational choice" by some economic standards. Formation in this perspective on rationality is encouraged in the market and within capitalist culture. In the case of this latter form of discrimination, then, we are also dealing with social sin—the sinful consequences of interpersonal moral malformation. With these distinctions and a very rudimentary theoretical analysis of racism in hand,[17] I can now survey existing experiments on discrimination in markets.

Experiments on Discrimination in Markets

The most extensive range of studies within the discipline of experimental economics pertaining to identity concerns discrimination in various markets. Typically, two kinds of experiments are performed.[18] In audit studies, social scientists send fake job applicants of different races, ethnicities, genders, or other relevant categories to interview for jobs or inquire about rent, testing labor and housing markets for discrimination.[19] In correspondence studies, applications and/or résumés of fictitious applicants who differ by race, ethnicity, gender, or other relevant categories are sent to jobs to see which ones result in callbacks for interviews. The evidence from such studies is consistent. As David Neumark and Judith Rich summarize, "Nearly every study focusing on race or ethnicity finds evidence of race or ethnic discrimination in the labor market or in the housing market, and the conclusions

---

17 This basic analysis does not consider the roles of culture, stereotyping, the psychological effects of discrimination, or the historical or genealogical rise of theories of race, to name only a few factors. Such subjects are important, but they are beyond the scope of this chapter.

18 For further details about these methods, see David Neumark and Judith Rich, "Do Field Experiments on Labor and Housing Markets Overestimate Discrimination? A Re-Examination of the Evidence," *ILR Review* 72, no. 1 (January 2019): 223–52.

19 Studies of labor and housing markets are the most extensive, though markets for automobiles and finance have also been studied. One notable study on automobile markets is by Ian Ares and Peter Siegelman, "Race and Gender Discrimination in Bargaining for a New Car," *American Economic Review* 85, no. 3 (June 1995): 304–21.

of the smaller number of studies of sexual orientation discrimination are equally consistent."[20] In the words of Marianne Bertrand and Esther Duflo, "This literature offers staggering evidence of pervasive discrimination against minority or under-represented groups all around the world."[21] Though I also consider the evidence of discrimination overwhelming, certain critiques can still be raised, so it is necessary to discuss the continued improvement of experimental methodology in this area before exploring the results of some specific studies.

Experimental economics has developed increasingly robust methods of identifying discrimination. The most basic method is a simple regression analysis that could find, for example, industries in which particular groups were underrepresented. However, such studies may not consider different variables not factored into the choices of employers and applicants.[22] Perhaps fewer women work in construction, for example, because fewer want to work in construction. Audit studies improved on regression analysis, but they are open to critique.[23] Audit studies are not double-blind, so auditors know that they are testing for discrimination. This may lead them, consciously or subconsciously, to try to act in ways that increase apparent discrimination to validate the results of the studies.[24] Audit studies also cannot eliminate the "intangibles" that are so important in hiring decisions. Though applicants from different demographic groups are often trained to act similarly, perhaps something outside of the training is the deciding factor.[25] Correspondence studies are therefore an improved method. Admittedly, since correspondence studies only explore interview rates, they cannot demonstrate the justice of

---

20 Neumark and Rich, "Field Experiments," 224.

21 Marianne Bertrand and Esther Duflo, "Field Experiments on Discrimination" (National Bureau of Economic Research Working Paper 22041, February 2016), 2, http://www.nber.org/papers/w22014/.

22 Bertrand and Duflo, "Field Experiments," 8.

23 One of the most robust critiques of the audit method grants as much: "The other major advantage of the audit technique is that it allows more control over the characteristics that are thought to be relevant to the employment decision than is possible in conventional ex-post regression analyses." James J. Heckman and Peter Siegelman, "The Urban Institute Audit Studies: Their Methods and Findings," in *Clear and Convincing Evidence: Measurement of Discrimination in America*, ed. Michael Fix and Raymond J. Struyk (Washington, DC: Urban Institute, 1993), 193.

24 Bertrand and Duflo, "Field Experiments," 11.

25 I find this an increasingly less plausible objection the more audit studies are performed.

final hiring rates or the equitability of resulting salaries.[26] Further, both audit and correspondence studies rely on jobs posted in newspapers or, later, online services, while most jobs are actually found through personal networks. This means the studies may not accurately reflect the economy as a whole; in fact, hirings made through personal networks may be even less equitable given the ethnic heterogeneity of many personal networks.[27] The largest objection to correspondence studies is known as the Heckman-Siegelman critique, to which I now turn.[28]

In a widely discussed paper from 1993, James Heckman and Peter Siegelman note that audit studies might be failing to account for certain other variables that might explain disparate outcomes. For example, Heckman and Siegelman note one study testing for discrimination against Hispanic applicants where all Hispanic participants in the audit had facial hair and accents, so "the hypotheses of discrimination against 'accents' or 'hair' are observationally equivalent to (indistinguishable from) the hypothesis of discrimination against Hispanics per se."[29] More commonly, this critique focuses on productivity. In a later paper, Heckman argues that most audit studies must assume that firms hire based on (a) variables in the interview or application that indicate productivity and are known to experimenters and (b) variables affecting productivity that are unobserved by the studies because they are not discernible in applications or interviews. For audit and correspondence studies to work in identifying discrimination, we must assume that "the mean of the unobserved productivity variable is the same for whites and blacks."[30] However, even if the mean is the same, Heckman argues that

---

26 Bertrand and Duflo, "Field Experiments," 25.

27 Heckman and Siegelman, "Urban Institute Audit Studies," 213–15. The case is well made in 1993 in this study, but the data is now dated, leaving me uncertain about the status of contemporary markets.

28 One argument I will not treat substantively is the possibility that some firms may have higher inherent costs to a multiethnic work group if the various ethnic groups have animosity toward one another or large cultural differences that hinder workplace cooperation. I will not examine data exploring this hypothesis, but my discussion of how identity in Christ eschews the profit motive will also apply to this perspective, which is found in Thomas Sowell, *Race and Culture: A Worldview* (New York: Basic, 1994), 84–87.

29 Heckman and Siegelman, "Urban Institute Audit Studies," 217–18. The authors note that an audit study in Denver involved men from both ethnic groups who were more similar in accent and facial hair and found little evidence of discrimination, suggesting that the "problem [of alternative hypotheses] is potentially serious."

30 James J. Heckman, "Detecting Discrimination," *Journal of Economic Perspectives* 12, no. 2 (spring 1998): 109.

there may in fact be greater variance in the unobserved variable within the Black community due to disparities in factors like education and the social environment of the applicant's neighborhood.[31] If we assume that hiring firms have a certain productivity threshold applicants must meet in order to be hired, then an applicant with a résumé that is questionable in terms of qualifications may be less likely to be hired if they come from a demographic with greater variance in their unobserved productivity variable.[32] In other words, where Black applicants receive lower callback rates on applications, it could be because human resources representatives or other individuals with the authority to hire are bigoted toward Black applicants. Or, as Heckman suggests, it could be that a Black applicant whose résumé appears to meet the threshold for being hired is less likely to receive a job opportunity because the Black community has a wider range of educational levels, and the human resources representative may not want to take the risk of hiring someone who might have had a weaker education and thus be less productive. In economic literature, discrimination due to bigotry is known as taste-based discrimination, while the latter form of discrimination is called statistical discrimination.[33] The Heckman-Siegelman critique could include statistical discrimination, but it also raises the possibility that neither taste-based racial discrimination nor statistical discrimination against a given ethnicity, race, or gender is occurring. The problem might be discrimination against an unconsidered factor like beards. One should also note that the line between statistical discrimination and taste-based discrimination can be quite fine. One might discriminate against a race or ethnic group under the belief that there are likely to be less productive workers, but belief may not be reality. If the differential in productivity is not real, then one is discriminating on the basis of prejudice yet simply without the animosity of bigotry.

It is important to be clear at this point of the argument: both taste-based discrimination and statistical discrimination are unacceptable from the standpoint of Christian ethics.[34] The former is condemnable for countless reasons; suffice it to say that bigotry does not honor the image of God present

---

31 Heckman, "Detecting Discrimination," 104.

32 Heckman, "Detecting Discrimination," 110–11.

33 See Bertrand and Duflo, "Economic Experiments," 2–3.

34 Disparate outcomes for hidden variables might also be morally problematic. For example, if the problem is not anti-Hispanic discrimination but a discrimination against accents found in candidates of any ethnicity, we could be dealing with nativism, which could also be challenged from the standpoint of Christian ethics.

in all human beings. Statistical discrimination is also condemnable as sin. Suppose, for example, that statistical discrimination entirely explains lower job offer rates and callback rates on applications from nonwhite job seekers. From the standpoint of some economic theory, statistical discrimination is not "irrational" but rather the reasonable pursuit of "profit maximization."[35] On utilitarian terms, one could argue that it is ethical.[36] Christian ethics cannot be utilitarian. Besides the typical objections against utilitarianism—how do we measure utility?[37]—there are several criticisms against utilitarianism that are particularly pointed for Christians. Where Christians are called to an ethic caring for "the least of these" (see Matt 25:31–46)[38] and manifest a "preferential option for the poor," utilitarianism risks harming minority groups for the benefit of the majority if overall utility increases.[39] Furthermore, if a central dimension of the Christian ethic is conformity to Christ, then that will often involve self-sacrifice in ways that are incompatible with utility maximization, as I will show below. Statistical discrimination is sin, but it is also social sin. Those who seek profit maximization at the expense of human beings have been trained to do so in universities, in job training programs, by

---

35 This is the language of George Akerlof in his famous article "The Market for 'Lemons,'" which contributed toward his earning a Nobel Prize in Economics. Akerlof, "The Market for 'Lemons,'" 494. Statistical discrimination is also said to be rational in Edmund S. Phelps, "The Statistical Theory of Racism and Sexism," *American Economic Review* 62, no. 4 (September 1972): 659–61. To his credit, Phelps argues that the "rational" statistical discrimination is still "damaging" and should be countered by "social policy." Phelps, "The Statistical Theory, 61.

36 This is noted by Bertrand and Duflo, "Economic Experiments," 3.

37 See chapter 2, notes 20 and 21, for further details of how this problem has been manifest in economic theory.

38 Some commentators argue that "the least of these" references Christians, not groups like poor people and immigrants. I have argued against this interpretation and in favor of a more widespread application of the term in Butner Jr., *Jesus the Refugee*, 148–52.

39 A typical classroom example of this problem faces the question of whether Jeff Bezos or some equivalent millionaire should be murdered to take his wealth and help the masses, but a similar principle applies to many proposals to act violently toward one individual or group for the benefit of others. Rule utilitarianism has made some progress in overcoming such issues by stipulating that we must follow those rules that lead to the greatest utility on average, as would the rule "do not murder." However, the form of utilitarianism typically incorporated into neoclassical economic theory is arguably the more basic act utilitarianism. For example, Pareto optimality might be met in a situation where one group is oppressed and harmed, while majorities experience high utility. If any increase in the utility of the oppressed group would decrease the utility of the majority, then the situation would remain Pareto optimal.

superiors, and subliminally in the marketplace. Much more could be said, but too long a critique would detract from the flow of my argument.

Returning to the issue of audit and correspondence studies, many more recent studies respond to the Heckman-Siegelman critique in a manner that provides stronger demonstrations of continued discrimination in both labor and housing markets. For example, Neumark and Rich adjusted ten earlier correspondence studies to include some of the unobserved variables of the sort that the Heckman-Siegelman critique is concerned about. The results found that, all considered, housing studies continued to show discrimination, and half of the remaining labor studies continued to show discrimination.[40] The authors conclude that they "have no doubt that in many countries discrimination occurs in labor and housing markets against many groups."[41] Other studies have been able to randomly assign signals of ethnicity to résumés while still finding evidence of discrimination, mitigating the problem of unobserved variables and overcoming Heckman and Siegelman's critique that the studies are not true experiments because they are not randomized.[42] One study on gender discrimination in Belgium found no evidence of a perceived difference in productivity between male and female applicants, undermining the applicability of the Heckman-Siegelman critique.[43] These and other studies provide evidence of discrimination that survives the Heckman-Siegelman critique.[44]

---

40 Neumark and Rich, "Field Experiments," 224–25. It is not surprising that correspondence studies in housing are more robust. As Heckman and Siegelman themselves note, fewer variables are relevant to housing markets than labor markets, making the former more suited to audit and correspondence studies anyway. Heckman and Siegelman, "Urban Institute Audit Studies," 191.

41 Neumark and Rich, "Field Experiments," 249.

42 One such study is Magnus Carlsson, Luca Fumarco, and Dan-Olof Rooth, "Ethnic Discrimination in Hiring, Labour Market Tightness and the Business Cycle—Evidence from Field Experiments," *Applied Economics* 50, no. 24 (2018): 2652–63. Carlsson, Fumarco, and Rooth find evidence of discrimination in Sweden, though this fluctuates with how tight the labor market is. The critique about randomization is found in Heckman and Siegelman, "Urban Institute Audit Studies," 188.

43 Stijn Baert, "Field Experimental Evidence on Gender Discrimination in Hiring: Biased as Heckman and Siegelman Predicted?" *Economics: The Open-Access, Open-Assessment E-Journal*, Discussion Paper 2015-44 (June 2015), http://www.economics-ejournal.org/economics/journalarticles/2015-25/.

44 Another example: one recent study of credit bureau records analyzed discrimination in automobile credit lending, finding that Black and Hispanic loan applicants' approval rates were 1.5 percentage points lower than white applicants despite being equally creditworthy and despite being less likely to default. See Alexander W. Butler, Erik J. Mayer, and James P. Weston, "Racial Discrimination in the Auto Loan Market," Social

One of the most telling studies was able to consider all variables known to those acting in the market to ensure that there were no unknown variables. Pope and Syndor analyzed historical transactions at Prosper.com, a peer-to-peer lending site and also a fascinating example of market design. Here is now Prosper.com works:

> Individuals wishing to borrow money create a listing that lasts for a prespecified length of time, usually between seven and 14 days. The listing includes the amount of money requested (up to $25,000), the maximum interest rate the borrower is willing to pay, credit information obtained by Prosper via a credit check, and voluntarily provided (and unverified) information, such as pictures and descriptions of what they plan to do with the money. Lenders browse the various listings and bid on specific loans by committing a portion of the principal (minimum of $50) and setting the lowest interest rate at which they are willing to provide those funds. The loan gets funded if and only if the total amount of money bid by lenders covers the size of the requested loan. Lenders get priority for the loan based on the minimum interest rate they are willing to accept, with low-rate bids getting higher priority.[45]

Prosper.com had kept all records of all transactions and was willing to make this available for academic studies. Potential lenders only knew the applicant's credit report, the requested loan value, and the unverified plan for using the funds. Applicants could also choose the option of uploading a photo. Pope and Syndor were therefore able to categorize all loan applications to find out whether the race of the individual in the photo had any impact on the likelihood of being approved for a loan, all else being held equal. The result was that the loan listings with a picture of a Black applicant were 30 percent less likely to be funded than white applicants with similar credit history.[46] The study finds this to be statistical discrimination, not bigotry, since Black applicants were also found to have a higher default rate. To offset this rate, Black applicants were typically charged a higher interest rate.[47]

The Pope and Syndor study provides strong evidence of statistical discrimination in one particular financial market, but their study also helps us

---

Science Research Network Scholarly Paper (Rochester, NY: Social Science Research Network, March 31, 2021), https://files.consumerfinance.gov/f/documents/cfpb_mayer_racial-discrimination-in-the-auto-loan-market.pdf.

45 Devin G. Pope and Justin R. Sydnor, "What's in a Picture? Evidence of Discrimination from Prosper.com," *Journal of Human Resources* 46, no. 1 (January 2011): 58.
46 Pope and Sydnor, "What's in a Picture?," 55.
47 Pope and Sydnor, "What's in a Picture?," 89–90.

to recognize the complexity of economic studies of discrimination. When the fact that Black loan applicants on Prosper.com are less likely to be approved is described as "statistical discrimination," we are dealing with another example of the fact/value distinction being blurred. The description appears to merely name the fact that Black applicants received fewer loans because of a higher degree of uncertainty as to whether the loans would be repaid given the higher default rate. Inclusion of the word *discrimination* carries an implied value judgment suggesting such discrimination is immoral. Attaching the adjective *statistical* fits a utilitarian value judgment that such discrimination could, in fact, be moral given the fact that it is economically rational, meaning that it seeks profit maximization for the lender. Framing things in this manner, however, adopts an individualistic perspective that ignores the larger context of the economy.[48] Lower rates of distributed loans for Black applicants are subtly justified as "economically rational" statistical discrimination because repayment rates are lower. However, the ability to repay a loan is certainly linked to one's employment status, and experimental studies are clear that Black job applicants have a harder time getting job interviews.[49] The language of *statistical discrimination* is then used to subtly defend the status quo by justifying the lower job offer rate on utilitarian grounds due to the statistical likelihood that Black applicants come from communities with worse public education outcomes. But the ability of Black families to move into better neighborhoods depends partly on their ability to get loans—notice the circularity here—and on their ability to actually secure housing in better neighborhoods, a possibility that was legally impossible historically and that is still apparently difficult as is seen in the various experiments demonstrating the same.

The basic point is that labeling the results of such experimental studies as "statistical discrimination" could be helpful insofar as it clarifies that we may not be dealing primarily with the sins of social groups (i.e., rampant anti-Black bigotry in housing and labor markets). Rather, we are dealing with structures of sin, markets that are structured such that Black Americans are caught in a

---

48 This individualistic mindset fits the basic individualistic "tool box" that tends to ignore systemic issues that was identified decades ago in the landmark study Michael O. Emerson and Christian Smith, *Divided by Faith: Evangelical Religion and the Problem of Race in America* (Oxford: Oxford University Press, 2000).

49 For an extensive survey of correspondence studies, see Eva Zschirnt and Didier Ruedin, "Ethnic Discrimination in Hiring Decisions: A Meta-Analysis of Correspondence Tests 1990–2015," *Journal of Ethnic and Migration Studies* 42, no. 7 (2016): 1115–34.

cycle of exclusion from the workforce, housing market, and world of finance. However, the language of *statistical discrimination* is deeply problematic insofar as it can provide cover for injustice in the market by suggesting that inequitable outcomes are a defensible outcome of utilitarian reason rather than a problem that we have a moral responsibility to change. While statistical discrimination does not prevent the possibility of individuals improving their situation through hard work or making decisions that harm themselves and others socially, such that individual Black market participants retain moral agency, it does tip the scales against the Black community in ways that are clearly harmful as a whole. The duration of this chapter will explore the implications of these studies for the moral formation of individual Christians in the market before turning to address ways that market design could either help resolve such injustices or contribute to perpetuating them.

Christian Identity and Unity in Christ

A fundamental feature of the apostle Paul's teaching is that our identity in Christ is the basis of Christian ethical action. Obviously, this is true in the theological sense that the infused virtues of faith, hope, and love come by impartation from the Spirit to those who are united to Christ. As such, our identity as those united in Christ is the basis for our ability to do the good acts we are called to do in working out our salvation (Phil 2:12). However, for the purposes of my current line of argument, I want to emphasize a second way in which our identity in Christ is the foundation for Christian ethical action. In the words of James Thompson, Paul establishes "a collective identity as the basis for the 'ought'" of our ethical action.[50] In other words, our identity in Christ both creates ethical obligations and establishes ethical parameters within which Christian moral deliberation is intelligible. To be united to Christ is, in part, to share his identity, and this identity governs the actions that are impermissible for Christians and those that are expected of Christians.

Our identity in Christ governs the actions that are impermissible for Christians partly by establishing a new community with new boundaries, resulting in a new self-understanding. Paul establishes a new community by speaking of Christians as a new family, using the term *adelphoi* 120 times in the undisputed letters, a number that Thompson calls "remarkable in comparison

---

50 James W. Thompson, *Moral Formation according to Paul: The Context and Coherence of Pauline Ethics* (Grand Rapids, MI: Baker Academic, 2011), 44.

with its frequency in Greco-Roman literature and the Old Testament."[51] The new family is called to be holy—literally set apart—and is said to be chosen, carrying on the mantle of Israel the holy chosen nation.[52] However, Paul has transformed the notions of holiness and election by rooting them in union with Christ (e.g., Eph 1:4–5; 1 Cor 1:30). In 1 Corinthians, for example, holiness entails not only sexual purity and avoiding idolatry but also, in Michael Gorman's words, "practicing Christlike, cruciform love that seeks the good of the other."[53] The distinctive boundaries of Christians do not prohibit care for those outside of the boundaries, but they do restructure social bonds into two fundamental categories: those being saved and those perishing (1 Cor 1:18; 2 Cor 2:15), believers (1 Cor 14:22; 1 Thess 1:7; 2:10) and unbelievers (1 Cor 7:12; 10:27; 14:22–23), and *koinonia* with the Lord or *koinonia* with demons (1 Cor 10:16–21).[54]

The fundamental restructuring of the boundaries of community in Corinth requires a relativizing of other identity markers. For example, note how Paul's claim that we are baptized into Christ, receiving a new ground for our identity (Gal 3:27), is followed immediately by the relativizing of other group memberships—"there is no Jew or Greek, slave or free, male and female; since you are all one in Christ Jesus" (Gal 3:28; cf. Col 3:10–11).[55] As audit and correspondence studies have shown, many market interactions heighten awareness of identity markers like race and ethnicity toward the end of producing a systemically unjust outcome. To clarify, the relativizing of identity through a more fundamental unity in Christ does not permit "color blindness" that ignores categories like race, ethnicity, and gender.[56] This fact should be obvious

---

51 Thompson, *Moral Formation*, 56. I extend my analysis to the canonical works attributed to Paul, setting aside disputes about historical authorship as important yet largely irrelevant to the theological and ethical question of how the moral formation outlined in Scripture is possible in a market context.

52 Thompson, *Moral Formation*, 53–56, 96.

53 Michael J. Gorman, *Inhabiting the Cruciform God: Kenosis, Justification, and Theosis in Paul's Narrative Soteriology* (Grand Rapids, MI: Eerdmans, 2009), 110; see also 118–25.

54 Thompson, *Moral Formation*, 46, 51.

55 Grant Macaskill, *Union with Christ in the New Testament* (Oxford: Oxford University Press, 2013), 196.

56 As Jarvis Williams explains, "God transforms the ethnic identities of this new people of God (Gal. 2:11–14), but he does not erase the old ethnic identities that once characterized or maybe even formerly defined the members (2:15). Natural ethnic identities and racialized identities are still apparent for those who are in Christ and still create real sociological advantages or disadvantages in the real world." Jarvis J. Williams, *Redemptive*

from the recurring discussions of relations between men and women (e.g., 1 Cor 11:2–16; Eph 5:21–33) and Jews and Gentiles (e.g., Gal 2–3) throughout Paul's letters. Ethnicity and gender remain important categories for analysis, but right Christian formation always relativizes them. We consider such distinctions to ensure justice while recognizing that differences matter, but identity in Christ does not permit a fundamental allegiance to one's gender or ethnicity as a basis for harming members of another gender or ethnicity. Such considerations bring us to the second aspect of unity in Christ as it relates to moral formation.

Those who are in Christ through union and share his identity in justification are expected to conform to the pattern of his life, establishing a new *telos* for the life of a Christian. This is evidenced through the various "epigrammatic statements" in which Paul draws an ethic out of theology (Rom 6:4; 1 Cor 5:7; Gal 5:1; 5:13; Phil 2:12–13).[57] Paul's personal moral theology is rooted in the claim "I have been crucified with Christ, and it is no longer I who live, but it is Christ who lives in me" (Gal 2:19b–20a).[58] His ethical teachings for the church call for following the pattern of the cruciform Son of God who humbled himself in service of others (Phil 2:5–11).[59] A narrative structure is important for the self-understanding of the community and identity formation, and Paul's central narrative for ethics focuses on our participation in Christ resulting in an other-regarding ethic.[60] In fact, Paul's choice of the word *dikaiosynē* to describe the status of the justified believer may have been an intentional challenge to the human-centered virtue ethic of much Greco-Roman ethical thinking, which used the word to depict the

---

Kingdom Diversity: A Biblical Theology of the People of God (Grand Rapids, MI: Baker, 2021), 150. Anthony Reddie helpfully notes that Galatians 3:28 "affirms difference" but "becomes a radical ideal in which distinctions between 'in groups' and 'out groups' are obliterated." Anthony G. Reddie, *Black Theology in Transatlantic Dialogue* (New York: Palgrave Macmillan, 2006), 202.

57 James D. G. Dunn, *The Theology of Paul the Apostle* (Grand Rapids, MI: Eerdmans, 1998), 627.

58 "Paul's identification with Jesus' life, death, and resurrection (the paschal mystery) constitutes both the beginning and the end (in the sense of 'goal') of his life project." Daniel J. Harrington and James F. Keenan, *Paul and Virtue Ethics: Building Bridges between New Testament Studies and Moral Theology* (Lanham, MD: Rowman and Littlefield, 2010), 16.

59 Michael J. Gorman, *Cruciformity: Paul's Narrative Spirituality of the Cross* (Grand Rapids, MI: Eerdmans, 2001), 43.

60 On the significance of narrative in Paul and in broader ethical theory, see Thompson, *Moral Formation*, 44–45.

concept of "virtue and moral character," particularly in the contexts of one esteemed for civic accomplishments or innate ability.[61] For Paul, the concept is indivisibly linked to Christ.

If virtue requires us to be conformed to Christ, then Christian behavior must always be other-regarding. Christians give to those in need as Christ gave to us (2 Cor 8:9). Even though there may be a particular obligation toward those in the family of believers (Gal 6:10), Christians soon earned renown for their care of non-Christian Romans, with the emperor Julian "the Apostate" famously lamenting the fact that Christians cared not only for their own poor but for the needs of pagans, while pagan priests themselves did little to alleviate the sufferings of their coreligionists.[62] Believers accommodate other Christians when their consciences are weak (Rom 14; 1 Cor 8:9–13), and they seek to serve all kinds of peoples, even when it calls for us to forsake our rights as Christ forsook his (1 Cor 9). Such self-sacrificial care for others, a regular theme of New Testament ethics,[63] is incommensurate with the utilitarian justifications offered in defense of statistical discrimination. Where the utilitarian may seek to defend statistical discrimination as a rational outcome of the logic of profit maximization,[64] the Christian's identity in Christ demands sacrificial love toward all people. Surely, this self-sacrifice extends to include sacrifice of profitability that could hypothetically occur if a member of a demographic group likely to have a weaker primary school education turned out to have slightly lower productivity rates.

---

61 Mark Strom, *Reframing Paul: Conversations in Grace and Community* (Downers Grove, IL: InterVarsity, 2000), 152–53.

62 See a brief summary in Henry Chadwick, *The Early Church: The Story of the Emergent Christianity from the Apostolic Age to the Dividing of the Ways between the Greek East and the Latin West*, rev. ed. (New York: Penguin, 1993), 157.

63 On the centrality of the cross in Paul, see Hays, *The Moral Vision of the New Testament*.

64 Though some profitability is required for any business to survive, and though profit does enable growth, maximization of profit is not a natural or necessary component of firms. In fact, though cases like *Dodge v. Ford* established a precedent in US case law for corporations' fiduciary duties toward their shareholders, all state laws recognize that other interests should be considered, including those of employees and customers. See Julie A. Nelson, *Economics for Humans* (Chicago: University of Chicago Press, 2010), 98–99. Once again, we are addressing an issue of market design. As Daniel Finn explains, under US corporate law, firms can choose to adopt "co-determination" requirements for corporate boards, including, for example, representatives of employees, which might change the overall goals of the corporation, shifting away from profit maximization for the benefit of shareholders. See Finn, *Moral Ecology of Markets*, 138.

Moral Formation in Racialized Markets

Thus far, I have argued that audit and correspondence studies reveal that markets tend to discriminate against a considerable variety of minority groups. Utilitarian perspectives rooted in the logic of profit maximization may reward acting in accordance with statistical discrimination, thereby reinforcing habits in market participants that are contrary to those actions demanded by the Christian's identity in Christ. Discrimination in such markets is condemnable as an injustice. However, as a further step of my argument, I propose two hypotheses. First, the processes of hiring, renting properties, lending money, or selling products that reward statistical discrimination train Christians to reify the social constructs of race in a manner that makes market participants more prone to what economists call taste-based discrimination, or, in common parlance, bigotry. Second, it is reasonable to hypothesize that habitual acts of statistical discrimination undermine the development of virtues like justice, prudence, and love. In other words, the evidence uncovered from correspondence and audit studies reveals that markets designed to encourage statistical discrimination undermine the moral formation expected of the Christian justified by and united with Christ.

Experimental economics has discovered evidence that any classification into groups, however arbitrary these are, can reinforce prejudicial behaviors toward members outside of the group. Perhaps this feature of fallen human psychology contributes to Paul's recurring admonition to act sacrificially toward others. Recall Insko and Schopler's study from chapter 1, which revealed that study participants sorted into arbitrary groups—in this study, based on preferences for the artists Klee or Kandinsky—tend to favor members of their own group while acting against members of another group. Multiple experimental studies have found similar outcomes, but it is reasonable to suppose that such effects are amplified where the social groupings are associated with existing social conflict. For example, studies with children participating in the prosocial game, which allows participants to share a good equitably or to favor themselves in distribution, found children equally generous to friends and unfamiliar children but less generous to nonfriends.[65] Another

---

[65] Nicola McGuigan, Ruth Fisher, and Rory Glasgow, "The Influence of Receiver Status on Donor Prosociality in 6- to 11-Year-Old Children," *Child Development* 87, no. 3 (May/June 2016): 856–57. McGuigan, Fisher, and Glasgow explain several similar studies in their article.

study ran the envy and dictator games with children from conflict zones, using candy instead of money. Specifically, they used Georgian and Russian participants following the 2008 war between these two nations. They found increased egalitarianism when children played with other children sharing their national identity but increased competition when children played with participants of another nationality.[66] In contexts where one racial or ethnic group has a long history of animosity toward others, it is reasonable to expect statistical discrimination's focus on ethnic, racial, gender, sexual, or national identity to foster an emphasis on in- and out-groups that eventually results in bigotry.

I am unaware of any experimental studies that would validate my second hypothesis, which claims that recurring practices of statistical discrimination on utilitarian grounds would undermine the development of virtues like prudence, justice, and love. However, it is standard fare of virtue theory to suggest that repeated action can contribute to the development of a *habitus*, which if moral would be virtue but if immoral would be vice.[67] More recently, some moral theologians have proposed the category of "corporate vice," suggesting that just like vices dwell in embodied individuals, vices may also be able to dwell in the body of the church.[68] Here, one could also imagine corporations, which are bodies with less of an ontological basis than the church but which nevertheless might incorporate similar collective patterns of embodied behavior. Discussion of corporate vice combines the fact that habits are shaped in a social context with the reality that social influence occurs within an institutional setting where structures of sin can also influence the development of vice.[69] Such institutional and social influence does not undermine moral freedom, but it does reveal that our freedom is morally conditioned. Whether one emphasizes an individualistic or a corporate view of vice, moral theology is clear that repeated acts of discrimination would undermine the development of virtue.

---

66 Baddeley, *Behavioural Economics*, 89.

67 For a brief and introductory presentation of this common understanding, see William C. Mattison III, *Introducing Moral Theology: True Happiness and the Virtues* (Grand Rapids, MI: Brazos, 2008), 57–65.

68 Katie Walker Grimes, *Christ Divided: Antiblackness as Corporate Vice* (Minneapolis: Fortress, 2017), 182.

69 Daniel J. Daly, "Structures of Virtue and Vice," *New Blackfriars* 92, no. 1039 (May 2011): 353.

MARKET DESIGN AND DISCRIMINATION

In chapter 4, I argued that God could use markets as a secondary cause for moral development, but the evidence explored so far in this chapter has pointed to the ways that markets can hinder moral development when they enable social sin or perpetuate acts that contribute to the development of a vicious character. Partly, my emphasis on malformation in markets is a reflection of my conviction that the primary context for sanctification is within the church. However, the duration of the chapter turns again to the topic of market design, demonstrating that other possible market formations can be better suited to our identity in Christ particularly in the context of a society plagued by past and current racism.

One of the most substantial connections between market design and discrimination in economics is redlining, the systematic exclusion of Black Americans from the market through the joint efforts of many groups.[70] For example, the federal government denied opportunities for Black potential homeowners to participate in Federal Housing Administration Loans or in housing programs in the Veterans Administration. In 1943, the National Association of Real Estate Brokers encouraged their brokers to work against "a colored man of means" trying to buy a property in a white neighborhood.[71] Meanwhile, local governments used claims of eminent domain to demolish properties belonging to nonwhite residents in white neighborhoods.[72] Private individuals would include "restrictive covenants" in their house's deed, declaring that their property could only be sold to other white property owners. Though the Supreme Court ruled in 1948 that the government could not enforce such private documents, many agencies continued to do so.[73]

Eventually the Housing and Urban Development Act passed with the included intention of ending housing discrimination partly through section 235 housing loans targeting Black applicants, but, as discussed in chapter 3, the end result was what Keeanga-Yamahtta Taylor has called "predatory inclusion": "Predatory inclusion describes how African American homebuyers were granted access to conventional real estate practices and mortgage financing,

---

70 I am here using the term in its colloquial sense, which extends beyond its more literal application to marking Black neighborhoods in red as poor targets for New Deal investments in housing.
71 Taylor, *Race for Profit*, 40.
72 Rothstein, *The Color of Law*, 128–29.
73 Rothstein, *The Color of Law*, 77–91.

but on more expensive and comparatively unequal terms."[74] In other words, government-mandated corrected measures (i.e., market design expanding market participants) did not correct inequities but rather further harmed the very communities that programs like section 235 were designed to help. In retrospect, it is obvious that this would be the outcome. The act kept the same moneylenders as financial gatekeepers who had discriminated on the basis of race, though they denied it.[75] The appraisals necessary to secure a HUD section 235 loan was often made by real estate agents who worried that nonwhite residents in a neighborhood would drop property values, and their commissions on sales, encouraging problematic appraisals.[76] Even within HUD, discrimination in promotional processes meant that programs designed to promote economic justice among Black and white Americans were often being run by white Americans who had benefited from and perpetuated injustice within HUD.[77] Taylor rightly concludes, "The imposition of a new law banning [discriminatory] practices could not undo the conditions that had helped constitute the market in the first place."[78]

The example of the end of redlining should serve as a cautionary warning to those involved in market design. Markets are clearly designed, but many social problems are so complex that a simple government mandate will be unable to successfully correct them. Redlining was a product of the coordinated efforts of governments, institutions like banks and real estate boards, neighborhood associations, and individuals. A change at only one level—that of government—was very unlikely to produce the corrective measures needed.[79] Corrective market design and residential planning can exist at multiple

---

74 Taylor, *Race for Profit*, 5.
75 Taylor, *Race for Profit*, 91.
76 Taylor, *Race for Profit*, 152–53. Rothstein provides some evidence that integration actually correlated with a rise in property values. See Rothstein, *The Color of Law*, 94.
77 In September 1970, "African Americans made up 75 percent of GS1 (General Schedule 1) through GS5 entry-level positions within HUD and only 5 percent of supervisory positions listed as GS14 through GS18." Taylor, *Race for Profit*, 160
78 Taylor, *Race for Profit*, 130.
79 Taylor agrees: "Statutory changes alone are rarely, if ever, enough to undo deeply ingrained cultural, social, economic, and political assumptions that shape our society." Taylor, *Race for Profit*, 254. Rothstein adds several additional social factors beyond those I have mentioned here that help explain why reversing housing segregation is not easy. Once one generation has an economic advantage, that tends to be passed down to subsequent generations through inheritance and as white homeowners' properties appreciated in wealth, while Black renters had no corresponding growth in wealth. Rothstein also notes the tax payments I discussed in chapter 7, where mortgage payment deductions provided

institutional levels.[80] Several lessons can thus be drawn from the aftermath of redlining: First, market design is a complex process, and central planners should not be overly optimistic about their capabilities. Second, design is best performed across multiple institutional levels. Individuals, communities, firms, institutions, and various levels of government can all be involved. Third, best practice would include as market designers those who will be affected by changes to the laws regulating markets. Liberation theologians refer to this as the oppressed being the agents of their own liberation, a necessary goal if the evidence from the elimination of redlining applies more widely, as it surely does. Fourth, design in one market likely will need to be connected to other markets. As Taylor points out, for example, it makes little sense to try to increase the access that Black Americans had to homeownership when they were "tied to a community with few prospects for reinvigorating its job market."[81] Without corresponding changes to labor markets and finance, the HUD plan faced insurmountable hurdles.

Admitting the complexity of the situation, I am still convinced that aspects of market design can be used to mitigate the injustices of discrimination, with the corresponding result of enabling actions in line with our identity in Christ. One means of corrective market design would be to modify what information is available on the labor market. For example, recent legislation in many US states prohibits prospective employers from asking about wage history. One stated reason for this prohibition is that "members of historically disadvantaged groups often start out their careers with unfair and artificially low wages compared to their white male counterparts, and the disparities are compounded from job to job throughout their careers."[82] Under the pressure

---

a government-designed wealth transfer to upper-class families. Finally, contemporary housing subsidy programs tend to target apartments. Rothstein, *The Color of Law*, 179–80.

80 For example, see June Manning Thomas, *Redevelopment and Race: Planning a Finer City in Postwar Detroit* (Detroit: Wayne State University Press, 2013), 193–97. Thomas provides a brief helpful summary of efforts by neighborhood associations to undertake urban planning themselves.

81 Taylor, *Race for Profit*, 169.

82 Orly Lobel, "Knowledge Pays: Reversing Information Flows and the Future of Pay Equity," *Columbia Law Review* 120, no. 3 (April 2020): 569. This is a statement from Rep. Norton during congressional debates on legislation. The authors of the study add that behavioral economics suggests that anchoring can be a problem linked to salary disclosure as well. Merely naming a lower salary rate can result in lower offered rates, even if the firm offering is aware of discrimination in salaries and intends to avoid such discrimination. Lobel, "Knowledge Pays," 571–72.

of activist shareholders, several large companies have made public disclosures of their gender-based pay gap, information that can also be effective in combatting pay discrimination in labor markets.[83] These specific measures apply to wage discrimination and not to the hiring discrimination uncovered in many audit and correspondence studies, but factors like the anonymizing of applications could also work to undermine discrimination in labor markets.

Market design can also be used to fight discrimination in markets by modifying the market mechanism used to establish prices. Many audit studies have found discriminatory pricing toward women and nonwhite customers in markets for cars.[84] After an audit of its own internal data where one family of dealerships found that their regular "back-and-forth negotiation model" tended to result in customers of lower socioeconomic status paying higher prices, the company switched to a fixed-pricing model, believing this better fit the Bible's mandate to not exploit those who are poor.[85] When dealership owners design their market to follow a fixed-price model, both the injustice of discrimination and the moral malformation that arises from salespersons participating in such practices would be largely eliminated.[86] Other data suggests that moving to online purchases of vehicles can eliminate the higher prices charged to nonwhite customers.[87] Of course, traditional solutions to

---

83 Erin M. Connell and Kathryn G. Mantoan, "Mind the Gap: Pay Audits, Pay Transparency, and the Public Disclosure of Pay Data," *ABA Journal of Labor and Employment Law* 33, no. 1 (Fall 2017): 17–19. The article considers specifically the advocacy of groups like Pax World Investments, Trillium Asset Management, and Arjuna Capital.

84 For example, see Ian Ayres, "Further Evidence of Discrimination in New Car Negotiations and Estimates of Its Cause," *Michigan Law Review* 94, no. 1 (October 1995): 109–47.

85 A full account of Flow Motors is found in Kenman L. Wong and Scott B. Rae, *Business for the Common Good: A Christian Vision for the Marketplace* (Downers Grove, IL: IVP Academic, 2011), 226–29. In 2007, the company had 900 employees and $650 million in annual sales.

86 Sadly, continued discrimination in access to financing cars could remain a problem without intentional design of this process as well. One recent audit study uncovered discrimination in auto finance, even though the nonwhite participants in the study were more creditworthy than the white participants. See Lisa Rice and Erich Schwartz Jr., "Discrimination When Buying a Car: How the Color of Your Skin Can Affect Your Car-Shopping Experience" (National Fair Housing Alliance, January 2018), https://nationalfairhousing.org/wp-content/uploads/2018/01/Discrimination-When-Buying-a-Car-FINAL-1-11-2018.pdf.

87 Fiona Scott Morton, Florian Zettelmeyer, and Jorge Silva-Risso, "Consumer Information and Discrimination: Does the Internet Affect the Pricing of New Cars to Women and Minorities?" *Quantitative Marketing and Economics* 1 (2003): 65–92.

discrimination in labor markets include a modified market mechanism of affirmative action, which would change the process of hiring labor to require or encourage greater diversity among hires.[88] Such market design occurs at all levels of government but could also be undertaken voluntarily by any organization.

Perhaps one of the largest theological challenges to discriminations in markets would be a direct theological critique of such practices as being out of line with the identity of the justified believer in Christ. Here, the church's proclamation and teaching ministry can challenge the ways that the market is imagined, including challenges to the related concept of markets as spheres of pure profit maximization, even if such profits require statistical discrimination. This is not the way for those who are in Christ, so those whom God has justified by special grace would do well to advocate for markets designed not to undermine their identity in Christ through rampant practices of discrimination. In other words, markets can be sites of common grace, where the concurrent work of God and humans helps the faithful grow morally into their identity in Christ. However, often markets pose the risk of undermining that identity by encouraging pursuit of the *telos* of profit rather than that of conformity to Christ.

---

88 See the brief discussion of affirmative action in Stanley H. Masters, "The Social Debt to Blacks: A Case for Affirmative Action," in *The Wealth of Races: The Present Value of Benefits from Past Injustices*, ed. Richard F. America (New York: Greenwood Press, 1990), 186–89. Masters argues that affirmative action is particularly necessary in the context of statistical discrimination, which might perpetuate productivity inequalities. Masters, "The Social Debt to Blacks," 183–84.

CHAPTER 9

The Sanctifying Spirit and the Market

Market-related activity, trade and other economic functionings have to be embedded in institutions and social norms. If we refuse to embed our models consciously, we will still be doing so, only unwittingly.

—Kaushik Basu[1]

The moral development of Christians occurs within the Father's sovereign plan as they act according to the identity they have received through union with Christ and justification, but such moral formation is especially associated with the sanctifying work of the Holy Spirit. After all, sanctification refers to Christians' progressive growth in holiness, so a study of the influence of markets on moral formation necessarily includes some discussion of sanctification. Sanctification involves "faith working through love" (Gal 5:6), which requires actions ordered toward the intrinsic good in God and neighbor and a commitment to act for the benefit of neighbor. Such love of God and neighbor fulfills the law (Matt 22:36–40). A move to the analysis of sanctification therefore requires a transition from analyzing how context conditions moral agency, such as economic inequality or culture, to the acts that occur in particular situations and contexts. Similarly, a theological analysis of sanctification moves from the question of identity, which determines self-understanding and the individuals or groups with which one will associate,

---

1 Kaushik Basu, *Prelude to Political Economy: A Study of the Social and Political Foundations of Economics* (Oxford: Oxford University Press, 2000), 68.

to the actions a Christian should take as a result of the identity received in Christ. Sanctification is logically subsequent to justification.

Markets serve as a potential context for the outworking of love, but the design of markets often risks replacing love with other motivations and goals. Because love must be freely given, the freedom of markets provides a context for the possibility of acts that consider others. Though economic theory can often neglect such aspects of human life, focusing instead on utility, which basically reduces to pleasure, certain contrarian accounts of markets prefer to emphasize the need of love. Luigino Bruni, for example, critiques neoclassical economic theory for having no account of noninstrumental relationships. Bruni advocates an emphasis on "relational goods," which are noncommodified sources of wellbeing[2] rooted in gratuitous, reciprocal relationships, including love.[3] Bruni argues that increases in income from lower levels of poverty also increases wellbeing and the quality of relational goods, a phenomenon I have already partly discussed in chapter 7. However, as pursuit of income and materialistic pleasure continues to increase, relational goods tend to decrease, harming the overall wellbeing of society.[4] Love, therefore, improves the wellbeing of society, though it ought not to be instrumentalized. Markets, however, can either enable relational goods like love or impede them.

This chapter will explore several ways that markets can by common grace enhance the sanctifying work of the Holy Spirit, which enables us to love. It will largely do this through exposing several potential market formations that can impede sanctification, especially incentives, theories of rational choice prioritizing self-interest, and harmful social norms. Drawing on an account of the Spirit's direct work in bringing about faith working through love and considering the indirect work of the Spirit through the means of grace, I will argue for a final time that the question of whether markets contribute to moral formation or undermine it will depend on the way in which markets are constructed and on the strategies that market participants are taught to use in markets.

---

2 I am using *wellbeing* as a rough translation of *eudaimonia*.

3 Bruni, *The Wound and the Blessing*, 85–90. Bruni traces the concept to four thinkers: Martha Nussbaum, Pierpaulo Donati, Benedetto Gui, and Carol Uhlahner. I am here simplifying his definition.

4 Bruni, *The Wound and the Blessing*, 94.

SANCTIFICATION IN THE HOLY SPIRIT

Space does not permit an exhaustive treatment of the Holy Spirit's work in sanctification as it relates to moral formation. A full treatment of this subject would require extended analysis of such questions as the nature of grace, the relationship between sanctification and virtue formation, and the extent to which the Holy Spirit facilitates moral improvement prior to the eschaton. My goal in this chapter is much more modest: I intend to demonstrate that there is broad consensus that the Holy Spirit works within human beings to develop morally positive desires and dispositions oriented toward the intrinsic good of God and God's creation. While different accounts of desire, virtue, and the Holy Spirit will persist, to name only several ongoing debates in moral theology, certain aspects of market design can be critiqued on the basis of shared fundamental commitments without resolving the many associated more technical debates.

A typical treatment of Galatians 5:6 in the works of many recent moral theologians reveals a basic consensus. In Galatians 5:6, Paul says, "For in Christ Jesus neither circumcision nor uncircumcision counts for anything; the only thing that counts is faith working through love." The statement serves as something of a hinge between Paul's treatment of identity in Christ—notably represented in Galatians 3:28, which played a role in chapter 8's discussion of identity—and Paul's treatment of life in the Spirit in 5:13–6:10.[5] As such, it is a helpful starting point for considering how the identity Christians have in Christ is worked out in the Spirit-empowered life. There is some consensus among ethicists regarding the passage's import. Consider first the perspective of Oliver O'Donovan. O'Donovan notes the parallel between Paul's use of "working through/in" (*energein*; Gal 5:6) and James's use of "faith operative with works" (*synergein*; Jas 2:22), claiming that both point in different ways to how sanctification "leads out the gift of righteous agency in Christ into reconciled participation in the world."[6] This righteous agency must be characterized by love, which is ordered by its object. Love "attempts to

---

5 David DeSilva calls the verse "an effective summary of Paul's preceding argument and a précis of the contribution that the following section (5:13–6:10) will yet make to his argument." David A. DeSilva, *The Letter to the Galatians* (Grand Rapids, MI: Eerdmans, 2018), 423.

6 Oliver O'Donovan, "Sanctification and Ethics," in *Sanctification: Explorations in Theology and Practice*, ed. Kelly M. Kapic (Downers Grove, IL: InterVarsity, 2014), 156.

act *for* any being only on the basis of an appreciation *of* that being."[7] Thus, love can be described as "inclination" and "attachment," spatial metaphors referencing Spirit-enabled love's movement toward the good in another.[8] In other words, for love to be love, it must recognize the intrinsic good of that which is the object of love.

Similar interpretations of Galatians 5:6 are found among ethicists Helmut Thielicke and Daniel Westberg. Writing in a particularly Lutheran idiom, Thielicke emphasizes faith in Galatians 5:6—"The subject of the 'evangelical' process is not 'man.' It is 'faith', and hence a fact to which every man is continually summoned." The summons is to the choice between the Spirit and the flesh, between faith and sin.[9] To have faith and be in the Spirit is thus to have a complete movement of the self in which we are simultaneously righteous by God's love for us and in our faith-enabled love to God.[10] Thielicke rejects any ethical goal that "subscribe[s] to the blasphemous idea of a 'self-creation of the ego'" but instead demands love as rooted in our faith in God.[11] Though Thielicke differs in detail from O'Donovan, at one point there is significant overlap—love is love only insofar as its end is viewed as an intrinsic good. In Thielicke's case, the intrinsic good is especially the God revealed in Christ who is the object of our faith, that foundation of all moral action. Daniel Westberg, drawing heavily on Aquinas, argues that faith acting in love (Gal 5:6) requires the Spirit-given gift of understanding. God's character is the standard, expressed through reason as natural law, but we judge an act by this character through the illumination of the Holy Spirit. Loving acts, then, are motivated by the Spirit's empowerment of our understanding as our understanding and action are directed toward the intrinsic good of God's character.[12] Again, inner motivation toward intrinsic goods is clearly present.

Faith working in love is made possible through the Holy Spirit, for Spirit-given faith manifests in the fruits of the Spirit, the first of which (Gal 5:22) and greatest of which (1 Cor 13:13) is love. This love "does not seek its own

---

7 Oliver O'Donovan, *Resurrection and Moral Order: An Outline for Evangelical Ethics* (Grand Rapids, MI: Eerdmans, 1986), 25–26.

8 O'Donovan, "Sanctification and Ethics," 158.

9 Helmut Thielicke, *Foundations*, vol. 1 of *Theological Ethics*, ed. William H. Lazareth (Grand Rapids, MI: Eerdmans, 1966), 57, 61.

10 Thielicke, *Foundations*, 60–64.

11 Thielicke, *Foundations*, 61.

12 Daniel A. Westberg, *Renewing Moral Theology: Christian Ethics as Action, Character, and Grace* (Downers Grove, IL: IVP Academic, 2015), 229–30.

benefit" (13:5 NASB),[13] meaning that love requires the right motivations. We must have the disposition of caring for and acting toward the benefit of others because we value them as image-bearers. To be sanctified is to have the habit of love, but possessing love requires several additional dimensions. To love another, one must know how to love, and this often requires moral deliberation. If the law is summarized in the commandments to love God and neighbor (Matt 22:37–40), then the law itself can be seen as a guidance whereby we can learn how to love others. Finally, for present purposes at least, sanctification is a communal reality. When Paul speaks of love in 1 Corinthians 13, he does so in the context of discussing spiritual gifts given for the "common good" (12:7).[14] Faith working through love thus requires us to have the wisdom to perform proper moral deliberation so that we can act toward others with their benefit in mind, recognizing their intrinsic value as members of the community. I turn now to consider how markets may enhance or impede our ability to act in this manner.

INCENTIVES AND MORAL FORMATION

One of the most prevalent aspects of modern market design is the use of incentives to shape the outcomes of market transactions. Incentives are intended to change the behavior of market participants. Because character is shaped by recurring behaviors, we can expect incentives to have some effect on the development of our character. Since incentives have been extensively studied by the field of experimental economics, we also have some empirical data to determine what sorts of effects incentives actually have on those who are incentivized by them.

It is necessary to define incentives before considering how they can play a role in moral formation. Ruth Grant helpfully explains the three basic components of an incentive: "Incentives 'strictly speaking' are a particular kind of offer: 1. an extrinsic benefit or bonus that is neither the natural or automatic consequence of an action nor a deserved reward or compensation; 2. a discrete prompt expected to elicit a particular response; and 3. an offer intentionally

---

13 New American Standard Bible®, Copyright © 1960, 1971, 1977, 1995, 2020 by The Lockman Foundation. All rights reserved.

14 Paul returns to a discussion of these gifts in 1 Corinthians 14 after concluding his discussion of love.

designed to alter the status quo by motivating a person to choose differently than he or she would be likely to choose in its absence."[15]

In most market design, whether centralized or decentralized, incentives play a major role. These incentives can be used to encourage market participants that would otherwise be absent, or they can be a component of the exchange mechanism, changing the equilibrium of the market. G. C. Archibald helpfully explains that designing a market process usually begins with a "qualitative rule" used to determine "what is optimal." In most cases, this rule will be derived at least in part from an economic model. These processes will also require some kind of implementation system that leads market participants to act in the optimal fashion as defined by the model, and this system usually consists of an incentive structure.[16] Archibald provides many examples, the most easily accessible of which is the example of television. Suppose at a given time 80 percent of the population favors a show of type A and 20 percent of type B and that there are three private television stations whose earnings come from advertising sales. All three will present shows of variety A to maximize viewership and ad revenue. This situation is not Pareto optimal, a standard economic model for welfare economics, because changes could be made to the market where some viewers would be better off without harming other viewers. A solution can be found in establishing a public channel, a new market participant whose goal is to maximize total viewership for the market, and that will therefore put on a type B show. Of course, the public channel's managers would need to be incentivized to ensure this outcome—perhaps their salaries will be linked to total consumers in the market for television shows, not to the number of people who watch their station's shows. The basic pattern illustrated here is the need to recognize a suboptimal outcome through an economic model; to design a market where it is possible to overcome the suboptimal outcome, perhaps through inviting new market participants; and then to incentivize the proper individuals so that they meet the objectives of the model.[17] Such incentives serve as a modification to the exchange mechanism. As such, they are an important aspect of market design.

---

15 Ruth W. Grant, *Strings Attached: Untangling the Ethics of Incentives* (Princeton, NJ: Princeton University Press, 2012), 43.
16 G. C. Archibald, *Information, Incentives, and the Economics of Control* (New York: Cambridge University Press, 2005), 30–31.
17 Archibald, *Information, Incentives*, 86–88.

The use of incentives sounds innocent enough until you begin to survey the literature of the impact of incentives on economic agents. Studies have time and again shown that when a particular action is incentivized, linking that action to an extrinsic benefit, two common problems occur. The first is known as crowding out. When external motivation is supplied for an action, internal motivation tends to wither.[18] For example, when blood donation was augmented by a system offering incentives for giving blood in the United States, donations significantly declined. More than this, "our internalized benevolence towards those unknown to us, who need blood, began to atrophy from nonuse." Over a similar time span, donations in the United Kingdom, where incentives for donations were not offered, remained strong, as did the general benevolence needed to motivate individuals to donate blood.[19] Several outstanding surveys of the literature come to similar conclusions: in whatever area incentives are offered, be it to encourage children to draw during recess or to persuade students to obtain high grades, internal motivation is reduced and often practically eliminated.[20] The second major problem with incentivizing is known as the spillover effect. When incentives eliminate internal motivation through crowding out, they tend to also eliminate internal motivation in other areas of human action. Incentivizing blood donations also harms the internal motivation to be honest; more donors will lie about their health status. Incentivizing teachers by test scores will cause a higher number of teachers to modify students' answers on exams. When students are incentivized, cheating goes up, but results on academic performance as a whole may be mixed.[21]

The most common use of incentives in the economy concerns employee and executive compensation. Interestingly, when surveyed, employees tend to state that financial incentives are not the best way to encourage employee

---

18 Grant, *Strings Attached*, 115–16. Cf. Long, Fox, and York, *Calculated Futures*, 67–68.

19 Charles K. Wilber, "Trust, Moral Hazards, and Social Economics: Incentives and the Organization of Work," in *Economics, Ethics, and Public Policy*, ed. Charles K. Wilber (Lanham, MD: Rowman and Littlefield, 1998), 99.

20 Deci, Ryan, and Costner surveyed 128 studies that demonstrate the same crowding-out effect for incentives. Edward L. Deci, Richard M. Ryan, and Richard Koestner, "A Meta-Analytic Review of Experiments Examining the Effects of Extrinsic Rewards on Intrinsic Motivation," *Psychological Bulletin* 125, no. 6 (1999): 627–68. See similar surveys in Robert E. Lane, *The Market Experience* (Cambridge: Cambridge University Press, 1991), 371–74.

21 Grant, *Strings Attached*, 117.

productivity. Most employees claim to prefer a sense of significant, challenging work and opportunity for growth and advancement over financial incentives.[22] Despite this, the use of incentives has become increasingly common, especially as a part of executive compensation packages.[23] If we consider the spillover effect and crowding-out effect so commonly observed in terms of compensation packages, we would expect a resulting decrease in internal motivation and a decline in various related intrinsic motivators rooted in the intrinsic good of an action. This should make incentives the subject of intense scrutiny, but this is rarely the case. For example, John Reynolds considers problems surrounding investment banking after the 2008 global financial crisis. He clearly explains how investment bankers' salaries are a mix of shares and salary "based on a review of an individual's contribution to the bank's profit or loss."[24] These incentives are designed to encourage bankers to be cautious and prudent, avoiding unnecessary risk and promoting the security of the bank because stability is in their own self-interest as they are stakeholders. Despite equity in the banks, sometimes worth hundreds of millions, many bank executives still prioritized high-risk, short-term gain to long-term gains and security leading up to the 2008 financial crisis. Reynolds attributes this to high turnover rates, particularly among junior bankers, that undermine any orientation toward long-term stability that incentives might provide.[25] He concludes by cautioning against any major change in the banking system, merely suggesting that incentives for ethical behavior may not "outweigh" those for unethical behavior.[26] In other words, the collapse was a mistake in judgment, not evidence of a decline in ethics. While I have no doubt that many virtuous bankers still work in firms across the globe, a response encouraging banks to double down on incentives by increasing them so that they outweigh

---

22 Frederick Herzberg, "One More Time: How Do You Motivate Employees?" *Harvard Business Review* 46, no. 1 (January/February 1968): 53–62.

23 This shift is partly the result of the Omnibus Budget Reconciliation Act of 1993, which limited corporations' deductions for executive salary to one million dollars, unless that pay was linked with performance. As a result, performance-based incentives have increased as a portion of executive pay, with fixed salary only making up 10 to 12 percent of executive pay for S&P 500 companies as of 2012. Robert W. Kolb, *Too Much Is Not Enough: Incentives in Executive Compensation* (Oxford: Oxford University Press, 2012), 12–14.

24 John Reynolds, "Investment Banking: The Inevitable Triumph of Incentives over Ethics," in *Crisis and Recovery: Ethics, Economics and Justice*, ed. Rowan Williams and Larry Elliott (New York: Palgrave Macmillan, 2010), 126.

25 Reynolds, "Investment Banking," 130–33.

26 Reynolds, "Investment Banking," 143–44.

unethical behavior misses the basic point: external motivations often kill the very intrinsic ethical factors that are necessary for financial stability.

Why does the crowding-out effect occur? Surveying relevant literature, Samuel Bowles presents four overlapping explanations.[27] First, framing a decision in terms of incentives may signal that the choice is an economic one more than an ethical one. Here, the problem would be one of moral deliberation, or rather the lack thereof, as the individual reflected on maximizing income and utility rather than focusing on the Spirit-revealed principles for moral deliberation found in Scripture, for example. Second, incentives may "induce long-term change in motivations."[28] In this case, the problem is allowing monetary gain to supplant Spirit-given motivations rooted in love. Third, the presence of incentives may "overjustify the activity," taking away individuals' sense of agency, resulting in an aversion to control that causes them to reject the incentivized action.[29] Fourth, incentives may convey information that dissuades moral action, conveying that the principal, the one utilizing incentives, "is seeking to profit at the expense of the agent, or that the principal believes the agent to be otherwise not committed to performing well, or that the job is onerous, or, as we have seen, that he does not trust the agent."[30] For these latter two explanations, the problem, in part, would be that incentives undermine community and the free actions for the common good taken within the beloved community. Incentives do not take away freedom and moral agency—persons acting in the economy have moral responsibility and a degree of moral autonomy, though much of this is hindered by sin. Yet each causal description explains incentives such that they appear to undermine sanctification.

It is important to be cautious when explaining the crowding-out effect, as it has sometimes been used to justify poor wages. For example, one economist has argued that increasing wages for nurses would be a bad idea because of something like the crowding-out effect—such wage increases would attract those who pursued nursing for money and not those who pursued it as a

---

27 Samuel Bowles, "Policies Designed for Self-Interested Citizens May Undermine 'the Moral Sentiments': Evidence from Economic Experiments," *Science* 320, no. 5883 (June 20, 2008): 1605–9.

28 Bowles, "Policies Designed for Self-Interested Citizens," 1607.

29 Bowles, "Policies Designed for Self-Interested Citizens," 1607–8.

30 Bowles, "Policies Designed for Self-Interested Citizens," 1608.

vocation out of the intrinsic motivation to do good.[31] Careful attention to the definition of an incentive reveals that the compensation within an incentive is not natural to the incentivized act and that incentives are designed to change behavior. Wages are a benefit to labor that is intrinsic to the act of working, a natural right even referenced in Scripture (1 Tim 5:18). Further, paying a nurse well is generally not done with the intent of changing how nurses act on the job. Wages are not incentives, and there are good moral and economic reasons to pay good wages.[32] Paying someone not to pollute is an incentive since payment is not natural to cleanliness and since such incentives are trying to change behavior. In such contexts, we can anticipate the crowding-out effect and have good moral reasons for suspicion about the use of incentives.

The crowding-out effect, though prevalent, may not be the only way that incentives can result in moral formation. Some economists have explored a less frequent result, crowding in, through which incentives may increase internal motivation. Part of the problem is that many theoretical analyses of the crowding-out effect assume that people are too homogenous. While many may have preexisting internal motivations that are crowded out by incentives, some market participants may lack such internal motivation. Further, it may be that incentives deter some behavior not due to the elimination of internal motivations but due to moral repugnance at receiving a financial reward for a good act.[33] In other words, the net result of incentives may be a decline in the total number of people undertaking the morally desirable action from crowding out, but some who may not have been doing the morally desirable action may begin to do so through incentives, and having begun, they could develop the necessary intrinsic motivation. Those who develop such motivations as a result of incentives experience what is known as crowding in.

Some have even advocated using market design to eliminate the crowding-out effect. In one fascinating study, Antoine Beretti, Charles Figuières, and Gilles Grolleau propose designing incentives where the incentive could either be pocketed or else donated to a charity. In such circumstances, the incentive may not undermine the intrinsic motivation of individuals already having

---

31 See Anthony Heyes, "The Economics of Vocation or 'Why Is a Badly Paid Nurse a Good Nurse'?" *Journal of Health Economics* 24, no. 3 (May 2005): 561–69.

32 For a direct response to Heyes, see Julie A. Nelson and Nancy Folbre, "Why a Well-Paid Nurse Is a Better Nurse," *Nursing Economics* 24, no. 3 (May–June 2006): 127–30.

33 Antoine Beretti, Charles Figuières, and Gilles Grolleau, "Using Money to Motivate Both 'Saints' and 'Sinners': A Field Experiment on Motivational Crowding-Out," *Kylos* 66, no. 1 (February 2013): 63–64.

one and could actually encourage intrinsic motivation in those who did not previously care about the issue at hand by exposing them to opportunities for charitable giving.[34] In a related experimental study, Beretti, Figuières, and Grolleau tested this proposed mechanism of exchange by sending out surveys on environmentally friendly behavior to nearly 1,500 French citizens. Some surveys included no incentive, while others promised direct incentives to the participants if they submitted the survey. A third option allowed participants to choose between donating to an environmental charity and accepting a monetary reward themselves, and a fourth only supported the environmental cause. Unsurprisingly, the small monetary incentive had a crowding-out effect. Surprisingly, however, directing the donation to the environmental cause displayed a small crowding-out effect as well, with fewer participating in the survey. Given the choice, however, total participation increased.[35] Further study is needed to confirm that these results consistently hold true.

THE HOLY SPIRIT, LITURGY, AND THE MEANS OF GRACE

God's work in sanctifying the church is appropriated to the Holy Spirit, who works directly within the Christian to bring about love of God and neighbor, a love oriented to the intrinsic good of each. The Spirit also works indirectly through the means of grace, such as sacraments, liturgy, and spiritual disciplines. The above section considered how incentives in markets might undermine the direct work of the Spirit through the crowding-out and spillover effects. This section will consider how the Holy Spirit's indirect work through the means of grace might be undermined by markets. In order to analyze markets, I must first attend to frequent Christian appeal to liturgy as source of moral formation for Christians. I will then consider the "liturgies" of markets and the possible social norms perpetuated by them, concluding with a brief consideration of how technology influences moral formation in markets. This brief survey will reveal markets to be a potential means of common grace, though also a potential site for social sin.

---

34 Antoine Beretti, Charles Figuières, and Gilles Grolleau, "How to Turn Crowding-Out into Crowding-In? An Innovative Instrument and Some Law-Related Examples," *European Journal of Law and Economics* 48 (August 2019): 417–38.
35 Beretti, Figuières, and Grolleau, "'Saints' and 'Sinners,'" 70–73.

Liturgies in Moral Theology

The concept of liturgy has played a prominent role in Christian ethics over the last half century. Liturgy is featured especially prominently in *The Blackwell Companion to Christian Ethics*, a text in which Stanley Hauerwas and Samuel Wells draw together an impressive list of contributors to teach the entire scope of Christian ethics through the liturgy. Hauerwas and Wells argue that "the liturgy offers ethics a series of ordered practices that shape the character and assumptions of Christians, and suggest habits and models that inform every aspect of common life."[36] Arguing that much of contemporary "Christian ethics" is a result of a "compromise" seeking to gain public hearing for Christian views as long as "they were detached from the Church's practices,"[37] Hauerwas and Wells instead pursue a vision of Christian ethics rooted in "the public formation of character through the rhythm of corporate practice," specifically liturgical worship focused on word and sacrament.[38]

Certainly, the Eucharist is the most discussed example of Christian liturgy as a force in the moral formation of Christians.[39] As a meal, the Eucharist already plays an important role in establishing identity in Christ, for table fellowship plays an important role in determining inclusion and exclusion in group membership,[40] a regular subject of discussion in Scripture's treatment of corporate worship (see 1 Cor 12:17–22; Gal 2:11–14; Jas 2:1–13). The formative nature of the Eucharist extends beyond normal meals, as is widely

---

36 Stanley Hauerwas and Samuel Wells, "Christian Ethics as Informed Prayer," in Hauerwas and Wells, *The Blackwell Companion to Christian Ethics*, 7. Hauerwas and Wells name the following liturgical habits that shape common life: "meeting people, acknowledging fault and failure, celebrating, thanking, reading, speaking with authority, reflecting on wisdom, naming truth, registering need, bringing about reconciliation, sharing food, renewing purpose."

37 Stanley Hauerwas and Samuel Wells, "Why Christian Ethics Was Invented," in Hauerwas and Wells, *The Blackwell Companion to Christian Ethics*, 28.

38 Stanley Hauerwas and Samuel Wells, "How the Church Managed before There Was Ethics," in Hauerwas and Wells, *The Blackwell Companion to Christian Ethics*, 49.

39 Hauerwas and Wells identify a Eucharistic emphasis at the start of their *Companion*, noting they focus "most particularly [on] the Eucharist." Hauerwas and Wells, "Christian Ethics as Informed Prayer," 3.

40 The issue of table fellowship is helpfully explored in George M. Soares-Prabhu, *The Dharma of Jesus*, ed. Francis X. D'Sa (Maryknoll, NY: Orbis, 2003), 117–30. Soares-Prabhu pays particular attention to the table fellowship of Christ in his earthly ministry, though he does connect table fellowship to the Eucharistic content of 1 Corinthians.

recognized. For example, Margaret Scott has argued that the anamnesis of Christ in the Eucharist is not a mere remembrance but a call to adopt the attitude of Christ (Phil 2:5), actualizing the past way of Christ in present circumstances.[41] Similarly, Victor Codina analyzes the Eucharist against the horizon of the kingdom of God, arguing that sacraments are "prophetic symbols of the kingdom" that announce the kingdom, denounce the sin of the world, and demand moral transformation.[42] Specifically, Codina explains that the Eucharist is the banquet of the Kingdom, a renewed celebration of the Passover "feast of the liberation from Egypt," demanding that we act for liberation as well.[43] Other examples related to the economy will be mentioned briefly below.

The Reformed concept of the means of grace can help articulate the work of the Spirit through liturgy and especially sacrament. A reformed account affirms the application of redemption through the direct work of the Spirit and indirectly through external means. William Ames notes that these external means "concur and operate in the preparation of [humans] to receive grace,"[44] but that properly speaking, the conveyance of grace belongs to the Holy Spirit. There is no reason to restrict the application of redemption to the sacramental application of special grace. Geerhardus Vos explains, "There is common grace and special grace. But what serves for receiving and granting the former must also count as a means of grace. What occurs in the sphere of God's providence cannot be excluded."[45] The concurrent work of God and humans in the world is often treated in Scripture as a basis for moral formation. For example, God can use suffering to build character (e.g., Rom 5:3–5). This fact does not entail that suffering is equally efficacious with word and sacrament. Nor does it make suffering intrinsically good. However, it does show that moral transformation is possible through common experiences like suffering in ways that are oriented to and a shadow of the formation available to Christians through the special graces of word and sacrament. The concept of

---

41 Margaret Scott, *The Eucharist and Social Justice* (New York: Paulist, 2009), 69–75.

42 Victor Codina, "Sacraments," in Ellacuría and Sobrino, *Mysterium Liberationis*, 666–67.

43 Codina, "Sacraments," 671–72.

44 William Ames, *The Marrow of Theology*, trans. John Dykstra Eusden (Durham, NC: Labyrinth, 1968), 33.3.

45 Geerhardus J. Vos, *Ecclesiology, the Means of Grace, Eschatology*, trans. and ed. Richard B. Gaffin Jr., vol. 5 of *Reformed Dogmatics* (Bellingham, WA: Lexham, 2016), 60.

the means of grace allows us to connect the concurrent work of humans and God in markets through common grace to the inseparable work of the Trinity in sanctifying through the means of grace, which is especially completed through the mission of the Holy Spirit.[46] Consideration of the role of the Holy Spirit in liturgy and worship also begins to expose a seeming imbalance in the use of liturgy in some Christian ethics: the potential overemphasis of liturgical practices with a corresponding underemphasis of the work of the Spirit in making present Christ, our intercessor before the Father.[47]

Valid insights regarding the formative nature of Christian liturgy have perhaps been overapplied in some corners of the theological landscape, where the Eucharist is thought to show the value of social goods in a manner that challenges exclusive notions of private property[48] and to resist consumerism by consuming the Christian through incorporation into the body of Christ.[49] The Eucharist is argued to secure the balance between the one and the many in the context of globalization,[50] to establish social bonds of greater depth than those offered in economic contracts,[51] and to provide a basis for analyzing hunger in the context of global poverty.[52] While I appreciate the depths of the significance of the Eucharist and other liturgical practices for moral formation that theological analysis of this kind has uncovered, I also remember my days in seminary, where the typical refrain in most student discussions in my ethics survey class pointed to the Eucharist as *the* solution to virtually any

---

46 I am here following Wollebius, who treats the efficient cause as the Trinity and the means of grace as instrumental causes, though efficient causation is especially associated with the mission of the Holy Spirit, and the external cause is especially associated with the mission of Christ in his atoning work. Johannes Wollebius, *Compendium Theologiae Christianae*, in *Reformed Dogmatics: Seventeenth-Century Reformed Theology through the Writings of Wollebius, Voetius, and Turretin*, ed. and trans. John W. Beardslee III (Grand Rapids, MI: Baker, 1965), 172.

47 Note that I am discussing a matter of emphasis and balance. None of the writers I consider in this section neglects altogether the work of the Spirit in this process. For example, see Stanley Hauerwas and Samuel Wells, "The Gift of the Church and the Gifts God Gives It," in Hauerwas and Wells, *The Blackwell Companion to Christian Ethics*, 18. Here, Hauerwas and Wells distinguish between God-given practices and Spirit-enabled charisms. Yet, their emphasis falls clearly on the side of liturgical practices.

48 Meeks, *God the Economist*, 178–80.
49 Cavanaugh, *Being Consumed*, 53–54.
50 Cavanaugh, *Being Consumed*, 83–85.
51 Long, Fox, and York, *Calculated Futures*, 185–205.
52 Robert Song, "Sharing Communion: Hunger, Food, and Genetically Modified Foods," in Hauerwas and Wells, *The Blackwell Companion to Christian Ethics*, 388–400.

ethical dilemma, which causes me to worry for the potential for imbalance in moral theology if liturgy is emphasized too highly.[53] Certainly, the Holy Spirit uses the sacraments, liturgy, and spiritual disciplines as means of (special) grace that enable sanctification. However, overapplication of the Eucharist as a solution in social ethics risks restricting the Spirit's formative work too sharply, denying the work of the Spirit in common grace and resulting in a restraint of sin that is also a source of development in sanctified Christians. If the efficacy of the Eucharist in moral formation extends beyond other formative practices, it is in large part because of the real presence of Christ. Yet, though Christ is uniquely present in the bread and the wine, he certainly is not only present there, nor do all who participate in communion necessarily benefit from his presence (see 1 Cor 11:29–30).

Several other concerns must qualify my use of liturgy here. First, overly optimistic views of the Eucharist can also ignore the problems that are intrinsic to ecclesial practices. Lauren Winner identifies the risk of affirming the theoretical good of a practice without testing such theories against ethnography, which might uncover malformation that is possible through them.[54] Practices sometimes cause damage because the practice has been deformed, but at other times risk of a certain variety of damage is intrinsic to the practice itself.[55] Winner is not speaking of causal necessity, and she rightly insists that moral agents retain moral responsibility, but practices do contain intrinsic risk: "Judas received the Eucharist and then he immediately betrayed the Lord; written into the rite from its Dominican inception, then, was the certainty of its going wrong."[56] Winner points to the medieval host desecration myths, in

---

53 Hauerwas and Wells recognize risks too: "Because the Eucharist incorporates so many practices, one could easily fall into the habit of using the term in a sweeping manner to suggest that the Eucharist is the answer to every question that arises in contemporary ethics. This is a danger because not only does it risk overlooking the detail of what those specific practices are and how they are best carried out, but also it can slip into making the Eucharist an abstraction, a theoretical panacea detached from embodied practice—the very opposite of the intention." Hauerwas and Wells, "Christian Ethics as Informed Prayer," 9.

54 Lauren F. Winner, *The Dangers of Christian Practice: On Wayward Gifts, Characteristic Damage, and Sin* (New Haven, CT: Yale University Press, 2018), 41–42.

55 Winner, *The Dangers of Christian Practice*, 5.

56 Winner, *The Dangers of Christian Practice*, 20. Winner acknowledges the debate concerning whether Judas actually partook of the Eucharist, arguing that the synoptics allow such an interpretation, which was regularly held in the tradition. See Winner, *The Dangers of Christian Practice*, 52–56.

which Jews were frequently accused of trying (unsuccessfully) to harm the host, the body of Christ. The result was frequent pogroms and mass killings. Winner argues that there is an intrinsic risk to the Eucharist that leads in such directions. This risk is a function of the supercessionist nature of the Eucharist as a replacement of Passover and is intrinsic to a theology of transubstantiation as a possible fear of what harm may befall Christ's body in the host.[57] Even the best of practices contains within it the risk of the worst of sins. Second, since much liturgy in most denominations is not sanctioned directly by Scripture,[58] centering liturgy too much can risk displacing Scripture in favor of tradition, a risk that runs contrary to the Protestant affirmation of the primacy of Scripture. Third, focus on liturgy could lead to a neglect of the formative nature of practices outside of the church. Thankfully, this third concern has been mitigated by recent work, especially that of James K. A. Smith on what he calls *cultural liturgies*.

Smith describes practices as rituals, "material, embodied routines that we do over and over again."[59] These rituals are oriented to a *telos* and become "part of the very fiber of our character." When rituals are especially "thick," when they are "rituals of ultimate concern," they serve as liturgies, shaping our identities, our desire, and the "visions of the good life" that we are pursuing."[60] Smith considers cultural liturgies of various sorts, including athletic events, political processes, and consumeristic practices like shopping. It is the role liturgies play in shaping desire that is particularly important to Smith,[61] a

---

57 Winner, *The Dangers of Christian Practice*, 37–38, 43. Winner notes that the theology of the time treated the host as "weirdly both strong and fragile," able to be effective on those who merely viewed it but at risk to harm from mice who might eat crumbs from it. Host desecration narratives play on such risks, viewing the host as vulnerable to being stolen from the church but invulnerable to imagined hostility from Jews. Winner, *The Dangers of Christian Practice*, 44.

58 Even those churches that follow the regulative principle are faced with questions about seating arrangements, the order of service, the tunes that will be used to sing the Psalms, and so forth. These choices cannot be governed by Scripture and always open up the possibility of the formative impact of liturgy moving away from the moral bounds of Scripture.

59 James K. A. Smith, *Desiring the Kingdom: Worship, Worldview, and Cultural Formation* (Grand Rapids, MI: Baker Academic, 2009), 85.

60 Smith, *Desiring the Kingdom*, 86.

61 See James K. A. Smith, *You Are What You Love: The Spiritual Power of Habit* (Grand Rapids, MI: Brazos, 2016), 27–38. In this work, which targets a popular-level audience, Smith tellingly summarizes his understanding of liturgies by focusing on desire, even going so far as to describe liturgies as "love-shaping practices."

fact that returns us to our focus on the Holy Spirit, who replaces the desires of the flesh with the desires of the Spirit (Gal 5:17). Here, we must be careful. It is not that sanctification is acquired by practices or liturgies as if by some work. Recall John Owen's remarks that any *habitus* infused by sanctification "is not acquired by any or many acts of duty or obedience, yet is it, in a way of duty, *preserved, increased, strengthened,* and *improved* thereby."[62] At the same time, if God has furnished means of grace, even smaller ignoble ones like work, then we must make use of them.[63] Smith agrees, recognizing that it is the Spirit who works primarily in the gifts of the sacraments and liturgy, and arguing that his teachings on the moral formation possible through the liturgy is not instrumentalizing worship but is fundamental to the Spirit-empowered missional *telos* of worship.[64]

Liturgy and sacraments, especially Eucharist, are thus an important locus of the Spirit's sanctifying agency in the church, but the cultural liturgies of markets are also sites of moral formation. This chapter has shown that the presence or absence of incentives can affect the extent to which participation in a market undermines faith working through love. However, the effect of markets on sanctification is also influenced by the social norms within which market activity occurs and by the deployment of technology in a market context. The remainder of this chapter turns to briefly considering these two points.

Liturgies and the Varied Social Norms of Markets

Social scientists and theologians alike tend to point to the various social norms pervasive in markets that influence persons involved in those markets. The term *social norm* refers to a shared expectation of behavior that is often socially enforced. Social norms are a subset of culture, while the concept of culture itself also includes additional dimensions such as values, artifacts, and the conceptual framework within which sensory input is processed. The connection between social norms and economics is quite complex, with many

---

[62] John Owen, *On the Holy Spirit, Part I*, in *The Works of John Owen*, vol. III, ed. William H. Goold (Philadelphia: Leighton, 1862), 476.

[63] To cite another reformed theologian, sanctification "is essentially a work of God, though in so far as He employs means, man can and is expected to co-operate by the proper use of these means." Berkhof, *Systematic Theology*, 532.

[64] James K. A. Smith, *Imagining the Kingdom: How Worship Works* (Grand Rapids, MI: Baker Academic, 2013), 151–54.

possible approaches for theoretical analysis. One might, for example, follow the approach of Max Weber, exploring the ways that the "protestant work ethic," one example of religious social norms, contributed to industrialization and the expansion of capitalism.[65] My focus will center on the conclusions of experimental economics.

The line between norms and culture is somewhat blurred, and so the theological response to each can be as well. In chapter 7, I framed a response to culture in terms of the Father's providence, noting how culture can be slow to change, but Christians can view culture as a providentially given contingent reality to which we respond in faith, hope, and love. Since norms are a subset of culture, we must recognize that changing norms is difficult, seeing problematic norms as a providential opportunity to witness to the faith, hope, and love that we have through the gospel. However, in this chapter, I argue that norms can also contribute to markets functioning as liturgies, embodied practices that we can resist through counter-liturgies and the means of grace, as enabled by the Holy Spirit. The blurred boundaries between culture and social norms are not problematic for my analysis given that I am appropriating providence to the Father and sanctification to the Spirit—technically, the doctrine of inseparable operations requires us to see Father, Son, and Spirit involved in providence and in sanctification, with one Person simply more clearly evident in each act. The fuzzy boundaries between norms and culture are thus not a problem for a trinitarian account of divine agency.

Chapter 1 discussed two sets of economic experiments that are particularly relevant for any analysis of social norms. The first was a series of experiments beginning with Ruth Ames and Gerald Marwell that considered the effects of students' majors on the likelihood that they would take advantage of the free rider problem in economic simulations. The second set of experiments concerns what is called the discontinuity effect and will be discussed below. Recall that Ames and Marwell found that economics students displayed the tendency to be free riders more prevalently than their peers.[66] Though there are some differences in how data from this and subsequent studies is interpreted,

---

65 Max Weber, *The Protestant Ethic and the Spirit of Capitalism*, trans. Talcott Parsons (Upper Saddle River, NJ: Prentice Hall, 1958).
66 See pages.

these experiments do seem to suggest that the study of economics influences the way that economics students think.[67]

The implications of these findings for the present work are considerable, for here again the strong fact/value distinction often manifest in standard economic theory's positive/normative distinction is untenable. Neoclassical economic theory often describes rational economic agency as the pursuit of utility maximization, a self-interest that, by the invisible hand, results in the maximal economic growth and the most wealth for all. Individuals who act in this manner, often labeled the *homo economicus*, are the subject of extensive debate. Neoclassical economics can treat the self-interest of the *homo economicus* as demonstrable through empirical confirmation of predictions made by models of self-interested agents, but the matter is not one of pure positive analysis. Dale Miller puts the matter nicely: "That the explanatory power of the self-interest assumption has been the major focus of the self-interest debate is understandable, but it has also proven limiting. In particular, it has forestalled consideration of the theory's causal power—a serious omission, as the assumption of self-interest is not simply an abstract theoretical concept but a collectively shared cultural ideology."[68] Quantitative analysis of economic actions that confirm predications made by the standard *homo economicus* view of human nature may still not demonstrate that the actual motives of economic agents can accurately be interpreted in light of utility maximization. Miller insists that it may instead merely reveal that social norms oriented toward self-interest are particularly strong.[69]

If self-interest-oriented models of economic behavior cause those who study these models to act in a more self-interested way, it is no surprise that there have been extensive theological critiques of the *homo economicus*. For example, the economic personalism from the turn of the millennium particularly emphasized the need to develop a more accurate understanding of human nature and behavior.[70] Such approaches tended to emphasize arguments that more realistic depictions of human beings who were motivated

---

67 Intuitively, this seems obvious, or what would the point of studying economics be? The most interesting, and difficult to resolve, portion of the debate concerns the extent to which education has an effect.

68 D. T. Miller, "The Norm of Self-Interest," *American Psychologist* 54, no. 12 (December 1999): 1053.

69 Miller, "The Norm of Self-Interest," 1056.

70 This critique has been especially central in the work of much economic personalism. See Edward J. O'Boyle, "Requiem for *Homo Economicus*," *Journal of Markets and*

by more factors than self-interest would result in more accurate economic predictions.[71] Though the point is well taken, studies like Ames and Marwell's indicate that the problem is deeper, for training students in models of market efficiency, equilibrium exchange, and rational choice that are rooted in such theories could lead them to act according to the theories' mandates. More than this, these theories may reinforce social norms toward selfishness and against other-regarding behavior.[72]

One important task for theological analysis of markets is therefore to identify alternative models of human agency and to encourage the use of such models in the classroom and in the contexts where market design is occurring. One notable alternative model is found in Amartya Sen, who critiques typical economic models for having no place for human actions that are not utility-maximizing. To make his point, Sen distinguishes between sympathy and commitment. Sympathy is "concern for others [that] directly affects one's own welfare."[73] So, for example, if it pains a person greatly to see someone in poverty, their gift of money to a poor beggar actually provides a utility or welfare benefit for them by reducing that pain. On the other hand, commitment addresses a situation in which the injustice "does not make you feel personally

---

Morality 10, no. 2 (Fall 2007): 321–37. See also Donohue-White et al., *Human Nature*, 73; Beabout et al., *Beyond Self-Interest*, 104.

71 Beabout et al., *Beyond Self-Interest*, 3, 12, 104; Donohue-White et al., *Human Nature*, 60, 94.

72 I was first introduced to these questions as an undergraduate student at the University of North Carolina in a class taught by Jürg Steiner. Steiner had focused considerable energy in attempting to identify examples of political actions that were selfless and in fact self-defeating from the standpoint of what offered political utility. The rational choice theory prevalent throughout the UNC political science department at the time had most students convinced that the actions of elected officials should be self-interested by pursuing vote maximization, for actions that maximized votes would also be those that represented the largest number of constituents. Beyond that, many had accepted a theory of psychological egoism that argued that it was impossible to act in non-selfish ways. In class, Steiner asked students in an honors seminar if I should be able to run for office with prior ethical commitments that may not pursue vote maximization. Every student in the class argued that I should not. Steiner alone dissented. In a sense, this entire book and the dissertation that preceded it are my attempts to understand the moral poverty found in much political and economic thought without falling into many of the simplistic responses that I encountered during my seminary years. For Steiner's work on conscience in politics, see Jürg Steiner, *Conscience in Politics: An Empirical Investigation of Swiss Decision Cases* (New York: Garland, 1996).

73 Amartya Sen, "Rational Fools: A Critique of the Behavioral Foundations of Economic Theory," *Philosophy and Public Affairs* 6, no. 4 (Summer 1977): 326.

worse off, but you think it is wrong and you are ready to do something to stop it."[74] The difference here is one of motivation. In a case of sympathy, at least part of the motive is the desire to alleviate one's own discomfort of suffering. In commitment, there is no such self-interested welfare motive.

Sen describes welfare, goal, and choice as the three aspects of economic choices. He suggests that self-interested behavior has three components: "self-centered welfare" indicates that a person's utility depends only on their own consumption, "self-welfare goal" indicates that a self-interested agent has the goal of maximizing utility, and "self-goal choice" indicates that a person's choices are guided by their own goals.[75] A self-interested individual therefore acts in such a way that goals and choices are joined with and subsumed to self-welfare maximization. Commitment, on the other hand, drives one "wedge" between welfare and choice and another between goal and choice.[76] The wedge between welfare and choice is fairly easy to understand if commitment motivates actions that provide no welfare benefit. The wedge between goal and choice is more controversial and warrants further consideration.

Sen's argument is that commitment can cause someone to make a choice contrary to their own goals, therefore driving a wedge between choice and goal. Hans Bernhard Schmid has critiqued this position, claiming that such a thing is impossible. Schmid suggests that this wedge is impossible according to John Searle's notion of "conditions of satisfaction." A condition of satisfaction is the requirement that must be fulfilled for me to have done what I intended to do. Schmid suggests that if a person intends something, then they must have chosen their goal, their own conditions of satisfaction.[77] I think Schmid overstates the case insofar as someone can, through commitment, find themselves in a situation where they intend to act according to the commitment, setting conditions of satisfaction on that intention, namely, the willingness to do whatever that commitment entails. What the commitment entails, however, may not be set by the agent but by some "other." Thus, to intend to adhere to a particular commitment is to intend to act according

---

74 Sen, "Rational Fools," 326.
75 Amartya Sen, *On Ethics and Economics* (New York: Basil Blackwell, 2007), 80.
76 Sen, "Rational Fools," 329; Amartya Sen, *The Idea of Justice* (Cambridge: Harvard University Press, 2009), 188–93.
77 Hans Bernhard Schmid, "Beyond Self-Goal Choice: Amartya Sen's Analysis of the Structure of Commitment and the Role of Shared Desires," in *Rationality and Commitment*, ed. Fabienne Peter and Hans Bernhard Schmid (New York: Oxford University Press, 2007), 214–15.

to some external standard that will have its own conditions of satisfaction, its own *telos*. Such a commitment would seem to fit the goal of "faith working through love," where faith commits one to following the Spirit's leading without necessarily knowing the purpose of sanctifying actions at any particular time. Sen's theory of commitment is, to my mind, a plausible account of agency that could resist accounts of rationality that are reducible to self-interest, with the resulting outcomes uncovered in experiments like Ames and Marwell's. A second set of experiments reveals another place where social norms may lead to behavior that is not in line with the Spirit's sanctifying work. I turn to consider those results now, albeit briefly.

Several sets of experiments in economics have considered the effects of running successive economic games, exploring how the nature of the first game might shape the outcomes of the second.[78] One set of researchers found that when individuals participated in a self-interested game before participating in a second game, the outcomes of the second game tended to be more self-interested than the outcomes were for a second control group that had not been primed by a self-interested game of this sort. One explanation of this outcome is the "social support for shared self-interest hypothesis," which suggests that group members support one another in acting selfishly.[79] In other words, social norms can reinforce selfishness, which would be contrary to the sacrificial love expected of someone being sanctified by the Holy Spirit. Here, we come to one of the clearest examples of social sin explored in this book. When a social norm is established that encourages selfish behavior in one context, that norm carries over into other contexts much like the spillover effect discussed above with respect to incentives. Sin begets more sin.

This section is merely a preliminary treatment of the ways that social norms can shape markets. In particular, I have considered how social pressures connected to models of rationality can compel students to act according to those models of rationality, but not all models of rationality need to challenge Christian ethical assumptions. Similarly, acts in markets may be shaped by prior social norms. Here, one can hope that the norms present within churches and by common grace throughout society can lead to more virtuous behavior in markets. The classroom and other quarters of society can serve as a cultural liturgy and a means of common grace. However, we must extend analysis beyond the interpersonal dimensions of social norms

---

78 See the discussion on pages 23–25.
79 Bornstein, "A Classification of Games by Player Type," 28.

into questions of technology to see the full dimensions of moral formation in the economy.

Technology and Social Action

Within modern markets, an impersonal structure can also play a powerful role in shaping market participants: technology. As I have already briefly suggested in chapter 2, economic models themselves can serve as an external means of regulating human behavior through what is known as *performativity*. Michel Callon in particular highlights this fact when he argues that "mathematical economics" can become "realistic under certain conditions," namely, when "calculative agencies are there to introduce interrelated calculations in decisions and in the formation of actions."[80] In other words, when firms, consumers, or other economic agents deliberately act according to an economic model, they can perform that model, making it a more realistic depiction of markets. Richard Thaler gives an example of the trades in the National Football League. After studying historical valuations of trades, Thaler noticed something peculiar:

> The individual trades, represented by the dots, lie very close to the estimated line. In empirical work you almost never get such orderly data. How could this happen? It turns out the data line up so well because everyone relies on something called the Chart, a table that lists the relative value of picks. Mike McCoy, a minority owner of the Dallas Cowboys who was an engineer by training, originally estimated the chart. The coach at the time, Jimmy Johnson, had asked him for help in deciding how to value potential trades, and McCoy eyeballed the historical trade data and came up with the Chart. Although the Chart was originally proprietary information only known by the Cowboys, eventually it spread around the league, and now everyone uses it.[81]

Thaler tested the value of players based on stats and found that Coach Johnson's model was not accurate—the valuations were not an example of efficient or rational markets but of performativity, where markets operate according to a model by following the calculations of that model.[82]

---

80 Michel Callon, *The Laws of Markets* (Malden, MA: Blackwell, 1998), 50. While my estimation of how much realism in mathematical economic models can be traced to the performative influence of models is more modest than Callon, his point is still well taken.
81 Thaler, *Misbehaving*, 281.
82 Thaler, *Misbehaving*, 283–85. Thaler remarks, "The trade market curve (and the chart) says you can trade the first pick for five early second-round picks, but we are finding

With the increasing role that technology plays in the marketplace, we can expect more and more performativity as individuals within markets rely on the recommended actions of computer programs.[83] Consider the example of the Black-Scholes-Merton (BSM) model for options pricing. At one point in time, stock options were not legally traded in US markets because they were thought to be too close to gambling. The BSM model for options pricing was developed, giving credibility to options and helping facilitate trade in the Chicago Board Options Exchange (CBOE). When options trading began, the model was actually a poor fit, but over time, human actions and option prices both converged on predictions made by the models. Initially, statistical sheets were circulated to traders, creating social pressure to conform to apparent standards of scientific rigor to maintain credibility as a professional trader.[84] In due time, statistical sheets were replaced by computer programs that facilitated trading according to an economic model depicting ideal options prices.[85] When the CBOE opened, options were initially 30–40 percent overvalued relative to the model.[86] Despite this discrepancy, and through a variety of factors, the model began to be widely used throughout the CBOE. Simplifying to a degree, whenever options prices differed from the "correct" price according to the model, arbitragers bought and sold options to make a profit until the price converged on the model. By June–August 1983, options' prices only departed from the BSM model by an average of 0.32 percent.[87] Many interviewed traders held the belief that "Black-Scholes was really what enabled the exchange to thrive."[88] However, in 1987, a financial

---

that each of these second-round picks yields more surplus to the team than the first-round pick they are together traded for! In all my years of studying market efficiency, this is the most blatant violation I have ever seen." Thaler, *Misbehaving*, 286–87.

83 In some cases, less relevant to the moral formation we are considering but perhaps more significant for questions of justice, software and AI will play an increasing role in market transactions where there is no direct human input into the purchase or sale of a good. This is already prevalent in the world of stocks, where platforms like e*trade can be set up to automatically sell stocks if the market drops beneath a certain floor, to cite only one such example.

84 Donald MacKenzie, *An Engine, Not a Camera: How Financial Models Shape Markets* (Cambridge: The MIT Press, 2006), 160–62.

85 MacKenzie, *An Engine*, 201. The Autoquote system technically used the Cox-Ross-Rubinstein model, which was closely related to the BSM.

86 MacKenzie, *An Engine*, 158.

87 MacKenzie, *An Engine*, 176.

88 Donald MacKenzie and Yuval Millo, "Constructing a Market, Performing Theory: The Historical Sociology of a Financial Derivatives Exchange," *American Journal of Sociology* 109, no. 1 (July 2003): 121.

crash led to a loss of faith in the BSM model, which is now permanently a poor fit as a result of what is known as the "volatility skew."[89] The BSM would no longer fulfill its performative function of coordinating agents within a market to act in a particular manner.

The BSM model is certainly not the only example of an economic model incorporated into technology in a manner that guides human action in markets. Consider, for example, critical path management (CPM), a form of linear programming that solves what economists call an optimization problem, in this case the problem of determining the quickest and most efficient path to completing a project. CPM is deployed in many industries, ranging from weapons contractors to software firms to architectural and construction companies. Both charts and software platforms are available to complete the calculations for companies.[90] Software incorporating the BSM model, CPM, or other economic models serves as part of a calculative network that encourages economic agents to act according to the normative economic notions concerning ideal economic behavior that are implicit in any economic model. The purportedly ideal behavior within a model may or may not cohere with the ideal that Christian ethics would put forward in a given situation. Repeated acts contrary to Christian ethics can contribute to the development of vice, even if those acts were merely following a model. Conversely, if models were to recommend behavior in line with Christian ethics, then they could contribute to the formation of virtue. While a full analysis of technology as such exceeds the scope of this chapter, clearly software can serve as a liturgy, a possible means of common grace used by the Holy Spirit, or else as a hindrance to sanctification. To my knowledge, few economists and programmers are considering such implications, which causes me to suspect the influence is largely negative. Furthermore, because performativity and the impact of software are not adequately studied, its role in the discipline of market design appears to this observer to be underdeveloped. Here is one of many points for growth in analysis of markets. Having made my case, I move now to conclude by summarizing my argument and identifying other areas of growth.

---

89 MacKenzie, *An Engine*, 202.
90 For a brief summary, see Litan, *Trillion Dollar Economists*, 82–84. For a more extensive example in terms of construction, see Jonathan F. Hutchings, *Project Scheduling Handbook* (New York: Marcel Dekker, 2004), 55–77.

Conclusion

Economists freely acknowledge that markets are not "free." Markets are highly regulated institutions of advanced societies. If markets fail to deliver what societies want from them, then they need to be redesigned and regulated appropriately.

—Michael G. Pollitt[1]

This book has explored the biblical exhortation to "work out your salvation" (Phil 2:12) with the conviction that such redemptive work must connect with the work in markets that occupies such a large fraction of many of our lives. I have endeavored to show that markets can be a context for God's transformative work in the life of the Christian, even as they can easily be sites of sinful resistance to God's transformative work. The effect of markets on our moral transformation is not a given and varies based on many features of market design. The preceding chapters have shown numerous factors that may influence the ways in which human beings are shaped by the markets in which they work. Do markets make us better human beings? Are they morally corrupting? To answer such questions, we must ask many others. What models of purportedly rational behavior are being taught to market participants, and what assumptions about ideal behavior are inscribed into the software on which such market participants rely? Is the market in question found in a society where there is great economic inequality or superfluous wealth? Does the market encourage those who exchange within it to adopt identities contrary to, or to treat others in a manner incongruent with, their identity in Christ?

---

1 Michael G. Pollitt, "What Do Theologians Need to Know about Economics?" in Kidwell and Doherty, *Theology and Economics*, 39.

CONCLUSION

How are incentives used within markets, what mechanism(s) of exchange is preferred, and in what cultural context are such exchanges found? Different answers to each of these questions would lead to different conclusions about the ways in which markets could corrupt or improve the behavior of those who buy, sell, produce, consume, loan, borrow, and invest in said markets.

Throughout this work, I have relied on two fields of economics that are often neglected in theological analysis of the economy. Experimental economics has provided concrete data regarding the possible outcomes of different market formations. Such experiments help the theologian or ethicist analyzing markets to attend to the concrete particularism of differing markets. I have also relied heavily on the field of market design, which brings to light what many have known all along—markets are not purely spontaneous or natural entities. Many features of markets are designed and regulated, and this is true even in the most "free market" contexts.

While these economic subdisciplines have enabled a more precise analysis than I could have otherwise provided, several limitations must be noted. First, the economic experiments considered rarely analyzed moral formation or the ethical outcomes of market transactions with an explicitly Christian ethic in mind. Though the results of the studies surveyed here more than prove the variability of markets, a more robust Christian use of experimental economics would need to incorporate the insights of moral theology at the stage of designing the experiments themselves. The blurriness of the line between positive and normative economics requires such attentiveness, and I hope, perhaps naively, that the arguments of this book inspire such study. Second, where I have argued that market design can occur through the work of governments, firms, economists, organized labor, and individual consumers and producers, I recognize that in many contexts, the clergy leading the local church will lack the detailed economic training to lead their congregants toward such changes. *Work Out Your Salvation* will not provide enough in the way of specific guidance for the local church. I hope it may suggest preliminary steps and perhaps even inspire others to develop the practical tools needed to implement market design through church work.

Where economics has aided the argument of this book, theology must play a more substantive role. Market design guided by experimental economics must be chastened by the realities of fallen humanity and by the recognition that only at the eschatological return of Christ to fully establish his Father's kingdom in the power of the Spirit will perfect justice exist in the created world. Yet Christians must continue to act in hope, recognizing the concurrent work of God in all our economic activities. Though the perils of individual and social sin are ever before us, so, too, is the grace of God, which works through common grace to benefit all humanity, even through markets. Through special grace, we come to see the providential work of the Father in markets, even as he mysteriously allows injustice to persist until the return of his Son. Thanks to special grace, Christians are in Christ, having been bestowed an identity through justification that is the basis for our good fruit, an identity that markets can either encourage or undermine. Further, it is in special grace that the Holy Spirit presents Christ to the church in word and sacrament, the means of grace, for the purpose of the sanctification of those who believe. Even so, markets can either hinder or encourage such sanctification.

So we are called to work out our salvation, yet never as those who hope to perfect ourselves or our markets through human effort. As G. C. Berkouwer remarks, "The progress of salvation never meant working out one's own salvation under one's own auspices; on the contrary, it meant working out one's own salvation with a rising sense of dependence on God's grace."[2] If the hope of improved markets that serve as better channels for God's common grace comes to fruition, then we can expect an even deeper sense of our dependence on the grace of the God who could improve on markets that are so often terribly broken: "For it is God who is at work in you, enabling you both to will and to work for his good pleasure" (Phil 2:13).

---

2 G. C. Berkouwer, *Faith and Sanctification*, trans. John Vriend (Grand Rapids, MI: Eerdmans, 1952), 112.

Bibliography

Akerlof, George A. "The Market for 'Lemons': Quality Uncertainty and the Market Mechanism." *Quarterly Journal of Economics* 84, no. 3 (August 1970): 488–500.

Akerlof, George A., and Rachel E. Kranton. *Identity Economics: How Our Identities Shape Our Work, Wages, and Well-Being*. Princeton, NJ: Princeton University Press, 2010.

Akerlof, George A., and Robert J. Shiller. *Phishing for Phools: The Economics of Manipulation and Deception*. Princeton, NJ: Princeton University Press, 2015.

Allen, Michael, and Scott R. Swain, eds. *Christian Dogmatics: Reformed Theology for the Catholic Church*. Grand Rapids, MI: Baker Academic, 2016.

Altman, Morris, ed. *Handbook of Contemporary Behavioral Economics: Foundations and Developments*. London: Routledge, 2006.

Ames, William. *The Marrow of Theology*. Translated by John Dykstra Eusden. Durham, NC: Labyrinth, 1968.

Ando, Amy W., and Donna Ramirez Harrington. "Tradable Discharge Permits: A Student-Friendly Game." *Journal of Economic Education* 37, no. 2 (Spring 2006): 187–201.

Anselm of Canterbury. *On Free Will*. In Davies and Evans, *Anselm of Canterbury*, 175–92.

———. *Why God Became a Man*. In Davies and Evans, *Anselm of Canterbury*, 260–356.

Aquinas, Thomas. *Summa Theologica*. 5 volumes. Translated by Fathers of the English Dominican province. Allen, TX: Christian Classics, 1981.

Archibald, G. C. *Information, Incentives, and the Economics of Control*. New York: Cambridge University Press, 2005.

Arendzen, J. P. *The Holy Trinity: A Theological Treatise for Modern Laymen*. New York: Sheed and Ward, 1937.

Ariely, Dan. *Predictably Irrational: The Hidden Forces That Shape Our Decisions*. Rev. ed. New York: HarperCollins, 2009.

Asch, Beth J., James C. Miller, III, and John T. Warner. "Economics and the All-Volunteer Military Force." In *Better Living through Economics*, edited by John J. Siegfried, 253–69. Cambridge: Harvard University Press, 2010.

Atherton, John. *Christianity and the Market: Christian Social Thought for Our Times*. London: SPCK, 1992.

Ayer, Alfred Jules. *Language, Truth and Logic*. London: Victor Gollancz, 1949.

Ayres, Ian. "Further Evidence of Discrimination in New Car Negotiations and Estimates of Its Cause." *Michigan Law Review* 94, no. 1 (Oct. 1995): 109–47.

Ayres, Ian, and Peter Siegelman. "Race and Gender Discrimination in Bargaining for a New Car." *American Economic Review* 85, no. 3 (June 1995): 304–21.

Ayres, Lewis. *Nicaea and Its Legacy: An Approach to Fourth-Century Trinitarian Theology*. Oxford: Oxford University Press, 2004.
Bac, J. Martin. *Perfect Will Theology: Divine Agency in Reformed Scholasticism as against Suárez, Episcopius, Descartes, and Spinoza*. Leiden: Brill, 2010.
Backhouse, Roger E. *The Puzzle of Modern Economics: Science or Ideology?* Cambridge: Cambridge University Press, 2010.
———. *Truth and Progress in Economic Knowledge*. Cheltenham, UK: Edward Elgar, 1997.
Baddeley, Michelle. *Behavioural Economics and Finance*. London: Routledge, 2013.
Baert, Stijn. "Field Experimental Evidence on Gender Discrimination in Hiring: Biased as Heckman and Siegelman Predicted?" *Economics: The Open-Access, Open-Assessment E-Journal*. Discussion Paper 2015-44, August 20, June 2015. http://www.economics-ejournal.org/economics/journalarticles/2015-25/.
Baker, Tom. "Health Insurance, Risk, and Responsibility after the Patient Protection and Affordable Care Act." *University of Pennsylvania Law Review* 159, no. 6 (June 2011): 1577–622.
Banuri, Sheheryar, and Catherine Eckel. "Experiments in Culture and Corruption: A Review." In *New Advances in Experimental Research on Corruption*, edited by Danilla Serra and Leonard Wantchekon, 51–76. Bingley, UK: Emerald Group, 2012.
Barnes, Kenneth J. *Redeeming Capitalism*. Grand Rapids, MI: Eerdmans, 2018.
Barnes, Michel René. *The Power of God: Δύναμις in Gregory of Nyssa's Trinitarian Theology*. Washington, DC: The Catholic University of America Press, 2001.
Barrera, Albino. *God and the Evil of Scarcity: Moral Foundations of Economic Agency*. Notre Dame, IN: University of Notre Dame Press, 2005.
Barrett, Matthew. "The Bondage and Liberation of the Will." In *Reformation Theology: A Systematic Summary*, edited by Matthew Barrett, 451–508. Wheaton, IL: Crossway, 2017.
Barth, Karl. *The Epistle to the Philippians*. Translated by James W. Leitch. Richmond, VA: John Knox, 1962.
Bartholomew, Craig G. *Contours of the Kuyperian Tradition: A Systematic Introduction*. Downers Grove, IL: IVP Academic, 2017.
Basu, Kaushik. *Prelude to Political Economy: A Study of the Social and Political Foundations of Economics*. Oxford: Oxford University Press, 2000.
Bauer, Michal, Julie Chytilová, and Barbara Pertold-Gebicka. "Parental Background and Other-Regarding Preferences in Children." *Experimental Economics* 17, no. 1 (2014): 24–46.
Bavinck, Herman. "Calvin and Common Grace." In *Calvin and the Reformation*, edited by William Park Armstrong, 99–130. Grand Rapids, MI: Baker, 1980.
———. "Common Grace." Translated by Raymond C. Van Leeuwen. *Calvin Theological Journal* 24, no. 1 (April 1989): 35–65.
———. *God and Creation*. Vol. 2 of *Reformed Dogmatics*, edited by John Bolt. Translated by John Vriend. Grand Rapids, MI: Baker Academic, 2004.
Bayer, Richard C. *Capitalism and Christianity: The Possibility of Christian Personalism*. Washington, DC: Georgetown University Press, 1999.
Beabout, Gregory, Ricardo F. Crespo, Kim Paffenroth, and Kyle Swan. *Beyond Self-Interest: A Personalist Approach to Human Action*. Lanham, MD: Lexington Books, 2002.
Beck, Andreas J. "Gisbertus Voetius (1589–1676): Basic Features of His Doctrine of

God." In van Asselt and Dekker, *Reformation and Scholasticism*, 205–26.
Becker, Gary S. *Economic Theory*. New York: Alfred A. Knopf, 1971.
Beckwith, Carl L. *The Holy Trinity*. Fort Wayne, IN: The Luther Academy, 2016.
Bell, Daniel M., Jr. *The Economy of Desire: Christianity and Capitalism in a Postmodern World*. Grand Rapids, MI: Baker Academic, 2012.
Berg, Natalie, and Miya Knights. *Amazon: How the World's Most Relentless Retailer Will Continue to Revolutionize Commerce*. 2nd ed. New York: Kogan Page, 2022.
Berger, Peter L., and Thomas Luckmann. *The Social Construction of Reality: A Treatise in the Sociology of Knowledge*. New York: Anchor, 1966.
Berkhof, Louis. *Systematic Theology*. 4th ed. Grand Rapids, MI: Eerdmans, 1941.
Berkouwer, G. C. *Faith and Sanctification*. Translated by John Vriend. Grand Rapids, MI: Eerdmans, 1952.
———. *Man: The Image of God*. Translated by Dirk W. Jellema. Grand Rapids, MI: Eerdmans, 1962.
Bernasek, Anna. *The Economics of Integrity: From Dairy Farmers to Toyota, How Wealth Is Built on Trust and What That Means for Our Future*. New York: HarperStudio, 2010.
Beretti, Antoine, Charles Figuières, and Gilles Grolleau. "How to Turn Crowding-Out into Crowding-In? An Innovative Instrument and Some Law-Related Examples." *European Journal of Law and Economics* 48 (August 2019): 417–38.
———. "Using Money to Motivate Both 'Saints' and 'Sinners': A Field Experiment on Motivational Crowding-Out." *Kylos* 66, no. 1 (Feb. 2013): 63–67.
Bertrand, Marianne, and Esther Duflo. "Field Experiments on Discrimination." National Bureau of Economic Research Working Paper 22014, February 2016. http://www.nber.org/papers/w22014/.
Blaug, Mark. *The Methodology of Economics: Or How Economists Explain*. 2nd ed. Cambridge: Cambridge University Press, 1992.
———. "Ugly Currents in Modern Economics." In *Fact and Fiction in Economics: Models, Realism, and Social Construction*, edited by Uskali Mäki, 35–56. Cambridge: Cambridge University Press, 2002.
Blomberg, Craig. *Neither Poverty nor Riches: A Biblical Theology of Possessions*. Downers Grove, IL: InterVarsity, 1999.
Boesak, Allan. *Black and Reformed: Apartheid, Liberation, and the Calvinist Tradition*. Maryknoll, NY: Orbis, 1986.
Boff, Clodovis. *Theology and Praxis: Epistemological Foundations*. Translated by Robert R. Barr. Maryknoll, NY: Orbis, 1978.
———. *Theology and Praxis: Epistemological Foundations*. Eugene, OR: Wipf and Stock, 2009.
Boff, Leonardo. *Faith on the Edge: Religion and Marginalized Existence*. San Francisco: Harper and Row, 1989.
———. "Trinity." In Ellacuría and Sobrino, *Mysterium Liberationis*, 389–404.
———. *Trinity and Society*. Translated by Paul Burns. Maryknoll, NY: Orbis, 1988.
Boff, Leonardo, and Clodovis Boff. *Introducing Liberation Theology*. Translated by Paul Burns. Maryknoll, NY: Orbis, 1988.
Bornstein, Gary. "A Classification of Games by Player Type." In *New Issues and Paradigms in Research on Social Dilemmas*, edited by Anders Biel, Daniel Eck, Tommy Gärling, and Mathias Gustafsson, 27–42. New York: Springer, 2008.

Bolt, John. *Economic Shalom: A Reformed Primer on Faith, Work, and Human Flourishing*. Grand Rapids, MI: Christian's Library Press, 2013.

Boot, Max. *The Savage Wars of Peace: Small Wars and the Rise of American Power*. New York: Basic Books, 2002.

Boulnois, Olivier. "From Divine Omnipotence to Operative Power." *Divus Thomas* 115, no. 2 (May/August 2012): 83–97.

Bowles, Samuel. "Policies Designed for Self-Interested Citizens May Undermine 'the Moral Sentiments': Evidence from Economic Experiments." *Science* 320, no. 5883 (June 20, 2008): 1605–9.

Brand, Chad, and Tom Pratt. *Seeking the City: Wealth, Poverty, and Political Economy in Christian Perspective*. Grand Rapids, MI: Kregel, 2013.

Bratt, James D. *Abraham Kuyper: Modern Calvinist, Christian Democrat*. Grand Rapids, MI: Eerdmans, 2013.

Brennan, H. Geoffrey. "The Impact of Theological Predispositions on Economics: A Commentary." In Brennan and Waterman, *Economics and Religion*, 163–77.

Brennan, H. Geoffrey, and A. M. C. Waterman, eds. *Economics and Religion: Are They Distinct?* Norwell, MA: Kluwer Academic, 1994.

Brennan, Jason. "Do Markets Corrupt?" In Baker and White, *Economics and the Virtues*, 236–56.

———. *Economics and the Virtues: Building a New Moral Foundation*. Edited by Jennifer A. Baker and Mark D. White. Oxford: Oxford University Press, 2016.

Brock, Cory C., and N. Gray Sutanto. *Neo-Calvinism: A Theological Introduction*. Bellingham, WA: Lexham, 2022.

Brown, Jennifer, and John Morgan. "Reputation in Online Auctions: The Market for Trust." *California Management Review* 49, no. 1 (Fall 2006): 61–81.

Bruni, Luigino. *The Wound and the Blessing: Economics, Relationships, and Happiness*. Translated by N. Michael Brennan. Hyde Park, NY: Hyde City Press, 2012.

Bryar, Colin, and Bill Carr. *Working Backwards: Insights, Stories, and Secrets from Inside Amazon*. New York: St. Martin's, 2021.

Bujo, Bénézet. *Foundations of an African Ethic: Beyond the Universal Claims of Western Morality*. Translated by Brian McNeil. New York: Herder and Herder, 2001.

Butler, Alexander W., Erik J. Mayer, and James P. Weston. "Racial Discrimination in the Auto Loan Market." Social Science Research Network Scholarly Paper. Rochester, NY: Social Science Research Network, March 31, 2021. https://files.consumerfinance.gov/f/documents/cfpb_mayer_racial-discrimination-in-the-auto-loan-market.pdf.

Butner, D. Glenn, Jr. *Jesus the Refugee: Ancient Injustice and Modern Solidarity*. Minneapolis: Fortress, 2023.

———. *The Son Who Learned Obedience: A Theological Case against the Eternal Submission of the Son*. Eugene, OR: Pickwick, 2018.

———. *Trinitarian Dogmatics: Exploring the Grammar of the Christian Doctrine of God*. Grand Rapids, MI: Baker Academic, 2022.

———. "The Trinity in the Theology of Economics." *Faith and Economics* 76 (Fall 2020): 29–42.

Callon, Michel. *The Laws of Markets*. Malden, MA: Blackwell, 1998.

———. "What Does It Mean to Say That Economics Is Performative?" In MacKenzie, Muniesa, and Siu, *Do Economists Make Markets?*, 311–57.

Calvin, John. *Commentaries on the First Book of Moses Called Genesis*. Translated by

John King. Grand Rapids, MI: Baker, 1979.

———. *Institutes of the Christian Religion*. Translated by Henry Beveridge. Peabody, MA: Hendrickson, 2008.

Campbell, Constantine R. *Paul and Union with Christ: An Exegetical and Theological Study*. Grand Rapids, MI: Zondervan, 2012.

Carlson, Allan C. *Third Ways: How Bulgarian Greens, Swedish Housewives, and Beer-Swilling Englishmen Created Family-Centered Economies—and Why They Disappeared*. Wilmington, DE: ISI, 2007.

Carlsson, Magnus, Luca Fumarco, and Dan-Olof Rooth. "Ethnic Discrimination in Hiring, Labour Market Tightness and the Business Cycle—Evidence from Field Experiments." *Applied Economics* 50, no. 24 (2018): 2652–63.

Carter, John R., and Michael D. Irons. "Are Economists Different, and If So, Why?" *Journal of Economic Perspectives* 5, no. 2 (Spring 1991): 171–77.

Cassar, Alessandra, Giovanna d'Adda, and Pauline Grosjean. "Institutional Quality, Culture, and Norms of Cooperation: Evidence from Behavioral Field Experiments." *Journal of Law and Economics* 57, no. 3 (August 2014): 821–63.

Cavanaugh, William T. *Being Consumed: Economics and Christian Desire*. Grand Rapids, MI: Eerdmans, 2008.

Chadwick, Henry. *The Early Church: The Story of the Emergent Christianity from the Apostolic Age to the Dividing of the Ways between the Greek East and the Latin West*. Rev. ed. New York: Penguin, 1993.

Chapman, Peter. *Bananas: How the United Fruit Company Shaped the World*. Edinburgh: Canongate, 2007.

Cheng, Patrick S. "A Three-Part Sinfonia: Queer Asian Reflections on the Trinity." *Journal of Race, Ethnicity, and Religion* 3, no. 2 (2012): 1–23.

Childs, Brevard S. *Biblical Theology of the Old and New Testaments: Theological Reflection in the Christian Bible*. Minneapolis: Fortress, 1992.

———. *The Book of Exodus*. Philadelphia: Westminster, 1974.

Choi, Seung Ginny, and Virgil Henry Storr. "Can Trust, Reciprocity, and Friendships Survive Contact with the Market?" In Baker and White, *Economics and the Virtues*, 217–35.

Chong, Siang Yew, Jan Humble, Graham Kendall, Jaiwei Li, and Xin Yao. "The Iterated Prisoner's Dilemma: 20 Years On." In *The Iterated Prisoner's Dilemma: 20 Years On*, edited by Siang Yew Chong, Xin Yao, and Graham Kendall, 1–22. Singapore: World Scientific Publishing, 2004.

Chua, Amy. *World on Fire: How Exporting Free Market Democracy Breeds Ethnic Hatred and Global Instability*. New York: Anchor, 2003.

Claar, Victor. "What I Wish Theologians Understood about Markets and the Economists Who Study Them." *Faith and Economics* 60 (Fall 2012): 32–39.

Clark, Charles M. A. "Foreword." In Bruni, *The Wound and the Blessing*.

Codina, Victor. "Sacraments." In Ellacuría and Sobrino, *Mysterium Liberationis*, 654–76.

Colander, David, and Huei-Chun Su. "Making Sense of Economists' Positive-Normative Distinction." *Journal of Economic Methodology* 22, no. 2 (June 2015): 157–70.

Connell, Erin M., and Kathryn G. Mantoan. "Mind the Gap: Pay Audits, Pay Transparency, and the Public Disclosure of Pay Data." *ABA Journal of Labor and Employment Law* 33, no. 1 (Fall 2017): 1–30.

Coolman, Boyd Taylor, and Dale M. Coulter, eds. *Trinity and Creation: A Selection of Works from Hugh, Richard and Adam of St. Victor*. Hyde Park, NY: New City Press, 2011.

Cooper, David J., and John H. Kagel. "Other-Regarding Preferences: A Selective Survey of Experimental Results." In *The Handbook of Experimental Economics*. Vol. 2, edited by John H. Kagel and Alvin E. Roth, 217–89. Princeton, NJ: Princeton University Press, 2015.

Côté, Stéphane, Julian House, and Robb Willer. "High Economic Inequality Leads Higher-Income Individuals to Be Less Generous." *Proceedings of the National Academy of Sciences of the United States of America* 112, no. 52 (December 29, 2015): 15838–43.

Crockett, Richard. *Thinking the Unthinkable: Think-Tanks and the Economic Counter-Revolution, 1931–1983*. London: HarperCollins, 1994.

Daly, Daniel J. "Structures of Virtue and Vice." *New Blackfriars* 92, no. 1039 (May 2011): 341–57.

Danner, Peter L. *The Economic Person: Acting and Analyzing*. Lanham, MD: Rowman and Littlefield, 2002.

Davies, Brian. *The Thought of Thomas Aquinas*. Oxford: Oxford University Press, 1992.

Davies, Brian, and G. R. Evans, eds. *Anselm of Canterbury: The Major Works*. Oxford: Oxford University Press, 1998.

Davis, John B. "Economists' Odd Stand on the Positive-Normative Distinction: A Behavioral Economics View." In *Oxford University Press Handbook on Professional Economic Ethics: Views from the Economics Profession and Beyond*, edited by G. DeMartino and D. McCloskey, 200–218. Oxford: Oxford University Press, 2015.

———. *Individuals and Identity in Economics*. New York: Cambridge University Press, 2011.

Davis, John B., and D. Wade Hands, eds. *The Elgar Companion to Recent Economic Methodology*. Northampton, MA: Edward Elgar, 2011.

De Caussade, Jean-Pierre. *Abandonment to Divine Providence*. Translated by John Beevers. New York: Doubleday, 1975.

De La Torre, Miguel A., and Edwin David Aponte. *Introducing Latino/a Theologies*. Maryknoll, NY: Orbis, 2001.

De Leeuw, Gawain. *The Body of Christ in a Market Economy: An Anglican Inquiry into Economic Thinking*. New York: Peter Lang, 2019.

De Lubac, Henri. *A Brief Catechesis on Nature and Grace*. Translated by Richard Arnandez. San Francisco: Ignatius, 1984.

———. *Catholicism: Christ and the Common Destiny of Man*. Translated by Lancelot C. Sheppard and Sister Elizabeth Englund. San Francisco: Ignatius Press, 1988.

———. *Surnaturel: Études historiques*. Paris: Desclée de Brouwer, 1946.

De Soto, Hernando. *The Mystery of Capital: Why Capitalism Triumphs in the West and Fails Everywhere Else*. New York: Basic, 2000.

De Swaan, J. C. *Seeking Virtue in Finance: Contributing to Society in a Conflicted Industry*. Cambridge: Cambridge University Press, 2020.

Deci, Edward L., Richard M. Ryan, and Richard Koestner. "A Meta-Analytic Review of Experiments Examining the Effects of Extrinsic Rewards on Intrinsic Motivation." *Psychological Bulletin* 125, no. 6 (1999): 627–68.

Dekker, Eef. "An Ecumenical Debate between Reformation and Counter-Reformation? Bellarmine and Ames on *liberum arbitrium*." In van Asselt and Dekker, *Reformation and Scholasticism*, 141–54.

Demarest, Bruce. *The Cross and Salvation: The Doctrine of Salvation*. Wheaton, IL: Crossway, 1997.

Dent, Martin, and Bill Peters. *The Crisis of Poverty and Debt in the Third World*. Brookfield, VT: Ashgate, 1999.
DeSilva, David A. *The Letter to the Galatians*. Grand Rapids, MI: Eerdmans, 2018.
Doherty, Sean. "The Kingdom of God and the Economic System: An Economics of Hope." In Kidwell and Doherty, *Theology and Economics*, 143–56.
Dolan, Edwin G. *Basic Economics*. 2nd ed. Hinsdale, IL: The Dryden Press, 1980.
Donohue-White, Patricia, Stephen J. Grabill, Christpher Westley, and Gloria Zúñiga. *Human Nature and the Discipline of Economics: Personalist Anthropology and Economic Methodology*. Lanham, MD: Lexington Books, 2002.
Doran, Robert M. *The Trinity in History: A Theology of the Divine Missions*. Vol. 1 of *Missions and Processions*. Toronto: University of Toronto Press, 2012.
Douma, Jochem. *Common Grace in Kuyper, Schilder, and Calvin: Exposition, Comparison, and Evaluation*. Edited by William Helder. Translated by Albert H. Oosterhoff. Hamilton: Lucerna, 2017.
Du Toit, Andre. "Puritans in Africa? Afrikaner 'Calvinism' and Kuyperian Neo-Calvinism in Late Nineteenth-Century South Africa." *Comparative Studies in Society and History* 27, no. 9 (April 1985): 209–40.
Dubois, Nicole. "Introduction: The Concept of a Norm." In *A Sociocognitive Approach to Social Norms*, edited by Nicole Dubois, 1–16. London: Routledge, 2002.
Dubow, Saul. "Afrikaner Nationalism, Apartheid, and the Conceptualization of 'Race.'" *Journal of African History* 33, no. 2 (1992): 209–37.
Dunn, James D. G. *The New Perspective on Paul: Collected Essays*. Tübingen: Mohr Siebeck, 2005.
———. *The Theology of Paul the Apostle*. Grand Rapids, MI: Eerdmans, 1998.
Dussel, Enrique D. "Theology of Liberation and Marxism." Translated by Robert Barr. In Ellacuría and Sobrino, *Mysterium Liberationis: Fundamental Concepts of Liberation Theology*, 85–102.
Eichrodt, Walther. *Theology of the Old Testament*. Vol. 2. Translated by J. A. Baker. Philadelphia: Westminster, 1967.
Eidem, Rolf, and Staffan Viotti. *Economic Systems: How Resources Are Allocated*. New York: John Wiley and Sons, 1978.
Ellacuría, Ignacio, and Jon Sobrino. *Mysterium Liberationis: Fundamental Concepts of Liberation Theology*. Maryknoll, NY: Orbis, 1993.
Ellerman, A. Danny. "Designing a Tradable Permit System to Control SO_2 Emissions in China: Principles and Practice." *Energy Journal* 23, no. 2 (2002): 1–26.
Elzinga, Kenneth G., and Daniel A. Crane. "Christianity and Antitrust: A Nexus." In *Christianity and Market Regulation: An Introduction*, edited by Daniel A. Crane and Samuel Gregg, 74–100. Cambridge: Cambridge University Press, 2001.
Emerson, Michael O., and Christian Smith. *Divided by Faith: Evangelical Religion and the Problem of Race in America*. Oxford: Oxford University Press, 2000.
Emery, Giles. *The Trinity: An Introduction to Catholic Doctrine on the Triune God*. Translated by Matthew Levering. Washington, DC: Catholic University of America Press, 2011.
Engel, Mary Potter. "Evil, Sin, and Violation of the Vulnerable." In *Lift Every Voice: Constructing Christian Theologies from the Underside,* edited by Susan Brooks Thistlethwaite and Mary Potter Engel, 152–64. San Francisco: Harper San Francisco, 1990.
Engelsma, David J. *Common Grace Revisited: A Response to Richard J. Mouw's He Shines in All That's Fair*. Grandville, MI: Reformed Free Publishing Association, 2003.

Enns, Peter. *Inspiration and Incarnation: Evangelicals and the Problem of the Old Testament*. Grand Rapids, MI: Baker Academic, 2005.

Erasmus, Desiderius. *On the Freedom of the Will: A Diatribe or Discourse*. In Rupp and Watson, *Luther and Erasmus*, 35–100.

Evans, David S., and Richard Schmalensee. *Matchmakers: The New Economics of Multisided Platforms*. Boston: Harvard Business Review Press, 2016.

Everhart, D. T. "Communal Reconciliation: Corporate Responsibility and Opposition to Systemic Sin." *International Journal of Systematic Theology* 25, no. 1 (January 2023): 134–56.

Finn, Daniel K. *The Moral Ecology of Markets: Assessing Claims about Markets and Justice*. Cambridge: Cambridge University Press, 2006.

Frank, Robert H., Thomas Gilovich, and Dennis T. Regan. "Does Studying Economics Inhibit Cooperation?" *Journal of Economic Perspectives* 7, no. 2 (Spring 1993): 159–71.

Friedman, Thomas L. *The World Is Flat: A Brief History of the Twenty-First Century*. 3rd ed. New York: Picador, 2007.

Gamble, Harry Y. *Books and Readers in the Early Church: A History of Early Christian Texts*. New Haven, CT: Yale University Press, 1995.

Giddens, Anthony. *The Consequences of Modernity*. Stanford, CA: Stanford University Press, 1990.

Gneezy, Uri, and Aldo Rustichini. "A Fine Is a Price." *Journal of Legal Studies* 29, no. 1 (January 2000): 1–17.

Goeree, Jacob K., Karen Palmer, Charles A. Holt, William Shobe, and Dallas Burtraw. "An Experimental Study of Auctions versus Grandfathering to Assign Pollution Permits." *Journal of the European Economic Association* 8, no. 2–3 (April–May 2010): 514–25.

Gold, Lorna. *New Financial Horizons: The Emergence of the Economy of Communion*. Hyde Park, NY: New City Press, 2010.

González Faus, José Ignacio. "Sin." In Sobrino and Ellacuría, *Systematic Theology*, 194–204.

González Fernández, Antonio. *God's Reign and the End of Empires*. Translated by Joseph V. Owens. Miami: Convivium, 2012.

González, Justo L. *A History of Christian Thought: From the Protestant Reformation to the Twentieth Century*. Rev. ed. Nashville, TN: Abingdon, 1987.

Goodchild, Philip. "Capitalism and Global Economics." In *The Cambridge Companion to Christian Political Theology*, edited by Craig Hovey and Elizabeth Phillips, 218–35. Cambridge: Cambridge University Press, 2015.

———. *Theology of Money*. Durham, NC: Duke University Press, 2009.

Goodwin, Neva, Julie A. Nelson, Frank Ackerman, and Thomas Weisskopf. *Microeconomics in Context*. 2nd ed. Amonk, NY: M. E. Sharpe, 2009.

Goodwin, Thomas. *The Work of the Holy Ghost in Our Salvation*. In *The Works of Thomas Goodwin*, vol. VI edited by Thomas Smith. Edinburgh: James Nichol, 1863.

Goold, William H., ed. *The Works of John Owen*. Vols. III and V. Philadelphia: Leighton Publications, 1862.

Gorman, Michael J. *Cruciformity: Paul's Narrative Spirituality of the Cross*. Grand Rapids, MI: Eerdmans, 2001.

———. *Inhabiting the Cruciform God: Kenosis, Justification, and Theosis in Paul's Narrative Soteriology*. Grand Rapids, MI: Eerdmans, 2009.

Gornall, Thomas. *A Philosophy of God: The Elements of Thomist Natural Theology*. London: Sheed and Ward, 1962.

Graafland, Johan J. *The Market, Happiness, and Solidarity: A Christian Perspective*. New York: Routledge, 2010.

Grant, Ruth W. *Strings Attached: Untangling the Ethics of Incentives*. Princeton, NJ: Princeton University Press, 2012.

Grant, W. Matthews. *Free Will and God's Universal Causality: The Dual Sources Account*. London: Bloomsbury, 2019.

Gregg, Samuel. *For God and Profit: How Banking and Finance Can Serve the Common Good*. New York: Crossroad, 2016.

Gregory of Nyssa. *An Answer to Ablabius: That We Should Not Think of Saying There Are Three Gods*. Edited and translated by Cyril C. Richardson. In *Christology of the Later Fathers*, edited by Edward R. Hardy, 256–67. Louisville: Westminster John Knox, 1954.

Grenz, Stanley J. *Rediscovering the Triune God: The Trinity in Contemporary Theology*. Minneapolis: Fortress, 2004.

Griffin, David Ray. *God, Power, and Evil: A Process Theodicy*. Philadelphia: Westminster, 1976.

Grimes, Katie Walker. *Antiblackness as Corporate Vice*. Minneapolis: Fortress, 2017.

Gronbacher, Gregory M. A. "The Humane Economy: Neither Right nor Left—A Response to Daniel Rush Finn." *Journal of Markets and Morality* 2, no. 2 (Fall 1999): 247–70.

———. "The Need for Economic Personalism." *Journal of Markets and Morality* 1, no. 1 (Spring 1998): 1–34.

Grundmann, Walter. "ἁμαρτάνω, ἁμάρτημα, ἁμαρτία." In *Theological Dictionary of the New Testament* vol. I, edited by Gerhard Kittel, translated by Geoffrey W. Bromiley, 267–316. Grand Rapids, MI: Eerdmans, 1964.

Gunton, Colin E. *The Promise of Trinitarian Theology*. Edinburgh: T & T Clark, 1991.

Haeringer, Guillaume. *Market Design: Auctions and Matching*. Cambridge: MIT Press, 2017.

Haight, Roger. "Sin and Grace." In *Systematic Theology: Roman Catholic Perspectives*, vol. 2, edited by Francis Schüssler Fiorenza and John P. Galvin, 75–142. Minneapolis: Fortress, 1991.

Hands, D. Wade. "The Positive-Normative Dichotomy and Economics." In *Philosophy of Economics*, edited by Uskali Mäki, 219–39. Amsterdam: Elsevier, 2012.

Hansen, G. Walter. *The Letter to the Philippians*. Grand Rapids, MI: Eerdmans, 2009.

Harper, Ian R., and Samuel Gregg, eds. *Christian Theology and Market Economics*. Northampton, MA: Edward Elgar, 2008.

Harper, Ian R., and Eric L. Jones. "Treating 'Affluenze': the Moral Challenge of Affluence." In Harper and Gregg, *Christian Theology and Market Economics*, 146–63.

Harrington, Daniel J., and James F. Keenan. *Paul and Virtue Ethics: Building Bridges between New Testament Studies and Moral Theology*. Lanham, MD: Rowman and Littlefield, 2010.

Hauerwas, Stanley, and Samuel Wells, eds. *The Blackwell Companion to Christian Ethics*. Malden: MA: Blackwell, 2006.

Hauerwas, Stanley, and Samuel Wells. "Christian Ethics as Informed Prayer." In Hauerwas and Wells, *The Blackwell Companion to Christian Ethics*, 3–12.

———. "How the Church Managed before There Was Ethics." In Hauerwas and Wells, *The Blackwell Companion to Christian Ethics*, 39–50.

———. "The Gift of the Church and the Gifts God Gives It." In Hauerwas and Wells, *The Blackwell Companion to Christian Ethics*, 13–27.

———. "Why Christian Ethics Was Invented." In Hauerwas and Wells, *The Blackwell Companion to Christian Ethics*, 28–38.

Hay, Donald A. "On Being a Christian Economist." In *Christianity and the Culture of Economics*, edited by Donald A. Hay and Alan Kreider, 166–90. Cardiff: University of Wales Press, 2001.

Hays, Richard B. *The Moral Vision of the New Testament: A Contemporary Introduction to New Testament Ethics*. New York: Harper Collins, 1996.

Heckman, James J. "Detecting Discrimination." *Journal of Economic Perspectives* 12, no. 2 (Spring 1998): 101–16.

Heckman, James J., and Peter Siegelman. "The Urban Institute Audit Studies: Their Methods and Findings." In *Clear and Convincing Evidence: Measurement of Discrimination in America*, edited by Michael Fix and Raymond J. Struyk, 187–258. Washington, DC: Urban Institute, 1993.

Henkel-Rieger, Rosemarie. "Deep Solidarity: A Pre-requisite to Resisting Capitalism and Building Economic Democracy." In *Faith, Class, and Labor: Intersectional Approaches in a Global Context*, edited by Jin Young Choi and Joerg Rieger, 185–211. Eugene, OR: Pickwick, 2020.

Henrich, Joseph, Robert Boyd, Samuel Bowles, Colin Camerer, Ernst Fehr, Herbert Gentis, and Richard McElreath. "In Search of *Homo Economicus*: Behavioral Experiments in Fifteen Small Scale Societies." *American Economic Review* 91, no. 2 (May 2001): 73–78.

Herzberg, Frederick. "One More Time: How Do You Motivate Employees?" *Harvard Business Review* 46, no. 1 (January/February 1968): 53–62.

Heyes, Anthony. "The Economics of Vocation or 'Why Is a Badly Paid Nurse a Good Nurse'?" *Journal of Health Economics* 24, no. 3 (May 2005): 561–69.

Hill, Daniel Lee, and Ty Kieser. "Social Sin and the Sinless Savior: Delineating Supra-Personal Sin in Continuity with Conciliar Christology." *Modern Theology* 38, no. 3 (July 2022): 568–91.

Hirschman, Albert O. "Rival Interpretations of Market Society: Civilizing, Destructive, or Feeble?" *Journal of Economic Literature* 20, no. 4 (December 1982): 1463–84.

Hodge, Charles. *Systematic Theology*. 3 vols. Grand Rapids, MI: Eerdmans, 1940.

Holm, Petter. "Which Way Is Up on Callon?" In MacKenzie, Muniesa, and Siu, *Do Economists Make Markets?*, 225–43.

Holmes, Stephen R. *The Quest for the Trinity: The Doctrine of God in Scripture, History, and Modernity*. Downers Grove, IL: IVP Academic, 2012.

Hubbard, Timothy P., and Harry J. Paarsch. *Auctions*. Cambridge: MIT Press, 2015.

Hübner, Jamin. "Owning Up to It: Why Cooperatives Create the Humane Economy Our World Needs." *Faith and Economics* 76, no. 2 (Fall 2020): 133–208.

Hugh of St. Victor. *On the Three Days*. In Coolman and Coulter, *Trinity and Creation: A Selection of Works from Hugh, Richard and Adam of St. Victor*, 49–102.

Hume, David. *A Treatise of Human Nature*. 2nd ed. Edited by L. A. Selby-Bigge. Oxford: Clarendon Press, 1978.

Hunsinger, George. "Justification and Mystical Union with Christ: Where Does Owen Stand?" In *The Ashgate Research Companion to John Owen's Theology*, edited by Kelly M. Kapic and Mark Jones, 199–211. New York: Routledge, 2016.

Hunter, James Davison. *To Change the World: The Irony, Tragedy, and Possibility of Christianity in the Late Modern World*. Oxford: Oxford University Press, 2010.

Hutchings, Jonathan F. *Project Scheduling Handbook*. New York: Marcel Dekker, 2004.

Insko, Chester A., and John Schopler. "Categorization, Competition, and Collectivity." In *Group Processes*, edited by Clyde Hendrick, 213–51. Newbury Park, CA: Sage Publications, 1987.

Johnson, Kelly S. "Praying: Poverty." In Hauerwas and Wells, *The Blackwell Companion to Christian Ethics*, 225–36.

Johnson, Richard R. "Ancient and Medieval Accounts of the 'Invention' of Parchment." *California Studies in Classical Antiquity* 3 (1970): 115–22.

The Joint Declaration on the Doctrine of Justification. Accessed August 29, 2023. https://www.lutheranworld.org/sites/default/files/2022-02/joint_declaration_2019_en.pdf.

Juselius, Katarina. "On the Role of Theory and Evidence in Macroeconomics." In Davis and Hands, *The Elgar Companion to Recent Economic Methodology*, 404–36.

Karlan, Dean, and Jacob Appel. *More than Good Intentions: How a New Economics Is Helping Solve Global Poverty*. New York: Dutton, 2011.

Keen, Karen R. *The Word of a Humble God: The Origins, Inspiration, and Interpretation of Scripture*. Grand Rapids, MI: Eerdmans, 2022.

Keener, Craig S. *The Gospel of John: A Commentary*. 2 vols. Grand Rapids, MI: Baker Academic, 2003.

Kelly, Conor M. "The Nature and Operation of Structural Sin: Additional Insights from Theology and Moral Psychology." *Theological Studies* 80, no. 2 (June 2019): 293–327.

Kerr, Suzi, James Sanchirico, and Richard Newell. "Fishing Quota Markets." *Journal of Environmental Economics and Management* 49, no. 3 (May 2005): 437–62.

Kidwell, Jeremy, and Sean Doherty, eds. *Theology and Economics: A Christian Vision of the Common Good*. New York: Palgrave MacMillan, 2015.

Kilby, Karen. "Perichoresis and Projection: Problems with Social Doctrines of the Trinity." *New Blackfriars* 81, no. 956 (2000): 432–45.

Kirkpatrick, Frank G. *The Mystery and Agency of God: Divine Being and Acting in the World*. Minneapolis: Fortress, 2014.

Kolb, Robert W. *Too Much Is Not Enough: Incentives in Executive Compensation*. Oxford: Oxford University Press, 2012.

Kuyper, Abraham. *Calvinism: Six Stone Foundation Lectures*. Grand Rapids, MI: Eerdmans, 1943.

———. *Common Grace: God's Gifts for a Fallen World*. Edited by Jordan J. Ballor and Stephen J. Grabill. Translated by Nelson D. Kloosterman and Ed M. van der Maas. Bellingham, WA: Lexham Press, 2019.

———. *Our Program: A Christian Political Manifesto*. Translated and edited by Harry Van Dyke. Bellingham, WA: Lexham, 2015.

———. *The South-African Crisis*. 4th ed. Translated by A. E. Fletcher. London: Stop the War Committee, 1900.

LaCugna, Catherine Mowry. *God for Us: The Trinity and Christian Life*. New York: HarperCollins, 1991.

Landy, Marc K., and Martin A. Levin. "Creating Competitive Markets: The Politics of Market Design." In Landy, Levin, and Shapiro, *Creating Competitive Markets*, 1–22.

Landy, Marc K., Martin A. Levin, and Martin Shapiro, eds. *Creating Competitive Markets: The Politics of Regulatory Reform*. Washington, DC: Brookings Institution Press, 2007.

Lane, Jan-Erik, and Svante Ersson. *Comparative Political Economy*. London: Pinter Publishers, 1990.

Lane, Robert E. *The Market Experience*. Cambridge: Cambridge University Press, 1991.

Lee, Hak Joon. *Christian Ethics: A New Covenant Model*. Grand Rapids, MI: Eerdmans, 2021.

Lefevre, Jürgen. "The EU Greenhouse Gas Emission Allowance Trading Scheme." In *Climate Change and Carbon Markets: A Handbook of Emission Reduction Mechanisms*, edited by Farhana Yamin, 75–150. New York: Earthscan, 2005.

Litan, Robert E. *Trillion Dollar Economists: How Economists and Their Ideas Have Transformed Business*. Hoboken, NJ: John Wiley and Sons, 2014.

Lobel, Orly. "Knowledge Pays: Reversing Information Flows and the Future of Pay Equity." *Columbia Law Review* 120, no. 3 (April 2020): 547–612.

Long, D. Stephen. *Divine Economy: Theology and the Market*. New York: Routledge, 2000.

Long, D. Stephen, and Nancy Ruth Fox, with Tripp York. *Calculated Futures: Theology, Ethics, and Economics*. Waco, TX: Baylor University Press, 2007.

Long, D. Stephen, and Tripp York. "Remembering: Offering Our Gifts." In Hauerwas and Wells, *The Blackwell Companion to Christian Ethics*, 332–45.

Lunn, John, and Robin Klay. "The Neoclassical Economic Model in a Postmodern World." *Christian Scholars Review* 24, no. 2 (1994): 143–62.

Luther, Martin. *On the Bondage of the Will*. In Rupp and Watson, *Luther and Erasmus*, 101–334.

Macaskill, Grant. *Union with Christ in the New Testament*. Oxford: Oxford University Press, 2013.

MacGillis, Alec. *Fulfillment: Winning and Losing in One-Click America*. New York: Farrar, Straus and Giroux, 2021.

MacKenzie, Donald. *An Engine, Not a Camera: How Financial Models Shape Markets*. Cambridge: The MIT Press, 2006.

Mackenzie, Donald, and Yuval Millo. "Constructing a Market, Performing Theory: The Historical Sociology of a Financial Derivatives Exchange." *American Journal of Sociology* 109, no. 1 (July 2003): 107–45.

MacKenzie, Donald, Fabian Muniesa, and Lucia Siu, eds. *Do Economists Make Markets?* Princeton, NJ: Princeton University Press, 2007.

Maital, Shlomo. "Moral Sentiments: Behavioral Economics and the Ethical Foundations of Capitalism." In Altman, *Handbook of Contemporary Behavioral Economics*, 202–17.

Malkiel, Burton G. *A Random Walk Down Wall Street: Including a Life-Cycle Guide to Personal Investing*. New York: Norton, 1990.

Marmot, Michael. *The Health Gap: The Challenge of an Unequal World*. New York: Bloomsbury, 2015.

Martin, Roderick. *Constructing Capitalisms: Transforming Business Systems in Central and Eastern Europe*. Oxford: Oxford University Press, 2013.

Marwell, Gerald, and Ruth E. Ames. "Economists Free Ride, Does Anyone Else? Experiments on the Provision of Public Goods, IV." *Journal of Public Economics* 15 (1981): 295–310.

Masters, Stanley H. "The Social Debt to Blacks: A Case for Affirmative Action." In *The Wealth of Races: The Present Value of Benefits from Past Injustices*, edited by Richard F. America, 179–89. New York: Greenwood Press, 1990.

Mattison, William C., III. *Introducing Moral Theology: True Happiness and the Virtues*. Grand Rapids, MI: Brazos, 2008.

McCloskey, Deirdre N. *The Bourgeois Virtues: Ethics for an Age of Commerce*. Chicago: University of Chicago Press, 2006.

McGuigan, Nicola, Ruth Fisher, and Rory Glasgow. "The Influence of Receiver Status on Donor Prosociality in 6- to 11-Year-Old Children." *Child Development* 87, no. 3 (May/June 2016): 855–69.

McMillan, John. *Reinventing the Bazaar*. New York: Norton, 2002.

McRorie, Christina. "Markets as Moral Contexts: An Account Based in Catholic Theological Anthropology." In *Democracy, Religion, and Commerce: Private Markets and the Public Regulation of Religion*, edited by Kathleen Flake and Nathan B. Oman, 162–76. London: Routledge, 2023.

———. "Rethinking Moral Agency in Markets: A Book Discussion of Behavioral Economics." *Journal of Religious Ethics* 44, no. 1 (March 2016): 195–206.

Médaille, John C. *Toward a Truly Free Market: A Distributist Perspective on the Role of Government, Taxes, Health Care, Deficits, and More*. Wilmington, DE: ISI Books, 2010.

Meeks, M. Douglas. *God the Economist: The Doctrine of God and Political Economy*. Minneapolis: Fortress, 1989.

Menzies, Gordon. "Economics as Identity." In Harper and Gregg, *Christian Theology and Market Economics*, 94–109.

Milbank, John. *Theology and Social Theory: Beyond Secular Reason*. 2nd ed. Malden, MA: Blackwell, 2006.

Miller, D. T. "The Norm of Self-Interest." *American Psychologist* 54, no. 12 (December 1999): 1053–60.

Miller, Vincent J. *Consuming Religion: Christian Faith and Practice in a Consumer Culture*. New York: Continuum, 2004.

Mirowski, Philip, and Edward Nik-Khah. "Markets Made Flesh: Performativity, and a Problem in Science Studies, Augmented with Consideration of the FCC Auctions." In MacKenzie, Muniesa, and Siu, *Do Economists Make Markets?*, 190–224.

Moltmann, Jürgen. *The Trinity and the Kingdom*. Translated by Margaret Kohl. San Francisco: Harper and Row Publishers, 1981.

Morton, Fiona Scott, Florian Zettelmeyer, and Jorge Silva-Risso. "Consumer Information and Discrimination: Does the Internet Affect the Pricing of New Cars to Women and Minorities?" *Quantitative Marketing and Economics* 1 (2003): 65–92.

Mouw, Richard J. "Calvin's Legacy for Public Theology." *Political Theology* 10, no. 3 (2009): 431–46.

Muller, Richard A. *Divine Will and Human Choice: Freedom, Contingency, and Necessity in Early Modern Reformed Thought*. Grand Rapids, MI: Baker, 2017.

Nelson, Julie A. *Economics for Humans*. Chicago: University of Chicago Press, 2010.

Nelson, Julie A., and Nancy Folbre. "Why a Well-Paid Nurse Is a Better Nurse." *Nursing Economics* 24, no. 3 (May–June 2006): 127–30.

Nelson, Derek R. *What's Wrong with Sin? Sin in Individual and Social Perspective from Schleiermacher to Theologies of Liberation*. London: T & T Clark, 2009.

Nelson, Robert H. *Economics as Religion: From Samuelson to Chicago and Beyond*. University Park: Pennsylvania State University Press, 2001.

Neumark, David, and Judith Rich. "Do Field Experiments on Labor and Housing Markets Overestimate Discrimination? A Re-Examination of the Evidence." *ILR Review* 72, no. 1 (January 2019): 223–52.

Noronha, Ernesto, and Premilla D'Cruz. *Employee Identity in Indian Call Centers: The Notion of Professionalism*. Los Angeles: Response, 2009.

Novak, Michael. "Seven Theological Facets." In *Capitalism and Socialism*, edited by Michael Novak, 109–23. Washington, DC: American Enterprise Institute for Public Policy Research, 1978.

———. *The Spirit of Democratic Capitalism*. Lanham, MD: Madison Books, 1991.

O'Boyle, Edward J. *Personalist Economics: Moral Convictions, Economic Realities, and Social Action*. Boston: Kluwer Academic Publishers, 1998.

———. "Requiem for *Homo Economicus*." *Journal of Markets and Morality* 10, no. 2 (Fall 2007): 321–37.

O'Donovan, Oliver. *Resurrection and Moral Order: An Outline for Evangelical Ethics*. Grand Rapids, MI: Eerdmans, 1986.

———. "Sanctification and Ethics." In *Sanctification: Explorations in Theology and Practice*, edited by Kelly M. Kapic, 150–66. Downers Grove, IL: InterVarsity, 2014.

O'Neill, Richard, and Udi Helman. "Regulatory Reform of the US Wholesale Electricity Markets." In Landy, Levin, and Shapiro, *Creating Competitive Markets*, 128–57.

Osborne, Martin J. *An Introduction to Game Theory*. New York: Oxford University Press, 2004.

Overby, Eric, and Sabyasachi Mitra. "Physical and Electronic Wholesale Markets: An Empirical Analysis of Product Sorting and Market Function." *Journal of Management Information Systems* 31, no. 2 (Fall 2014): 11–45.

Owen, John. *The Doctrine of Justification by Faith*. In Goold, *The Works of John Owen*. Vol. V.

———. *The Holy Spirit: His Gifts and Power*. Grand Rapids, MI: Kregel, 1954.

———. *On the Holy Spirit, Part I*. In Goold, *The Works of John Owen*—. Vol. III.

Palmer, Phoebe. *Entire Devotion to God*. In *Phoebe Palmer: Selected Writings*, edited by Thomas C. Oden, 185–207. New York: Paulist, 1988.

Pemberton, Prentiss L., and Daniel Rush Finn. *Toward a Christian Economic Ethic: Stewardship and Social Power*. Minneapolis: Winston Press, 1985.

Pérez Henríquez, Blas Luis. *Environmental Commodities Markets and Emissions Trading: Towards a Low-Carbon Future*. New York: Routledge, 2013.

Petrella, Ivan. *The Future of Liberation Theology: An Argument and a Manifesto*. Burlington, VT: Ashgate, 2004.

Phelps, Edmund S. "The Statistical Theory of Racism and Sexism." *American Economic Review* 62, no. 4 (September 1972): 659–61.

Piff, Paul K., Daniel M. Stancato, Stéphane Côté, Rodolfo Mendoza-Denton, and Dacher Keltner. "Having Less, Giving More: The Influence of Social Class on Prosocial Behavior." *Journal of Personality and Social Psychology* 99, no. 5 (2010): 771–84.

Piff, Paul K., Michael W. Kraus, Stéphane Côté, Bonnie Hayden Cheng, and Dacher Keltner. "Higher Social Class Predicts Increased Unethical Behavior." *Proceedings of the National Academy of Sciences of the United States of America* 109, no. 11 (March 13, 2012): 4086–91.

Plantinga, Alvin. *God and Other Minds: A Study of the Rational Justification of Belief in God*. Ithaca, NY: Cornell University Press, 1967.

Plantinga, Cornelius, Jr. *Not the Way It's Supposed to Be: A Breviary of Sin*. Grand Rapids, MI: Eerdmans, 1995.

Pollitt, Michael G. "What Do Theologians Need to Know about Economics?" In Kidwell and Doherty, *Theology and Economics*, 27–46.

Pope, Devin G., and Justin R. Sydnor. "What's in a Picture? Evidence of Discrimination from Prosper.com." *Journal of Human Resources* 46, no. 1 (January 2011): 53–92.

Prestige, G. L. *God in Patristic Thought*. 2nd ed. London: SPCK, 1952.

Putnam, Hilary. *The Collapse of the Fact/Value Dichotomy and Other Essays*. Cambridge: Harvard University Press, 2002.

Radin, Margaret Jane. *Contested Commodities: The Trouble with Trade in Sex, Children, Body Parts, and Other Things*. Cambridge: Harvard University Press, 1996.

Ragazzi, Maurizio. "The Concept of Social Sin in Its Thomistic Roots." *Journal of Markets and Morality* 7, no. 2 (Fall 2004): 363–408.

Rahner, Karl. *Foundations of Christian Faith: An Introduction to the Idea of Christianity*. New York: Seabury, 1978.

Rasell, Edith. *The Way of Abundance: Economic Justice in Scripture and Society*. Minneapolis: Fortress, 2022.

Ray, Stephen. "Structural Sin." In *T & T Clark Companion to the Doctrine of Sin*, edited by Keith L. Johnson and David Lauber, 417–32. London: Bloomsbury T & T Clark, 2016.

Reddie, Anthony G. *Black Theology in Transatlantic Dialogue*. New York: Palgrave Macmillan, 2006.

Reynolds, John. "Investment Banking: The Inevitable Triumph of Incentives Over Ethics." In *Crisis and Recovery: Ethics, Economics and Justice*, edited by Rowan Williams and Larry Elliott, 123–46. New York: Palgrave Macmillan, 2010.

Rieger, Joerg. *No Rising Tide: Theology, Economics, and the Future*. Minneapolis: Fortress, 2009.

Rice, Lisa, and Erich Schwartz Jr. "Discrimination When Buying a Car: How the Color of Your Skin Can Affect Your Car-Shopping Experience." National Fair Housing Alliance, January 2018. https://nationalfairhousing.org/wp-content/uploads/2018/01/Discrimination-When-Buying-a-Car-FINAL-1-11-2018.pdf.

Richard of St. Victor. *On the Trinity*. In Coolman and Coulter, *Trinity and Creation*, 195–382.

Richards, Jay W. *Money, Greed, and God: Why Capitalism Is the Solution and Not the Problem*. New York: Harper Collins, 2009.

Rittenhouse, Bruce P. *Shopping for Meaningful Lives: The Religious Motive of Consumerism*. Eugene, OR: Cascade Books, 2013.

Robbins, Lionel. *An Essay on the Nature and Significance of Economic Science*. London: Macmillan, 1932.

———. "Interpersonal Comparisons of Utility: A Comment." *Economic Journal* 48 (1938): 625–41.

Rollston, Christopher A. *Writing and Literacy in the World of Ancient Israel: Epigraphic Evidence from the Iron Age*. Atlanta: Society of Biblical Literature, 2010.

Rommen, Edward. *Get Real: On Evangelism in the Late Modern World*. Pasadena, CA: William Carey, 2010.

Rosefielde, Steven. *Comparative Economic Systems: Culture, Wealth, and Power in the 21st Century*. Malden, MA: Blackwell, 2002.

Roth, Alvin E. "The Art of Designing Markets." *Harvard Business Review* 85, no. 10 (October 2007): 118–26.

———. *Who Gets What—and Why? The New Economics of Matchmaking and Market Design*. Boston: Houghton Mifflin, 2015.

Roth, Timothy P. *The Present State of Consumer Theory: The Implications for Social Welfare Theory*. 3rd ed. Lanham, MD: University Press of America, 1998.

Rothstein, Richard. *The Color of Law: A Forgotten History of How Our Government Segregated America*. New York: Liveright, 2017.

Sachs, Jeffrey D. *The End of Poverty: Economic Possibilities for Our Time*. New York: Penguin, 2005.

Salant, David J. *A Primer on Auction Design, Management, and Strategy*. Cambridge: MIT Press, 2014.

Salehnejad, Reza. *Rationality, Bounded Rationality and Microfoundations: Foundations of Theoretical Economics*. New York: Palgrave Macmillan, 2007.

Samuelson, Paul Anthony. *Foundations of Economic Analysis*. Cambridge: Harvard University Press, 1947.

Sanders, Fred. *The Triune God*. Grand Rapids, MI: Zondervan, 2016.

Santelli, Anthony J., Jr., Jeffrey Sikkenga, Robert A. Sirico, Steven Yates, and Gloria Zúñiga. *The Free Person and the Free Economy: A Personalist View of Market Economics*. Lanham, MD: Lexington Books, 2002.

Santos, Ana. "Experimental Economics." In Davis and Hands, *The Elgar Companion to Recent Economic Methodology*, 39–60.

Schlefer, Jonathan. *The Assumptions Economists Make*. Cambridge: Harvard University Press, 2012.

Schmid, Hans Bernhard. "Beyond Self-Goal Choice: Amartya Sen's Analysis of the Structure of Commitment and the Role of Shared Desires." In *Rationality and Commitment*, edited by Fabienne Peter and Hans Bernhard Schmid, 211–26. New York: Oxford University Press, 2007.

Schnitzer, Martin C., and James W. Nordyke. *Comparative Economic Systems*. 3rd ed. Cincinnati: South-Western Publishing, 1983.

Schreiner, Thomas R. *Paul, Apostle of God's Glory in Christ: A Pauline Theology*. Downers Grove, IL: IVP Academic, 2001.

Scott, Margaret. *The Eucharist and Social Justice*. New York: Paulist, 2009.

Searle, John R. *The Construction of Social Reality*. New York: The Free Press, 1995.

Sen, Amartya K. *The Idea of Justice*. Cambridge: Harvard University Press, 2009.

———. *On Ethics and Economics*. New York: Basil Blackwell, 2007.

———. "Rational Fools: A Critique of the Behavioral Foundations of Economic Theory." *Philosophy and Public Affairs* 6, no. 4 (Summer 1977): 317–44.

Skaff, Jeffrey. "Common Grace and the Ends of Creation in Abraham Kuyper and Herman Bavinck." *Journal of Reformed Theology* 9, no. 1 (2015): 3–18.

Smith, James K. A. *Desiring the Kingdom: Worship, Worldview, and Cultural Formation*. Grand Rapids, MI: Baker Academic, 2009.

———. "The 'Ecclesial Critique' of Globalization: Rethinking the Questions." *Faith and Economics* 56 (Fall 2010): 5–19.
———. *Imagining the Kingdom: How Worship Works*. Grand Rapids, MI: Baker Academic, 2013.
———. *You Are What You Love: The Spiritual Power of Habit*. Grand Rapids, MI: Brazos, 2016.
Soares-Prabhu, George M. *The Dharma of Jesus*. Edited by Francis X. D'Sa. Maryknoll, NY: Orbis, 2003.
Sobrino, Jon. "Central Position of the Reign of God in Theology." In Sobrino and Ellacuría, *Systematic Theology*, 38–74.
———. *Spirituality of Liberation: Toward Political Holiness*. Translated by Robert R. Barr. Maryknoll, NY: Orbis, 1988.
———. *The True Church and the Poor*. Translated by Matthew J. O'Connell. Maryknoll, NY: Orbis, 1999.
Sobrino, John, and Ignacio Ellacuría, eds. *Systematic Theology: Perspectives from Liberation Theology*. Translated by Robert R. Barr. Maryknoll, NY: Orbis, 1996.
Song, Robert. "Sharing Communion: Hunger, Food, and Genetically Modified Foods." In Hauerwas and Wells, *The Blackwell Companion to Christian Ethics*, 388–400.
Sönmez, Tayfun, and M. Utku Ünver. "Market Design for Kidney Exchange." In *The Handbook of Market Design*, edited by Nir Vulkan, Alvin E. Roth, and Zvika Neeman, 93–137. Oxford: Oxford University Press, 2013.
Sontheimer, Kevin. "Behavioral versus Neoclassical Economics: Paradigm Shift or Generalization?" In Altman, *Handbook of Contemporary Behavioral Economics*, 237–56.
Sowell, Thomas. *Race and Culture: A Worldview*. New York: Basic, 1994.
Stackhouse, Max L. *Globalization and Grace: A Christian Public Theology for a Global Future*. New York: Continuum, 2007.
Stapleford, John E. *Bulls, Bears, and Golden Calves: Applying Christian Ethics in Economics*. Downers Grove, IL: InterVarsity, 2002.
Steiner, Jürg. *Conscience in Politics: An Empirical Investigation of Swiss Decision Cases*. New York: Garland, 1996.
Stiglitz, Joseph E. *Making Globalization Work*. New York: Norton, 2007.
Stone, Brad. *The Everything Store: Jeff Bezos and the Age of Amazon*. New York: Little, Brown and Company, 2013.
Strom, Mark. *Reframing Paul: Conversations in Grace and Community*. Downers Grove, IL: InterVarsity, 2000.
Stump, Eleonore. "Augustine on Free Will." In *The Cambridge Companion to Augustine*, edited by Eleonore Stump and Norman Kretzmann, 124–47. Cambridge: Cambridge University Press, 2001.
Swain, Scott. R. "Divine Trinity." In Allen and Swain, *Christian Dogmatics*, 78–106.
Sung, Jung Mo. *Desire, Market, and Religion*. London, SCM Press, 2007.
———. *The Subject, Capitalism, and Religion: Horizons of Hope in Complex Societies*. New York: Palgrave Macmillan, 2011.
Tanner, Kathryn. *Christianity and the New Spirit of Capitalism*. New Haven, CT: Yale University Press, 2019.
———. *Economy of Grace*. Minneapolis: Fortress, 2005.

BIBLIOGRAPHY

———. *God and Creation in Christian Theology: Tyranny or Empowerment?* Minneapolis: Fortress, 1988.
———. "Human Freedom, Human Sin, and God the Creator." In Tracy, *The God Who Acts*, 111–35.
———. "Is God in Charge? Creation and Providence." In *Essentials of Christian Theology*, edited by William C. Placher, 116–31. Louisville, KY: Westminster John Knox, 2003.
———. *Jesus, Humanity, and the Trinity: A Brief Systematic Theology*. Minneapolis: Fortress, 2001.
Taylor, Charles. *Sources of the Self: The Making of Modern Identity*. Cambridge: Harvard University Press, 1989.
Taylor, Keeanga-Yamahtta. *Race for Profit: How Banks and the Real Estate Industry Undermined Black Homeownership*. Chapel Hill: University of North Carolina Press, 2019.
Thaler, Richard H. *Misbehaving: The Making of Behavioral Economics*. New York: Norton, 2015.
Thielicke, Helmut. *Foundations*. Vol. 1 of *Theological Ethics*, edited by William H. Lazareth. Grand Rapids, MI: Eerdmans, 1966.
Thomas, June Manning. *Redevelopment and Race: Planning a Finer City in Postwar Detroit*. Detroit: Wayne State University Press, 2013.
Thompson, James W. *Moral Formation According to Paul: The Context and Coherence of Pauline Ethics*. Grand Rapids, MI: Baker Academic, 2011.
Tiemstra, John P., W. Fred Graham, George N. Monsma Jr., Carl J. Sinke, and Alan Storkey. *Reforming Economics: Calvinist Studies on Methods and Institutions*. Lewiston, NY: Edwin Mellen Press, 1990.
Torrance, Thomas F. *The Christian Doctrine of God: One Being, Three Persons*. London: T & T Clark, 1996.
Tracy, Thomas F. "Divine Action, Created Causes, and Human Freedom." In Tracy, *The God Who Acts*, 77–102.
Tracy, Thomas F., ed. *The God Who Acts: Philosophical and Theological Explorations*. University Park: Pennsylvania State University Press, 1994.
Turretin, Francis. *Institutes of Elenctic Theology*. Translated by George Musgrave Giger. Three vos. Edited by James T. Dennison Jr. Philipsburg, NJ: P and R, 1992.
Tutu, Desmond. "Spirituality: Christian and African." In *Resistance and Hope: South African Essays in Honour of Beyers Naudé*, edited by Charles Villa-Vicencio and John W. De Gruchy, 159–64. Grand Rapids, MI: Eerdmans, 1985.
Tversky, Amos, and Daniel Kahneman. "The Framing of Decisions and the Psychology of Choice." *Science* New Series 211, no. 4481 (January 30, 1981): 453–58.
Van Asselt, Willem J., J. Martin Bac, and Roelf T. te Velde. *Reformed Thought on Freedom: The Concept of Free Choice in Early Modern Reformed Theology*. Grand Rapids, MI: Baker Academic, 2010.
Van Asselt, Willem J., and Eef Dekker. *Reformation and Scholasticism: An Ecumenical Enterprise*. Grand Rapids, MI: Baker Academic, 2001.
Van der Kooi, Cornelis. "A Theology of Culture. A Critical Appraisal of Kuyper's Doctrine of Common Grace." In *Kuyper Reconsidered: Aspects of His Life and Work*, edited by Cornelis van der Kooi and Jan de Bruijn, 95–101. Amsterdam: VU Uitgeverij, 1999.

Van Eijkel, Remko, Niels Hermes, and Robert Lensink. "Group Lending and the Role of the Group Leader." *Small Business Economics* 36, no. 3 (April 2011): 299–321.
Vella, Danielle. *Dying to Live: Stories from Refugees on the Road to Freedom*. Lanham, MD: Rowman and Littlefield, 2020.
Vidu, Adonis. *The Same God Who Works in All Things: Inseparable Operations in Trinitarian Theology*. Grand Rapids, MI: Eerdmans, 2021.
Volf, Miroslav. "'The Trinity Is Our Social Program': The Doctrine of the Trinity and the Shape of Social Engagement." *Modern Theology* 14, no. 3 (July 1998): 403–23.
Von Balthasar, Hans Urs. *Dare We Hope That All May be Saved?* 2nd ed. Translated by David Kipp and Lothar Krauth. San Francisco: Ignatius, 2014.
Vos, Geerhardus J. *Ecclesiology, the Means of Grace, Eschatology*. Translated and edited by Richard B. Gaffin Jr. Vol. 5 of *Reformed Dogmatics*. Bellingham, WA: Lexham, 2016.
Wade, Robert. "The System of Administrative and Political Corruption: Canal Irrigation in South India." *Journal of Development Studies* 18 (1982): 287–328.
Walbert, Mark S., and Thomas J. Bierma. "The Permits Game: Conveying the Logic of Marketable Pollution Permits." *Journal of Economic Education* 19, no. 4 (Fall 1988): 383–89.
Wallace, James D. *Norms and Practices*. Ithaca, NY: Cornell University Press, 2009.
Walras, Léon. *Elements of Pure Economics: Or the Theory of Social Wealth*. Translated by William Jaffé. London: Routledge, 1954.
Ward, Kate. *Wealth, Virtue, and Moral Luck: Christian Ethics in an Age of Inequality*. Washington, DC: Georgetown University Press, 2021.
Ware, Bruce A. *Father, Son and Holy Spirit: Relationships, Roles, and Relevance*. Wheaton, IL: Crossway Books, 2005.
Waterman, A. M. C. "Whately, Senior, and the Methodology of Classical Economics." In Brennan and Waterman, *Economics and Religion*, 41–60.
Waters, Brent. *Just Capitalism: A Christian Ethic of Economic Globalization*. Louisville, KY: Westminster John Knox, 2016.
Weber, Max. *The Protestant Ethic and the Spirit of Capitalism*. Translated by Talcott Parsons. Upper Saddle River, NJ: Prentice Hall, 1958.
Webster, John. "Providence." In Allen and Swain, *Christian Dogmatics*, 148–64.
Westberg, Daniel A. *Renewing Moral Theology: Christian Ethics as Action, Character, and Grace*. Downers Grove, IL: IVP Academic, 2015.
Wilber, Charles K. "Trust, Moral Hazards, and Social Economics: Incentives and the Organization of Work." In *Economics, Ethics, and Public Policy*, edited by Charles K. Wilber, 93–105. Lanham, MD: Rowman and Littlefield, 1998.
Wiley, Tatha. *Original Sin: Origins, Developments, Contemporary Meanings*. New York: Paulist, 2002.
Wilkinson, Richard. "The Impact of Inequality: Empirical Evidence." In *Social Inequality and Public Health*, edited by Salvatore J. Babones, 159–68. Chicago: Policy Press, 2009.
Williams, Delores S. "The Color of Feminism." In *Feminist Theological Ethics: A Reader*, edited by Lois K. Daly, 42–58. Louisville, KY: Westminster John Knox, 1994.
Williams, Jarvis J. *Redemptive Kingdom Diversity: A Biblical Theology of the People of God*. Grand Rapids, MI: Baker, 2021.
Winner, Lauren F. *The Dangers of Christian Practice: On Wayward Gifts, Characteristic Damage, and Sin*. New Haven, CT: Yale University Press, 2018.

Wogaman, J. Philip. *Economics and Ethics: A Christian Inquiry*. Philadelphia: Fortress, 1985.
Wollebius, Johannes. *Compendium Theologiae Christianae*. In *Reformed Dogmatics: Seventeenth-Century Reformed Theology through the Writings of Wollebius, Voetius, and Turretin*, edited and translated by John W. Beardslee III, 26–262. Grand Rapids, MI: Baker, 1965.
Wong, Kenman L., and Scott B. Rae. *Business for the Common Good: A Christian Vision for the Marketplace*. Downers Grove, IL: IVP Academic, 2011.
Wood, Susan K. "Catholic Reception of the Joint Declaration on the Doctrine of Justification." In *Rereading Paul Together: Protestant and Catholic Perspectives on Justification*, edited by David E. Aune, 43–59. Grand Rapids, MI: Baker Academic, 2006.
Wright, Christopher J. H. *God's People in God's Land: Family, Land, and Property in the Old Testament*. Grand Rapids, MI: Eerdmans, 1990.
———. *Old Testament Ethics for the People of God*. Downers Grove, IL: IVP Academic, 2004.
Wright, Tom. *Justification: God's Plan and Paul's Vision*. London: SPCK, 2009.
Yunus, Muhammad. *Banker to the Poor: Micro-Lending and the Battle against World Poverty*. New York: Public Affairs, 1999.
Zschirnt, Eva, and Didier Ruedin. "Ethnic Discrimination in Hiring Decisions: A Meta-Analysis of Correspondence Tests 1990–2015." *Journal of Ethnic and Migration Studies* 42, no. 7 (2016): 1115–34.

Name Index

Agamben, Giorgio, 130n3
Akerlof, George, 69–71
Ames, Ruth, 15–16, 55, 222, 224, 226
Ames, William, 217
Anselm of Canterbury, 98
Aquinas, Thomas, 96, 147, 148, 208
Archibald, G. C., 210
Atherton, John, 42
Ayer, A. J., 40–41

Bac, J. Martin, 99n47
Barnes, Kenneth, 60
Barrera, Albino, 94–95
Basu, Kaushik, 205
Bavinck, Herman, 97n117, 122–24
Becker, Gary, 5n12
Bell, Daniel, 3–5, 15
Beretii, Antoine, 214–15
Berger, Peter, 143
Berkouwer, G. C., 233
Bernasek, Anna, 21
Bertrand, Marianne, 186
Bezos, Jeff, 77
Blaug, Mark, 46, 54
Boff, Clodovis, 38, 50–52
Boff, Leonardo, 50, 131–33
Bowles, Samuel, 213
Brand, Chad, 30, 42
Brennan, Geoffrey, 45–46
Brock, Cory, 105
Bruni, Luigini, 206
Buchanan, James, 5n12
Bujo, Bénézet, 114

Callon, Michel, 54, 227
Calvin, John, 96

Carter, John, 16–17
Cavanaugh, William, 3–4, 63
Choi, Ginny, 19
Chua, Amy, 162
Claar, Victor, 132
Clark, Charles, 154
Codina, Victor, 217
Condorcet, Nicolas, 6
Crockett, Richard, 5n12

Danner, Peter, 52n49
De Caussade, Jean-Pierre, 166–67, 169, 172
De Leeuw, Gawain, 183
De Lubac, Henri, 124
Dolan, Edwin, 48n36
Donahue-White, Patricia, 52–53
Dubois, Nicole, 146
Duflo, Esther, 186
Dunn, James D. G., 144
Dussel, Enrique, 50n39

Ellacuría, Ignacio, 109n13
Engelsma, David, 117n45
Evans, David, 68

Faus, Ignacio González, 112
Fernández, Antonio González, 62n13, 112n32, 183
Figuières, Charles, 214–15
Finn, Daniel, 43nn75–76, 82
Flake, Kathleen, 1n1
Fletcher, Joseph, 114
Friedman, Milton, 5n12

Gneezy, Uri, 24–25
Goodchild, Philip, 8n31

NAME INDEX

Goodwin, Thomas, 147–48
Gorman, Michael, 194
Graafland, Johan, 7–8
Grabill, Stephen, 52–53
Grant, Ruth, 209
Grant, W. Matthews, 93, 100–101
Greene, Joshua, 114n38
Gregory of Nyssa, 136
Grolleau, Gilles, 214–15
Gronbacher, Gregory, 54–56
Grenz, Stanley, 110–11, 131n5
Guala, Francesco, 71
Gunton, Colin, 129

Haeringer, Guillaume, 60, 66
Harper, Ian, 156
Hauerwas, Stanley, 216
Hayek, Friedrich, 5n12, 55
Heckman, James, 187–88, 190
Henkel-Rieger, Rosemarie, 173n75
Henrich, Joseph, 2n2
Hill, Daniel Lee, 108, 114
Hirschman, Albert, 6
Hodge, Charles, 142
Holm, Peter, 65
Hübner, Jamin, 174
Hugh of St. Victor, 141
Hume, David, 40

Insko, Chester, 197
Irons, Michael, 16–17

Johnson, Jimmy, 227
Jones, Eric, 156
Julian "the Apostate," 196
Juselius, Katarina, 54

Kahneman, Daniel, 27–28
Kelly, Conor, 109n13, 114
Kennedy, John F., 30
Kierkegaard, Søren, 114
Kieser, Ty, 108, 114
Klay, Robin, 47–48
Knight, Frank, 5n12
Kuyper, Abraham, 117–19, 122, 124–27, 165

Landy, Marc, 61
Levin, Martin, 61
Litan, Robert, 65
Long, D. Stephen, 8n30, 33–34, 47, 117
Luckmann, Thomas, 143
Lunn, John, 47–48
Luther, Martin, 98

Maital, Shlomo, 37
MacMillan, John, 163
Marmot, Michael, 160
Marwell, Gerald, 15–16, 55, 222, 224, 226
McClosky, Deirdre, 6–7
McCoy, Mike, 227
McRorie, Christina, 1, 9, 28n42
Menzies, Gordon, 181
Milbank, John, 52, 130n3
Miller, Dale, 223
Miller, Vincent, 25–27
Mises, Ludwig von, 55
Montesquieu, 6
Mori, Nobuchika, 73
Muller, Richard, 101

Nakano, Haruhiro, 73
Nelson, Derek, 109, 111
Nelson, Robert, 44n18
Neumark, David, 185, 190
Novak, Michael, 5n12, 19, 82–83, 116n41, 132, 165

O'Boyle, Edward, 52n49
O'Donovan, Oliver, 207–8
Owen, John, 87, 144–45, 221

Paine, Thomas, 6
Palmer, Phoebe, 148
Pemberton, Prentiss, 43
Petrella, Ivan, 50, 52, 60, 133
Pollitt, Michael, 231
Pope, Devin, 191
Pratt, Tom, 30
Putnam, Hilary, 46

Rahner, Karl, 113, 131n5
Radin, Margaret, 176–78

NAME INDEX

Rassell, Edith, 173–74, 175
Ray, Stephen, 109–10
Reddie, Anthony, 195n56
Reynolds, John, 212
Rich, Judith, 185, 190
Richard of St. Victor, 141
Richards, Jay, 30, 83n100
Rieger, Joerg, 30–31
Rittenhouse, Bruce, 26n37
Robbins, Lionel, 41, 44
Robinson, John A. T., 114
Rommen, Edward, 182
Roth, Alvin, 31, 32–33

Sachs, Jeffrey, 61n11
Samuelson, Paul, 41
Sanders, Fred, 139
Santos, Ana, 18n10
Sawakami, Atsuto, 73
Schmalensee, Richard, 68
Schmid, Hans Bernhard, 225
Schopler, John, 197
Schreiner, Thomas, 88n3, 144
Scott, Margaret, 217
Searle, John, 26–27, 225
Sen, Amartya, 5n12, 225
Shaw, David, 77
Siegelman, Peter, 187–88, 190
Simon, Julian, 65
Smith, Adam, 5n12, 60
Smith, James K. A., 3–4, 47, 220–21
Smith, Vernon, 6n22
Sobrino, Jon, 29, 168–69, 172
Storr, Virgil, 19
Stump, Eleanor, 99
Sung, Jung Mo, 30, 116, 134
Sutanto, Gray, 105
Swain, Scott, 138
Syndor, Justin, 191

Tanner, Kathryn, 60n3, 89–93, 102, 123, 171n67, 181–82
Taylor, Charles, 143
Taylor, Keeanga-Yamahtta, 74, 83, 199–201
Thaler, Richard, 16n5, 227
Thatcher, Margaret, 5n12
Thielicke, Helmut, 208
Thompson, James, 193
Torrance, T. F., 137n30
Tracy, Thomas, 91n13
Turretin, Francis, 102
Tutu, Desmond, 128n82
Tversky, Amos, 27–28

Unger, Roberto, 60

Vidu, Adonis, 137
Volf, Miroslav, 133
Vos, Geerhardus, 217

Wade, Robert, 164
Wallace, James, 146
Walras, Léon, 63
Ward, Kate, 156, 161
Waters, Brent, 19, 158–59
Weber, Max, 222
Webster, John, 98
Wells, Samuel, 216
Westberg, Daniel, 208
Westley, Christopher, 52
Whately, Richard, 41–42, 47
Wilkinson, Richard, 159
Williams, Delores, 110
Williams, Jarvis, 194n56
Winner, Lauren, 219–20
Wogaman, Philip, 42

Yunus, Muhammad, 31, 69

Zuñiga, Gloria, 52

Subject Index

abandonment to divine providence, 166–69
accommodation, 90
adverse selection, 69–70
affirmative action, 203
affluence, 158–59, 160
Affordable Care Act, 70–71
algorithms, 33, 68, 78
altruism, 18, 158, 163
analogy, 91, 131, 133
appropriations, 137–38, 140
auctions, 66–67, 71, 80–81. *See also* electromagnetic spectrum auctions
    varieties of, 67
audit studies. *See* experiments
Austrian economics, 5

behavioral economics, 44n18. *See also* experimental economics; framing; phishing
    theological responses to, 28n42

capitalism, 3–8, 25, 29–30, 52, 59–60, 62, 83, 116, 131, 173, 181
    superiority of markets as analytic concept, 35, 59–60, 173
Chicago School of Economics, 5
Christ Jesus, 142, 156, 171, 193–96, 197, 201, 203, 205. *See also* Son
    righteousness of, 144–45
    sinlessness of, 108
    and social sin, 108
church, 118, 121, 128, 178, 203
class, socioeconomic, 153–55, 157

commodification, 25–26, 33, 63–64, 75, 176–78
    complete and incomplete, 176–78
    definition of, 176
common grace, 97, 105, 117–28, 139, 140, 149, 162, 165, 167, 203
    and eschatology, 127
    and racism, 125–29
    and special grace, 118, 122–25, 140
    unknowability of the full workings of, 126
concurrence, 93–94, 99n47, 102, 149, 155, 162, 166, 203. *See also* free will; secondary causes
    definition, 92
    immediate, 92
    mediate, 92
    and supervenience, 96
conscience, 113, 114, 116
cooperatives, 174–75
correspondence studies. *See* experiments
corruption, 164
culpability. *See* responsibility
culture, 1–2, 57, 64, 141, 163–65, 166, 169, 176
    definition of, 163

decretive will of God, 103, 166
deregulation, 61
determinism, 87, 96, 103
dictator game. *See* experiments
discontinuity effect, 23–24
    and schema-based distrust hypothesis, 23
    and social-support for self-interest hypothesis, 23

SUBJECT INDEX

discrimination, 70n41, 184–93, 197, 201. *See also* racism; redlining
  and development of virtue, 197–98
  statistical, 188–89, 191–92, 196, 197, 198, 203
  taste-based, 188, 197
distributive justice, 29–30, 32, 67, 116, 176
distributivism, 49
divine agency, 88, 90, 129, 134–39. *See also* common grace; concurrence; providence; special grace
divine nature, 38, 88
doux commerce thesis, 6–8, 18, 19, 49, 95, 134

ecclesial ethics, 3–6, 8, 18, 49, 130, 134
electromagnetic spectrum auctions, 66–67, 71–72
eschatology, 127–28, 167
Eucharist, 14
exchange mechanisms. *See* mechanism of exchange
experiments, 15–18, 26n37, 57, 112, 153–55, 157, 160, 178, 197
  audit studies, 185–87, 197, 202
  bribery experiments, 164
  correspondence studies, 185–87, 197
  dictator game, 17n7, 19n15, 29, 153, 161, 198
  envy game, 198
  limits to experiments, 18
  mere categorization, 22–23
  prisoner's dilemma, 17, 21–23
  prosocial game, 197
  trust game, 154
  ultimatum game, 16–17, 19n15, 163

fact/value distinction, 37–42, 45–49, 51, 52, 56, 192
  and market design, 64–65
  and strong or weak versions of positive/normative distinction, 48, 57, 126
fairness, 1–2, 16–17, 29
  actuarial vs. equal access, 70
  definition of, 49

Father, 135, 141–42, 148, 166, 169, 176, 178–79, 205
  as Creator, 138
feminist ethics, 49
framing, 27–28, 35, 112
free rider problem, 15–16
free will, 96–102, 112, 113, 116, 198
fungibility, 80, 177

gender, 12, 185, 190, 194–95
Gini coefficient, 126–27
God, 162, 172, 199. *See also* divine agency; divine nature; providence; Trinity
  aseity, 100
  as cause, 93–94, 96
  goodness of, 88, 102–3
  holiness of, 88
  not part of a kind/genus, 89–90, 95
  sovereignty, 88
grace, 142, 147. *See also* common grace; special grace
  gratuitous nature of salvation, 88, 140

Heckman-Siegelman critique, 187–88, 190
holiness, 194
Holy Spirit, 118, 119, 126, 135, 141, 142, 146–49, 205
homo economicus, 4, 55
human nature, 53, 147
Hume's guillotine, 40

identity, 142–46, 181–84, 194–96, 201, 203
  as basis for moral deliberation, 193–94
  definition of, 182
image of God, 94, 133, 183, 188
incentives, 19, 158, 175
individual transferrable quotas (ITQs), 64–65
inequality, 153–55, 159–63, 166, 169–76, 178–79
  and health, 160–61
  in Scripture, 170–73
information asymmetry, 20, 69, 71
inseparable operations, 135–36
institutional facts, 26–27

SUBJECT INDEX

institutions, 23–24, 109, 200–201
intrinsic good, 205

justification, 142–46, 147, 195–96, 197, 203, 206
self-justification, 183

kidney exchanges, 32–35, 75
kingdom of God, 95n33, 167

labor unions, 173–74, 182
liberation theology, 29–30, 38, 50–52, 60, 83, 130, 201
spirituality of, 168–69
liturgy, 3
logical positivism, 40–41

market design, 9–10, 31–32, 59–61, 72–73, 82, 133, 140, 178, 199–203. *See also* auctions; electromagnetic spectrum auctions; individual transferable quotas; kidney exchange; mechanism of exchange
ethical dimensions of, 64–65, 67, 70, 73, 82–84, 200–201
explained through examples, 76–82
and inequality, 173–76
limits to, 169, 200–201
markets, 2, 25–27, 29, 75–76, 167, 169. *See also* commodification; distributive justice; market design; myth of the spontaneous and natural market
causing sin, 115
and deception, 20, 35
definition of, 62–63
and identity, 181–83
as imagined spaces, 63–65, 77, 115, 176
material dimensions of, 49, 63, 79, 115
and moral formation, 3–8, 83–84, 95, 140, 176, 206. *See also* market design, ethical dimensions of; sanctification; virtue
thickness of, 72, 77
variability of, 60, 82
Marxism, 50, 52
matchmakers. *See* multisided platforms
means of grace, 94

mechanism of exchange, 63, 65–69, 78, 173–75, 202
definition of, 65–66
method in theological economics, 49–56
methodological individualism, 52, 55–56
microfinance, 31–32, 69, 71
missions, divine. *See* Trinity
models, 43, 54–55
predictive power of, 53
moral individualism, 55–56, 114
moral luck, 156
multisided platforms, 68, 72, 76
myth of the spontaneous and natural market, 61, 83n100

nationality, 162
Noahic covenant, 119–20
normative economics. *See* fact/value distinction
norms. *See* social norms
nouvelle théologie, 123–25

oikonomia, 134, 139
original sin, 106, 111, 113, 165

Pelagianism, 84, 162, 167
performativity, 54–55
perichoresis, 131–33
personalism, 50, 52–56
phishing, 20–21
pollution markets, 79–82
positive economics. *See* fact/value distinction
poverty, 30–31, 156–59, 170, 202
absolute poverty, 159
definition of, 156
relative poverty, 159
preceptive will, 103, 158, 166
predatory inclusion, 74, 83, 199
prisoner's dilemma. *See* experiments
private property, 173
profit maximization, 60n2, 184–85, 189, 196n64, 203
providence, 87–88, 141–42, 155, 162, 166, 169, 176
and moral luck, 156
public goods, 15

261

SUBJECT INDEX

race, 109, 162, 194
racism, 125–28, 165, 184. *See also* discrimination; predatory inclusion; redlining
rationality (economic), 16–17, 25, 43–45, 72, 189, 192
    as normative, 45, 55
redlining, 73–74, 199–201
    definition of, 199
responsibility, 24, 87, 88, 95, 107, 112, 162

sacraments, 121. *See also* eucharist
sanctification, 2, 43, 118, 146–49, 205
    as faith working through love, 205
secondary causes, 94–95, 96, 128, 149, 199. *See also* concurrence
self-interest, 22–23, 34
sexual orientation, 185, 186
sin, 95, 116, 118, 124, 127, 165, 183, 189. *See also* original sin; social sin; structures of sin; vices
    of social groups, 107–8, 115, 165, 184, 192
social imaginary, 56
social norms, 23–24, 25, 109, 146–49, 205
social sin, 106, 113–14, 162, 185, 189
    definition of, 115
socialism, 60, 131, 173
socioanalytic mediation, 50
sola fide, 97
sola gratia, 97
solus Christus, 142
Son, 135, 139, 141, 142–46, 148. *See also* Christ Jesus
special grace, 106, 118, 122–25, 127, 140
structures of sin, 109–13, 116, 167, 184, 192, 198
    causing sin, 111–12
    definition of, 115
    and demonology, 110–11
subsidiarity, 117

technology, 55
thickness. *See* markets

transcendence, 89, 168
    Christology and, 91
    contrastive, 90, 102
    noncontrastive, 90–92, 103, 140, 166
Trinity. *See also* appropriations; Father; Holy Spirit; inseparable operations; perichoresis; Son
    exemplary approach to, 130–34, 141
    genealogical approach to, 130n3
    missions, 135, 138–39, 140, 147
    processions, 132, 137, 139
trust, 18, 19–24, 34, 77, 155, 174, 182n7
    definition of, 57
truth, 38–39, 46

ultimatum game. *See* experiments
unions. *See* labor unions
universal destination of goods, 171
univocity, 91, 133
utilitarianism, 43, 189–90, 193, 196

vices, 116, 156
    avarice, 156
    corporate vices, 198
    definitions of, 49
    envy, 7
virtues, 146–48, 162, 183, 195–96
    definitions of, 49, 57
    diligence, 7
    faith, 7, 168, 172, 178, 183, 193
    fidelity, 157
    generosity, 161
    honesty, 19–20, 23, 168
    hope, 7, 168, 172, 178, 193
    humility, 7
    justice, 18, 57, 197, 198
    love/charity, 21, 33–34, 168, 172, 178, 193, 197, 198, 206
    prudence, 6, 19, 197, 198

Washington consensus capitalism, 60n2
wealth, 156–59. *See also* affluence
    definition of, 156